Representation
and
Revelation

Representation and Revelation

Victorian Realism from Carlyle to Yeats

John P. McGowan

University of Missouri Press
Columbia, 1986

Copyright © 1986 by
The Curators of the University of Missouri
University of Missouri Press, Columbia, Missouri 65211
Printed and bound in the United States of America

Library of Congress Cataloging-in-Publication Data
McGowan, John P.
    Representation and Revelation.

        Includes index.
        1. English literature—19th century—History and
criticism. 2. Realism in literature. 3. Dualism in
literature. I. Title.
    PR468.R42M34 1986   820'.9'12   85-20117
    ISBN 0-8262-0492-9 (alk. paper)

⊛" This paper meets the minimum requirements of
the American National Standard for Permanence of Paper
for Printed Library Materials, Z39.48, 1984.

Passages from *The Collected Poems of William Butler Yeats,* and
from his *Autobiography* and *Essays and Introductions,* are
reprinted here with the kind permission of Michael B. Yeats,
Macmillan London Ltd., and the Macmillan Publishing
Company, New York.

Acknowledgments

Writing a book is a solitary affair, and as I face the finished product of my labors, images of libraries in Buffalo, Ann Arbor, Chicago, Berkeley, and San Francisco come first to mind. But there were classrooms and student unions adjacent to all those libraries, and sometimes coffeehouses and always bars in the immediate neighborhoods, where my pent-up thoughts found audiences that were invariably polite and often enough downright enthusiastic and where the measured responses of others engaged in similar work served to shift the current of my own thought.

Of teachers, Keith Fort of Georgetown University, Joseph Fradin of the State University of New York at Buffalo, Carol Christ of Berkeley, and Charles Altieri of the University of Washington will recognize mutated versions of their own insights sprinkled throughout these pages in ways that only their generous giving can absolve from the charge of outright theft. What they may not recognize is how their interest in my work sustained my own ability to believe in its worth.

My fellow students in Carol Christ's NEH seminar on Victorian and Modern Poetics will remember essays on Rossetti, Browning, and Yeats that discussions with them helped to engender and criticism from them led me to revise. I must also thank the Endowment for the opportunity to study with such an enlivening group.

Portions of chapters five and six originally appeared in *Nineteenth-Century Fiction,* while earlier versions of the Rossetti and Browning chapters appeared in *Victorian Poetry* and the *South Carolina Review* respectively.

Technical assistance (so necessary these days) in getting my book onto the computer and then off it again was rendered by Ken Jarboe in Ann Arbor and Hans Kellner in Rochester, with the help of generous amounts of computer time and money provided by the University of Michigan and the University of Rochester.

Assistance of an even more vital nature came from Peter Allan Dale, whose kind, but sharp, criticism of the first version of this book led to extensive rewriting, reorganization, deletion, and addition, making it, I believe, a much better book in the process. Additional suggestions from Roger Henkle have also been gratefully accepted. I must humbly admit that the flaws which remain are to be laid at my own door; my sympathetic readers indicated some shortcomings that I found neither the ability nor the energy to correct.

Personal debts reveal me less able to find words. I trust that Janet Patzman, Dan Hayes, John Marien, and Jane Danielewicz already know this book would never have been written without their love. And my wide-flung, generous family continues to defy mere geographical logic by always managing to be there.

J. P. M.
Rochester, New York
September 1985

Contents

Introduction

The subject of this book is the way the Victorians tried to connect mind with world. Each of the writers I discuss strives to identify a "reality" that exists prior to and independent of any thought or speech, and strives to guarantee literature's ability to represent that reality.

The exact nature of the real and the extent to which the human mind can comprehend it are, of course, issues that arose in literature and philosophy long before the Victorian period. But the question of the real possesses a special urgency in the nineteenth century, an urgency that explains the dominance of realism as the literary mode of the era. Writers do not begin to broadcast their works' faithfulness to reality until the very possibility of such faithfulness has been put into question. Victorian realism concerns itself with identifying the essential nature of a reality whose identity remains elusive. The Victorians' penchant to locate spiritual or moral truths as the most fundamental reality marks their distance from the realism found in France during the same period and explains my somewhat startling connection of the names Carlyle and Yeats with the word *realism* in my title.

Michel Foucault has argued that the real is especially hard to determine in the nineteenth century,[1] and the word *reality* is used by both materialists and their opponents in an effort to convince audiences of what is truly significant. Often enough, Victorian realism appears little more than a battle to capture the word *reality* and make its referent the particular values the writer cherishes. Having reality on the side of one's moral or social argument bolsters confidence wonderfully.

My design here is not to reduce realism to a rhetorical sleight of hand; my premise is that the Victorian writer's attempt to make reality apparent to himself and his readers displays the anxieties, desires, and achievements of the period. In other words, this book shares the Victorian faith that the ways we

1. See *The Order of Things* (New York: Vintage Books, 1973), esp. chap. 7. For Foucault, at the end of the eighteenth century a revolutionary change in the bases of European thought results in "the withdrawal of knowledge and thought outside the space of representation" (242). A new "metaphysics" arises, "one whose purpose will be to question, apart from representation, all that is the source and origin of representation; it makes possible those philosophies of Life, of Will, and of the Word, that the nineteenth century is to deploy in the wake of criticism" (243). Foucault's general description of this change, and of the relation between representation and its mysterious sources (Life, Will, or other hidden primal forces) during the nineteenth century, has greatly influenced my attention to similar issues in this study of Victorian literature.

think and talk about the world do make a difference, as distinct from the modern viewpoint (discussed in the chapter on Yeats) that mind's activities can make no impact on a brutal, indifferent, and unthinking reality. Victorian literature is firmly entrenched within the dualism characteristic of Western thought since Descartes, and the specter of mind's complete divorce from reality haunts the writers of the period. But comedy, with its eventual union of mind and world, remains the characteristic genre of the period, even when the anticipated union only occurs within the human order of culture and not between man and the material world. (Exceptions to comedy's reign, like *The Mill on the Floss* or "Empedocles on Etna," were taken by author and audience alike as failures of will and imagination that later texts should avoid.)

The Victorian approach to the problems raised by dualism can be recognized as a synthesis of eighteenth-century and romantic theories of mind's position in the world, and I want to use this introduction to outline briefly the legacy inherited by the Victorians from the empiricists and romantics. John Stuart Mill's famous essays on Bentham and Coleridge reveal how self-consciously the Victorians attempted to synthesize these two traditions. Well aware that the romantics viewed themselves as repudiating all of eighteenth-century thought, the Victorians still felt confident that they could make use of the strengths of empiricism and romanticism while rejecting the excesses of each.[2] Certainly the Victorians found themselves grappling with the same basic epistemological question that plagued both Locke and Coleridge: how can mind know nature when the two are distinct substances?

In this study I discuss the Victorian approach to this epistemological issue by distinguishing between two fundamental sources of knowledge: representation and revelation. Representational theories of knowledge posit the necessity for some intermediary that stands between mind and the world, serving as their point of contact. Revelation, on the other hand, is the basis of a model that asserts that immediate knowledge of the real, either through direct sensory perception or through an intuitive grasp of essential principles, can be attained. Obviously, the kinds of representation or revelation to which a writer will appeal depends on how he defines the reality that is to be known, but each of the writers I discuss relies on both models at various times and must come to grips with determining the benefits of each. In presenting reality to his readers, the writer must explain the process by which he came to know the real and afford his readers a similar mode of access.

Literary theory most often confines discussion of representation to the question of the ways in which language can be said to represent something other than itself. But Lockean epistemology, in large part through Locke's

2. See "Coleridge," in "Essays on Ethics, Religion and Society," vol. 10 of *The Collected Works of John Stuart Mill*, ed. John M. Robson (Toronto: University of Toronto Press, 1981), esp. pp. 123–25.

apparently inadvertent use of the word *idea* to mean two quite distinct things,[3] offers a representational theory of perception as well as of language. The analogies between perceptual and linguistic representation in this schema link Victorian discussions of how the mind knows the world to Victorian understandings of the way words represent things. Because the two are so closely linked for the Victorians, I have taken both the epistemological and the linguistic issues for my subject throughout this book.

The sources for Locke's representationalism are a matter of dispute among scholars,[4] but there is little reason to doubt that for the Victorians Locke was the origin of what John W. Yolton describes as "the 'new' doctrine" that "knowledge [occurs] by means of ideas which are causally connected with, but only representative of, objects distinct from the mind."[5] When considering knowledge received from sensory perception, Locke uses the word *idea* to mean *sense-data*.[6] Perceptual knowledge is representational in Locke because what we perceive is our "idea" of the thing, not the thing itself. Locke takes this position as a way of explaining the obvious "errors" in perception that also troubled Descartes. When we look at a tree from a distance, it appears quite different from the way it looks close up. So our "idea" of the tree (that is, what we see) is different at different times, even though it is the same tree, which is of a constant size, that causes that idea in us. (How we know it is the same tree, or that its reality is constant, or that it causes our ideas of it, are all problems that Locke wrestles with at various points in the *Essay Concerning Human Understanding,* without ever, as Berkeley and Hume were quick to point out, really solving them.[7]) Our visual "idea," then, is not identical to the object, but instead must be understood as a representative of

3. For a consideration of how Locke uses the word *idea,* see Jonathan Bennett, *Locke, Berkeley, Hume: Central Themes* (Oxford: Clarendon Press, 1971), pp. 25–30; Gilbert Ryle, "John Locke on the Human Understanding," in *Locke and Berkeley: A Collection of Critical Essays,* ed. C. B. Martin and D. M. Armstrong (Notre Dame: University of Notre Dame Press, 1968), pp. 16–25; and Richard I. Aaron, *John Locke* (2d ed.; Oxford: Clarendon Press, 1955), pp. 110–13.

4. Aaron, *John Locke,* pp. 102–3, offers a short summary of the sources mentioned most often.

5. *John Locke and the Way of Ideas* (Oxford: Oxford University Press, 1956), p. ix.

6. Bennett, *Locke, Berkeley, Hume,* p. 25.

7. To what extent Hume and, especially, Berkeley really addressed themselves to fundamental problems in Locke's philosophy has become a crucial issue in recent studies of Locke and the empiricist tradition. One school of thought on the subject holds that Berkeley misinterpreted Locke almost completely, and in so doing succeeded in guaranteeing that Locke would be misunderstood for two hundred years. Berkeley set up the terms and the questions by which Locke is judged (and found wanting), but they are the wrong terms and questions. Be that as it may, the Victorians usually interpreted Locke through the objections raised by Berkeley. On the relation of Berkeley to Locke, see the introduction to *Locke on Human Understanding: Selected Essays,* ed. I. C. Tipton (Oxford: Oxford University Press, 1977), pp. 3–4, and Winston H. F. Barnes, "Did Berkeley Misunderstand Locke?," in Armstrong and Martin, *Locke and Berkeley,* pp. 78–85.

it. When strictly faithful to this representationalism (which is not always the case), Locke describes knowledge as being of ideas only, not of things themselves. A representative theory makes knowledge of real entities mediate. "'Tis evident, the Mind knows not Things immediately, but only by the intervention of the *Ideas* it has of them."[8]

Locke is certainly aware of, and uneasy with, the difficulties raised by making knowledge of the world indirect. He follows the sentence just quoted by considering the basic problem his account of knowledge leaves unsolved. "*Our Knowledge* therefore is *real,* only so far as there is a conformity between our *Ideas* and the reality of Things. But what shall be here the Criterion? How shall the Mind, when it perceives nothing but its own *Ideas,* know that they agree with Things themselves?" (ECHU, 4.4.3). Locke goes on to answer his question by claiming that the ideas of perception are caused by things in the world. But such a link is difficult to prove, as Hume's attack on the notion of causation demonstrated. And even if an unproblematic causal link is assumed, there is still no explanation for how we know the *difference* between an "idea" and the thing itself. "Conformity between our simple *Ideas,* and the existence of Things" is the basis of "real Knowledge" (ECHU, 4.4.4), but Locke cannot explain how we can know when this conformity exists as distinct from times when our senses are deceiving us.

Modern commentators on Locke generally agree that his theory of knowledge gets him into difficulties he cannot solve.[9] Locke's modern defenders have usually made the argument that the representational model is so unworkable that Locke certainly never believed anything so patently absurd, and we owe our notion of Locke as representationalist to Berkeley's misreading of the Lockean position.[10] This current controversy is of little significance here. Even if we accept Hans Aarsleff's argument that the Victorians totally misunderstood Locke, what is crucial for my discussion is that the empirical and representationalist Locke is the Locke the Victorians knew and responded to.[11] Understood as making all knowledge mediate and as making the link of mind

8. *An Essay Concerning Human Understanding,* ed. Peter H. Nidditch (Oxford: Clarendon Press, 1975), bk. 4, chap. 4, par. 3. Subsequent references to the *Essay* are taken from this edition and are cited parenthetically in the text, with ECHU used to identify the text; book, chapter, and paragraph numbers are listed in the order given above.

9. See Bennett, *Locke, Berkeley, Hume,* pp. 64–77; and Reginald Jackson, "Locke's Version of the Doctrine of Representative Perception," in Armstrong and Martin, *Locke and Berkeley,* pp. 125–54.

10. See the introduction to Tipton, *Locke on Human Understanding,* pp. 4–7, and Douglas Greenlee, "Locke's Idea of 'Idea,'" also in Tipton, pp. 41–47.

11. Hans Aarsleff has argued that the nineteenth century consistently misinterpreted Locke for its own reasons and that many of our received opinions about Locke's work are based on those misinterpretations. Aarsleff singles out the Victorians as particularly guilty of such misinterpretation. See "Locke's Reputation in Nineteenth-Century England," in *From Locke to Saussure* (Minneapolis: University of Minnesota Press, 1982), pp. 120–45, and "Language and Victorian Ideology," *The American Scholar* 52 (1983): 365–72.

(and its perceptions) to world extremely tenuous, the theory of representational knowledge (almost always tied to Locke's name) established the terms of epistemological theorizing for the Victorians.

What is of significance in the recent controversy over the extent to which Locke was actually a representationalist is the attention focused on those aspects of Locke's work that explain how he became the leading figure for two contrary traditions. Berkeley and Hume, by emphasizing that mind only perceives "ideas," developed the latent subjectivism of Locke's representationalist theories. But Locke's work also inspired various forms of empiricism and materialism, which rested all claims to knowledge on the apprehension (seen as unproblematic) of objective facts independent of the perceiver. The writers I discuss in this book almost always ignore the intricacies of Locke's representationalism and take him as the exemplar of the "common sense" opinion that what we perceive is really there in the world. The Victorian argument with Locke usually takes the form of insisting that information received from the senses is not enough to give us an adequate understanding of reality; other kinds (nonsensual and nonmaterial) of information are also necessary, and Locke is attacked for seeming to deny the validity of those other kinds. Locke's representationalism directly influenced the Victorians only insofar as they experienced a general uneasiness about mind's ability to connect with reality. Hume's work, which developed the full consequences of the representational position, had little impact on the Victorians, who viewed it primarily as a convincing demonstration of the fruitlessness of empiricist thought. The Victorian encounter with representation rarely took the form of doubting the immediacy of sensory perception.

However, Locke's uneasiness with his own representationalism can be recognized as the source of interpretations that identify him as a believer in direct sensory knowledge, while his retreat to theories of immediacy as a response to the difficulties posed by representation offers an earlier instance of a pattern found repeatedly in Victorian literature. The Victorians continually tried to evade the necessity of representation and its indirections in favor of immediate access to the real. Locke evidences the same impatience with the subtleties and difficulties of mediation and "finds himself compelled to assert that knowledge, on occasion at least, is a direct apprehension of the real without the intervention of ideas."[12] Recent studies of Locke show that there is, in Douglas Greenlee's words, "a deep-lying vein of direct realism in the *Essay*, quite opposed to the representationalism."[13] In Locke, then, we do find, side by side with his representational theory of knowledge, what becomes the materialist solution to the dualism introduced by representationalism: a belief in the absolute accuracy of perception. Metaphors of sight become the model

12. Aaron, *John Locke*, p. 239.
13. "Idea and Object in the *Essay*," in Tipton, *Locke on Human Understanding*, p. 53.

for immediate knowledge, and both Locke and the Victorians use such metaphors to describe the knowledge of which we can be most certain.[14] But the
traditional puzzles about the inaccuracy of perception remain, even if ignored
at times, and finally Locke can only guarantee perception's adequacy by
appealing to a Creator who would not have given men a mind unable to gain
accurate knowledge of the rest of creation. Our vision of things "must necessarily be the product of Things operating on the Mind in a natural way, and
producing therein those Perceptions which by the Wisdom and Will of our
Maker they are ordained and adapted to" (ECHU, 4.4.4).

While perception reveals the physical world to us, Locke also gives some
attention to revelation as a source of information about things not accessible
to the senses.[15] The *Essay* has outlined the limits of human knowledge—how
difficult it is for men to obtain certain knowledge of the physical world—and
the author draws the following conclusion from his inquiry: "Since our
Faculties are not fitted to penetrate into the internal Fabrick and real Essences
of Bodies . . . 'tis rational to conclude, that our proper Imployment lies in those
Enquiries, and in that sort of Knowledge, which is most suited to our natural
Capacities . . . i.e., the Condition of our eternal Estate" (ECHU, 4.12.11). It
makes sense to turn our attention to spiritual matters because reason is given
extra help when it considers such things. "*Reason* is natural *Revelation*,
whereby the eternal Father of Light, and Fountain of all Knowledge communi-
cates to Mankind that portion of Truth, which he has laid within the reach
of natural Faculties: *Revelation* is natural *Reason* enlarged by a new set of
Discoveries communicated by God immediately" (ECHU, 4.19.4). Revelation
bypasses the torturous paths natural reason must follow to obtain knowledge·
revelation, like perception naively understood, does not involve representatives but affords a direct apprehension of the truth. Locke's discussion of
revelation can be played down as mere lip service to the religious prejudices
of his time, but I think the appeal to revelation is better understood as another
way to escape the consequences of a strict representationalism. My pairing of
revelation with representation in my title points toward a continual oscillation
between the two as sources of knowledge in the writers I discuss.

14. On metaphors of sight in Locke, see Ernest Lee Tuveson, *The Imagination as a Means
of Grace* (New York: Gordian Press, 1974), pp. 18–23. Eugenio Donato, in an essay that has
influenced my discussion in this study of the distinction between sight as a model of immediate
knowledge as contrasted to the mediations entailed in representation, has considered the practices
of contemporary literary critics in terms of whether they favor metaphors of sight or attempt
to avoid them. See "The Two Languages of Criticism," in *The Structuralist Controversy*, ed.
Richard Macksey and Eugenio Donato (Baltimore: Johns Hopkins University Press, 1972), pp.
89–97.

15. For an excellent discussion of revelation in Locke and its relation to the rest of the
Essay, see Richard Ashcraft, "Faith and Knowledge in Locke's Philosophy," in *John Locke:
Problems and Perspectives*, ed. John W. Yolton (Cambridge: Cambridge University Press, 1969),
pp. 194–223.

While inconsistent in adhering to a representational theory of knowledge, Locke always insists that words function as representatives. Locke's theory of knowledge rests on his using the word *idea* to mean *sense-data*. His theory of reflection and, crucially for our purposes, his description of language depend on understanding *idea* to mean *concept*. [16] In this sense of the term, the "idea" we have of a tree is our mental image of it. Thus, we can have an idea of a tree when the tree is not present to our senses, and we can have an idea of love even though love does not correspond to any definable sensory impression or set of impressions. In Locke's theory of language, words represent ideas, and are useful because they allow the communication of ideas from one mind to another.[17] "Words in their primary or immediate Signification, stand for nothing, but the *Ideas* in the Mind of him that uses them, how imperfectly soever, or carelessly those *Ideas* are collected from the Things, which they are supposed to represent. When a Man speaks to another, it is, that he may be understood; and the end of speech is, that those Sounds, as Marks, may make known his *Ideas* to the Hearer" (ECHU, 3.2.2).

We now have a representational system that has two parts, the second of which depends on the first. Our ideas represent the real world to us, and then our words represent our ideas to others. The danger in the first system is that ideas will not be accurate representatives of things; the danger in the second system is that words will not faithfully communicate the ideas they are meant to convey. Success in the whole enterprise (that is, obtaining knowledge and then being able to share it with others) depends on a "double conformity."[18]

> But this . . . *Idea*, being something in the Mind between the thing that exists, and the Name that is given to it; it is in our *Ideas*, that both the Rightness of our Knowledge, and the Propriety or Intelligibleness of our Speaking consists. And hence it is, that Men are so forward to suppose, that the abstract *Ideas* they have in their Minds, are such, as agree to the Things existing without them, to which they are refer'd; and are the same also, to which the Names they give them, do by the Use and Propriety of that Language belong. For without this *double Conformity of their Ideas*, they find, they should both think amiss of Things in themselves, and talk of them unintelligibly to others. (ECHU, 2.32.8)

The third book of Locke's *Essay* is devoted to ensuring that men talk intelligibly to one another. Hans Aarsleff has argued convincingly that the theory of language presented there rests on declaring representation "conventional" and "functional," not "natural." For Locke, "the relation between

---

16. Bennett, *Locke, Berkeley, Hume*, p. 25.
17. For descriptions of Locke's theory of language see Norman Kretzmann, "The Main Thesis of Locke's Semantic Theory," in Tipton, *Locke on Human Understanding*, pp. 123–40; and Stephen K. Land, *From Signs to Propositions: The Concept of Form in Eighteenth-Century Semantic Theory* (London: Longman, 1974), chap. 1.
18. See Aarsleff, *From Locke to Saussure*, pp. 24–28.

signifier and signified is arbitrary."[19] And this arbitrariness necessitates the continual warnings against the misuse of words. "Since Sounds have no natural connexion with our *Ideas,* but have all their signification from the arbitrary imposition of Men, the *doubtfulness* and uncertainty *of their signification,* which *is the imperfection* we here are speaking of, has its cause more in the *Ideas* they stand for, than in any incapacity there is in one Sound" (ECHU, 3.9.4). The best safeguard against this imperfection is to keep the idea a word represents firmly in mind while using the word; the difference between the representative (the word) and the represented (the idea) becomes disastrous when the word is allowed to function independently of the idea. And since the connection between word and idea is not natural or, we might add, necessary from an ontological point of view (Locke did not consider the social necessity of the connection within a given language), the possibility of the word's floating free is ever present. "There are several *wilful Faults and Neglects,* which Men are guilty of, in this way of Communication, whereby they render these signs less clear and distinct in their signification. . . . The First and most palpable abuse is, the using of Words, without clear and distinct *Ideas;* or, which is worse, signs without any thing signified" (ECHU, 3.10.1–2). The sign's possible independence from the signified explains Locke's famous hostility to figurative language and his suggestion that many philosophical and legal disputes can be explained as misunderstandings generated by an imprecise use of words.

Clearly, positivist attempts to purge language of its impurities and ambiguities can be traced to Locke's theory of language. But we should recognize that Locke's insistence that the sign is arbitrary makes him the forerunner of Saussurean linguistics and even of the structuralism and post-structuralism that is derived from Saussure's work.[20] Just as Locke's theory of knowledge reinforced the Cartesian distancing of mind from world, the Lockean theory of language opened up the gap between word and thing. Locke, of course, strove mightily to keep the distance between mind and world, word and thing, as small as possible—an effort that subsequent positivist thought continued. But the logic of Locke's theories also led subsequent writers to emphasize these distances instead of minimizing them. Thus, it seems to me that Jacques Derrida's work is strictly analogous to Hume's, although Derrida, of course, is not as directly concerned with Locke's thought as Hume was. Where Hume emphasized that empiricism divorces mind from world absolutely, Derrida argues that the difference between the signifier and the signified releases the signifier into a realm of "free play" that precludes any determinable link between words and the meanings they are traditionally thought to represent.[21]

19. Ibid., p. 27.
20. Hans Aarsleff's work has been devoted to showing how modern linguistics is derived from Locke through the intervention of the French *philosophes.* The introduction to *From Locke to Saussure* offers an overview of his position.
21. The aspect of Derrida's work described here is best illustrated in the essay "Structure,

While we tend to think of the extremity of Hume's and Derrida's positions as "modern," the fundamental issues their work addresses were of deep concern to the romantics and the Victorians. Romanticism can be defined as a particular set of responses to the problems raised by the dualism Locke's work introduced into England. The romantics, like Locke himself, wanted to lessen the distance between mind and nature, but wanted to reject what they saw as Locke's materialism (with the menacing figure of Hobbes standing as a shadow behind Locke's more benign appearance). We should recognize that the romantics for the most part accepted the *terms* as established by Descartes and Locke,[22] and that, as various studies of Locke and his influence have revealed, Locke's own attempts to overcome the distance between subject and object often anticipated romantic solutions.[23] In short, the romantics were very far from rejecting the whole of Locke's philosophy, despite their own pronouncements on the subject. But significant differences between romanticism and empiricism do exist, and my short account of romanticism here will try to indicate how the work of Wordsworth and Coleridge afforded the Victorians certain ways, not found in eighteenth-century thought, to understand the relation of mind to world and words to reality. I will begin with romantic theories of language and move on to their theories of knowledge.

Romantic theories of language are committed to closing the gap between the word and the thing it names.[24] Poetry, for Wordsworth, should be written in "the real language of nature,"[25] as opposed to an artificial and cultivated "diction . . . either peculiar to . . . [the] individual Poet or belonging simply to Poets in general" (P, 142). The poet's subject, if noble, can be expected to provide "naturally" the language in which it should be expressed. "If the Poet's

---

Sign, and Play in the Discourse of the Human Sciences," in *Writing and Difference,* trans. Alan Bass (Chicago: University of Chicago Press, 1978), pp. 278–94. Gerald Bruns, *Modern Poetry and the Idea of Language* (New Haven: Yale University Press, 1974), has discussed at length the "hermetic" tradition in modern literature, which he describes as attempting to make the "literary work . . . a self-contained linguistic structure (the ideal or absolute form of which would be Flaubert's imaginary 'book about nothing,' a book dependent on nothing external)" (1). Derrida's work is clearly an instance of the hermetic view.

22. Coleridge, in fact, was one of the first writers to stress the similarities between Descartes and Locke, going so far as to claim that everything Locke had to say could be found already in Descartes. See *The Collected Letters of Samuel Taylor Coleridge,* ed. Earl Leslie Griggs (Oxford: Clarendon Press, 1956), 2 vols., pp. 677–703. Further references to the *Letters* will be identified by the abbreviation CL, with page numbers given parenthetically in the text.

23. Tuveson's work is the most extended study of the romantics' debt to Locke; see also "Wordsworth, Language, and Romanticism" in Aarsleff, *From Locke to Saussure,* pp. 372–81.

24. On Wordsworth's and Coleridge's notions of poetic language, see Bruns, *Modern Poetry and the Idea of Language,* pp. 42–59; M. H. Abrams, *The Mirror and the Lamp* (New York: Oxford University Press, 1953), pp. 290–97; and A. C. Goodson, "Coleridge on Language: A Poetic Paradigm," *Philological Quarterly* 62 (1983): 45–68.

25. "Preface to *Lyrical Ballads,*" in *The Prose Works of William Wordsworth,* ed. W. J. B. Owen and J. W. Smyser (Oxford: Clarendon Press, 1974), 1:142. Subsequent references to the "Preface" are from this edition, with page numbers given parenthetically in the text and the source identified as P.

subject be judiciously chosen, it will naturally, and upon fit occasion, lead him to passions the language of which, if selected truly and judiciously, must necessarily be dignified and variegated, and alive with metaphors and figures. I forbear to speak of an incongruity which would shock the intelligent Reader, should the Poet interweave any foreign splendour of his own with that which the passion naturally suggests: it is sufficient to say that such addition is unnecessary" (P, 137). The well-chosen subject is completely adequate; it "naturally suggests" the appropriate response ("passion") and the proper expression of that response. The distinction between a natural language and the more artificial one of sophisticated urban man justifies Wordsworth's preference for "humble and rustic life" (P, 125). Against the "arbitrary and capricious habits of expression" found in the city, Wordsworth poses the "more permanent, and . . . far more philosophical language" characteristic of "rural life" (P, 125). Wordsworth aspires to make this "plain and more emphatic language" the basis of his own style, and locates the origins of language in the closer union with nature enjoyed by men before "the increasing accumulation of men in cities" (P, 129) began "to blunt the discriminating powers of the mind . . . [and] reduce it to a state of almost savage torpor" (P, 129).

Coleridge objects strenuously to Wordsworth's claims for the language used by rustics, but not, it is important to note, because he objects to the ideal Wordsworth presents. Coleridge merely thinks it is unlikely that the speech of uneducated country folk will provide examples of the "best part of language." The rustic is far too likely to concentrate on "insulated facts" whereas it is the "*connections* of things" that we really need to uncover (BL, 17).[26] But this shift in emphasis from perceivable objects to invisible relationships only serves to make the choice of the proper word all the more important. Poetic language is differentiated sharply from "words used as the *arbitrary marks* of thought, [the] smooth market-coin of intercourse with the image and superscription worn out by currency" (BL, 22). The famous distinction between allegory and symbol has its basis in denigrating allegory's artificial union of representative with idea in favor of the symbol's necessary conjunction.[27]

> An Allegory is but a translation of abstract notions into a picture-language which is itself nothing but an abstraction from objects of the senses; the principal being more worthless even than its phantom proxy, both alike unsubstantial, and the former shapeless to boot. On the other hand a Symbol . . . is characterized by a translucence of the Special in the Individual or the General in the Especial or

26. *Biographia Literaria*, ed. James Engell and W. Jackson Bate, in *The Collected Works of Samuel Taylor Coleridge* (Princeton: Princeton University Press, 1983), vol. 7. Passages from the *Biographia Literaria*, which will be abbreviated BL, are taken from this edition with chapter numbers given parenthetically in the text.

27. See Jean-Pierre Mileur, *Vision & Revision: Coleridge's Art of Immanence* (Berkeley: University of California Press, 1982), pp. 29–32, for an excellent discussion of the distinction between symbol and allegory in Coleridge.

of the Universal in the General. Above all by the translucence of the Eternal
through and in the Temporal. It always partakes of the Reality which it renders
intelligible; and while it enunciates the whole, abides itself as a living part in
that Unity, of which it is the representative.[28]

The symbol is no arbitrary representative, but something that manifests
the whole because it partakes of that whole. The absent eternal is represented
by the present symbol because the symbol's being rests on its connection to
that which it represents. The symbol, then, becomes our best access to that
"Reality . . . it renders intelligible." Symbolic language does not, like the
words described by Locke, divorce itself from reality and lead its users away
from adequate knowledge. Rather, language becomes a crucial source of
knowledge, a place where the real manifests itself. In Jean-Pierre Mileur's
words, "Coleridge's symbol is far less a specific kind of figure than an epistemological category coming into being—a category of mediation."[29] Language becomes the means by which a marriage of mind and world is
achieved.[30]

The issue of how successfully Wordsworth and Coleridge enacted their
theories in practice need not detain us here. In Coleridge's case, especially, the
poetry would seem to indicate that his usual experience was not the discovery
of translucent symbols but frustrating encounters with opaque words and an
unrevealing natural world. We could easily conclude that the theory of the
symbol expresses a desire impossible to satisfy, particularly because it is based
on a mistaken attempt to evade the "difference" between the sign and what
it stands for.[31] I do not find such an approach very fruitful. I will be considering in detail the gaps between theory and practice in Victorian texts, and my
attempt will be to show what desires generate the theories and how the
difficulties of practice feed back into the tenets of theory. The Victorians, like
the romantics, were well aware that the linguistic sign was conventional and
arbitrary, but they also experienced the force words carried, a force which
seemed inexplicable without appealing to theories of association, primitive
power, or cultural history. While perhaps unable to achieve everything they

28. "The Statesman's Manual," in *The Collected Works of Samuel Taylor Coleridge,* 6:30.
Passages from "The Statesman's Manual," abbreviated SM, are taken from this edition and are
cited parenthetically in the text.
29. Mileur, *Vision and Revision,* p. 21.
30. M. H. Abrams, *Natural Supernaturalism* (New York: W. W. Norton, 1971), pp.
21–37, describes the recurrent use of marriage imagery by the romantics as they tried to join
mind to nature and the temporal to the eternal.
31. The most influential "deconstruction" of romantic theories of the symbol has been
Paul de Man's "The Rhetoric of Temporality," in *Interpretation: Theory and Practice,* ed. Charles
S. Singleton (Baltimore: Johns Hopkins University Press, 1969), pp. 173–209. In *Blindness and
Insight* (New York: Oxford University Press, 1971), de Man calls "the recurrent confusion of
sign and substance" the "archetypal error" (136). On the relation of de Man's view of language
to Coleridge's, see Mileur, *Vision and Revision,* pp. 21–24 and 87.

desired, both the romantics and the Victorians, I would argue, did manage to discover, through the very act of writing, various ways to ensure that the word functioned as a force that established the writer's bond to his audience and to his world. To assert that such claims for success (either complete or partial) were illusory, as "deconstructionists" often do, is to underestimate the extent to which the romantics and Victorians were aware of the issues that dominate modern perspectives on epistemological and linguistic questions, and to over-emphasize the extent to which mediation (through language) must be inherently frustrating.[32]

Given the modern fascination with failure and impossible desires, it is no surprise that Coleridge seems more interesting than Wordsworth to us now, while the opposite was true of the Victorians.[33] The various romantic theories of poetic language, like the pure languages proposed by positivism, function as an ideal and a standard, not as a description of everyday talk. Coleridge's experience—in "The Nightingale" for example—may be that men continually misname things and are thus led to misunderstand them, but his notion of appropriate language provides him with the basis for identifying the act of misnaming as an error. For the Victorians, the romantic ideal functioned as a living pressure in spite of any shortcomings in romantic practice. Furthermore, the Victorians—as the assessments of Wordsworth by Carlyle, Arnold, and Pater reveal—were much more willing than modern critics to describe a poet's career in terms of what the poet himself understood as his accomplishments. The Victorians assumed, in a way that is now impossible, that the romantics did achieve that union between mind and reality in the symbol that romantic theorizing celebrated. When the Victorians ran into difficulties during the attempt to reenact romantic solutions (as I describe in my discussions

32. My approach is much closer to a critic like George Levine's, whose first chapter in *The Realistic Imagination* (Chicago: University of Chicago Press, 1981) admirably describes the extent to which the Victorians were concerned with the same problems raised in the current debates within literary theory, while also recognizing the ways in which the Victorians approached those problems rather differently than we do.

33. For examples of the Victorian willingness to accept Wordsworth's claims for his own poetry, see Thomas Carlyle, "Wordsworth's Poetical Works," in *Selected Prose and Poetry of the Romantic Period,* ed. George R. Creeger and Joseph W. Reed, Jr. (New York: Holt, Rinehart, and Winston, 1964), pp. 186–92; Matthew Arnold, "Wordsworth," in *The Complete Prose Works of Matthew Arnold,* ed. R. H. Super (Ann Arbor: University of Michigan Press, 1973), 9:36–55; and Walter Pater, "Wordsworth" and "Coleridge," in *Appreciations* (London: Macmillan, 1897), pp. 37–63 and 64–106. Pater's comparison of Wordsworth to Coleridge, and his greater admiration for the former, can be taken as fairly representative of the Victorian understanding of the two writers. Speaking of the *Lyrical Ballads,* Pater writes: "What Wordsworth then wrote already vibrates with that blithe impulse which carried him to final happiness and self-possession. In Coleridge we feel already that faintness and obscure dejection which clung like some contagious damp to all his work. Wordsworth was to be distinguished by a joyful and penetrative conviction of the existence of certain latent affinities between nature and the human mind, which reciprocally gild the mind and nature with a kind of 'heavenly alchemy' " (85).

of Rossetti, Carlyle, and Ruskin), they invariably ascribed their problems to their own shortcomings and not to any deficiency in romantic thought.

Coleridge's description of a happy moment when words and things did coalesce for him can serve to move us from romantic theories of language to romantic theories of knowledge. Significantly, Coleridge describes this experience in the third person and in the context of explaining how he lost the insight it yielded him so that he can now only offer the unfinished poem "Kubla Khan." In Coleridge's moment of vision "all the images rose up before him as things, with a parallel production of the correspondent expressions, without any sensation or consciousness of effort."[34] The elements here are similar to those present in Wordsworth's Preface, and are reminiscent of Locke's notion of "double conformity." In Wordsworth, nature generates the appropriate passions that, in turn, must be expressed in fitting words. Coleridge is closer to Locke, since he speaks of "images," not "passion." But the premise is the same for all three writers. "Passion" in Wordsworth, "image" in Coleridge, and "idea" in Locke, all convey the notion that mind's response to reality is not identical to reality itself, and therefore the issue of the "correspondence" between the mental state and reality is raised. For Coleridge, the mystical vision allows "images" to become "*as* things," with the "as" indicating that the two are normally distinct. For this reason, I think the usual designation of Coleridge as a monist is a mistake.[35] The Coleridgean imagination "struggles to . . . unify" (BL, 13) because ordinary experience is of distance and difference. Our ideas (to use Locke's word in a statement he would endorse) are distinct entities from things. In Coleridge's words, "All *our* thoughts are in the language of the old Logicians *inadequate:* i.e. no *Thought,* which I have, of any *thing* comprizes the whole of that Thing. I have a distinct thought of a Rose-Tree; but what countless properties and goings-on of that plant are there, not included in my *Thought* of it" (CL, 1195). When Wordsworth makes "the appropriate business of poetry . . . to treat of things not as they *are,* but as they *appear;* not as they exist in themselves, but as they *seem* to exist to the *senses,* and to the *passions,*"[36] he accepts the same firm distinction between the mind's image of a thing and the thing itself.

The romantic theory of knowledge differentiates itself from Locke's in the ways it strives to overcome this gap between mind and world. We have seen that Locke, at times, succumbs to the temptation to accept sensory evidence as absolutely reliable and as a source of immediate knowledge. The

34. "Kubla Khan," in *The Complete Poetical Works of Samuel Taylor Coleridge,* ed. E. H. Coleridge (Oxford: Clarendon Press, 1975), 1:296.
35. See Abrams, *Natural Supernaturalism,* pp. 267–68, for a good description of Coleridge's position. Abrams identifies Coleridge as a "compulsive monist," but recognizes that "dualism" is the primary experience of things in nature in Coleridge's view (267).
36. "Essay, Supplementary to the Preface," in *The Prose Works of William Wordsworth,* 3:63.

adequacy of our "ideas" is guaranteed by our passivity in receiving the impressions of outward nature. "In this part, the *Understanding* is merely *passive;* and whether or no, it will have these Beginnings, and as it were materials of Knowledge, is not in its own Power. For the Objects of our Senses, do, many of them, obtrude their particular *Ideas* upon our minds, whether we will or no" (ECHU, 2.1.25). If the mind performs no operation on the incoming data, we can at least be sure that all men perceive the same ideas. Locke uses the traditional metaphor of the mirror to assert that the mind does not "alter" the impressions it receives from without. "These *simple Ideas,* when offered to the mind, *the Understanding* can no more refuse to have, nor alter, when they are imprinted, nor blot them out, and make new ones in it self, than a mirror can refuse, alter, or obliterate the Images or *Ideas,* which, the Objects set before it, do therein produce" (ECHU, 2.1.25). For Locke, our vision of objects in the world serves as the primary model of all knowledge.[37] Just as the mind experiences objects, it experiences its own processes in reflection, and these two experiences are the source of all knowledge.

The romantics understood themselves as rejecting completely the empiricist effort to connect mind to world through a passive reception of impressions. Coleridge inveighs against both parts of the Lockean scheme: passivity and the primacy of sight. "Newton was a mere materialist—*Mind* in his system is always passive—a lazy Looker-on on an external World. . . . There is ground for suspicion that any system built on the passiveness of the mind must be false, as a system" (CL, 709). Coleridge is determined to overthrow a materialism that "reduce[s] all things to impressions, ideas and sensations" (BL, 12). M. H. Abrams describes Coleridge's objection to the empiricists' dependence on sight: "Coleridge . . . came to identify that condition in which the mind is a slave and the physical eye its master—the inner state that he called the 'despotism of the eye,' or 'the despotism of outward impressions,' or the 'Slavery of the Mind to the Eye and [to] the visual Imagination, or Fancy'—as the index and prime cause of the intellectual, moral, political, and aesthetic errors of post-Lockean sensationalist philosophy."[38]

Against empiricist passivity and vision, the romantics posed the mind's activity and powers of insight. The issue here, as it will be in so many Victorian texts, is what deserves the title of "reality": perceivable appearances or some substratum beyond the realm of the senses. The romantics objected that empiricism reduced the world to the motions of matter and insisted that such a reduction did not account for the most significant truths of existence. Those nonmaterial truths were invisible, and so the romantics had to reject any theory of knowledge that based knowledge on perception. Where Locke used the notion of a harmony between mind and world to ensure that perception

37. See Tuveson, *The Imagination as a Means of Grace,* p. 21.
38. Abrams, *Natural Supernaturalism,* p. 366.

conformed with the reality of things, the romantics asserted that mind's harmony with the world demonstrated that the material was everywhere infused with the nonmaterial.[39] The perceiving mind is active because it must bring to (add to) a material world the apprehension of how appearances are connected to the true reality of (to use Platonic language) eternal forms. This active part of the mind is called the imagination, and is distinguished (on the basis of a passage from *Paradise Lost)* by both Wordsworth and Coleridge from the Lockean mind's ability to restructure the images received from the senses, an ability now called "fancy."[40] Romantic Platonism makes reality more difficult to apprehend, and sets the stage for the battle over the proper referent of the word *reality* during the Victorian period.[41]

Coleridge's theories of the symbol and of the imagination offer the fullest theory of knowledge developed by the English romantics. We should note that Coleridge uses the word *symbol* in a way that does not distinguish between a material thing of this world and an image found in a poem. This collapsing of two meanings is based on the traditional metaphor of "the great book of . . . Nature" in which "gentle and pious minds read . . . [and] find therein correspondences and symbols of the spiritual world" (SM, 70). Words and material things become equivalent in that both serve as symbols of something beyond themselves which is the basis of their meaning. So that when Coleridge talks of "elevating . . . words into Things,"[42] he wants words, like natural things, to function as representatives of the divine. And since the symbol's meaning is not apparent from the material physical properties it portrays to the senses, the mind must be given the power called imagination to make interpretation possible. The mind, then, is in closer touch with the underlying reality of the universe than is matter, and the mind's task is to reconnect matter to its spiritual base by comprehending matter's relationship to the originating spirit. This reincorporation of matter into spirit constitutes Coleridge's solution to dualism. "Body and spirit are therefore no longer absolutely heterogeneous, but *may* without any *absurdity* be supposed to be different modes, or degrees in perfection, of a common substratum" (BL, 13).

But such monism is not easy to maintain. Coleridge must still explain the problem of the gap between appearances and reality, or, to revert to the terms of the letter quoted above, the gap between the "thought . . . I have

39. See BL, 8, and the Second Preface, 488–89.

40. Coleridge's distinction between imagination and fancy is found in BL, chaps. 12 and 13; Wordsworth's in the "Preface of 1815," in *The Prose Works of William Wordsworth,* 3:26–39.

41. On romantic Platonism, see Abrams, *Natural Supernaturalism,* pp. 146–54. Such Platonism, with its appeal to hidden principles that govern the world of appearances, is clearly aligned with those philosophies of "Life and the Will" that Foucault identifies as typical of nineteenth-century thought and indicative of the era's conviction that reality was hidden from perception.

42. *The Collected Works of Samuel Taylor Coleridge,* 5:53.

of any *thing*" and the thing itself. Why are our thoughts "inadequate"? Why must we deal in symbols and not in things themselves? Coleridge offers a traditional answer: "The Thoughts of God, in the strict nomenclature of Plato, are all Ideas, archetypal, and anterior to all but himself alone: therefore consummately *adequate:* and therefore according to our common habits of conception and expression, incomparably more *real* than all things besides, & which do all depend on and proceed from them in some sort perhaps as our Thoughts from those Things" (CL, 1195). Even if the dualist distinction between mind and matter has been overcome, this account establishes an absolute distinction between the eternal mind of God and the minds of men in time. The crucial point for my purposes is that Coleridge's system never allows him to dispense with representation, with its reliance on symbols that mediate between mind and that which is to be known. Redefining the object of knowledge, even redefining it as of essentially the same substance as the human mind, does not free Coleridge from a representationalism as irksome and logically inescapable as Locke's.[43]

As we would expect, the romantics, like Locke, are not rigorously faithful to the acceptance of the necessity of indirection. Wordsworth claims for the poet "a certain quantity of immediate knowledge" (P, 140), while Coleridge distinguishes between Understanding and Reason in order to restore the possibility of direct insight into truth. David Keppel-Jones has described the Coleridgean distinction in terms relevant to my discussion here: "Reason, unlike the Understanding which deals with truths derived from the senses, is concerned with truths of a higher kind, that can be defined as truths above sense, and are named *ideas.* . . . In approaching these truths, Reason (unlike the Understanding, which remains in contact with the concrete worlds through the medium of the senses) needs no intermediate organ."[44] The Understanding is "discursive" whereas Reason is "intuitive" (BL, 10), and, at his most exuberant, Coleridge can insist that "intuition," with its immediate insight into the nature of things, provides the only firm basis of knowledge. "On the *Immediate,* which dwells in every man, and on the original intuition, or absolute affirmation of it, (which is likewise in every man, but does not in every man rise into consciousness) all the *certainty* of our knowledge depends" (BL, 12). Reason is "not the effect of any Experience, but the condition of all Experience, & that indeed without which Experience itself would be inconceivable. . . . Reason is therefore most eminently the Revelation of an immortal soul" (CL, 1198). "All Truth," Coleridge writes, "is a species of Revelation" (CL, 709).

This appeal to revelation is required to explain how men know the

43. See Mileur, *Vision and Revision,* pp. 15–21.
44. Quoted from *Imagination in Coleridge,* ed. John Spencer Hill (Totowa, N.J.: Rowman and Littlefield, 1978), p. 152.

principles by which material things are to be interpreted, but revelation also serves romantic thought as an explanation for intuitive knowledge of a less theoretical sort. Coleridge explicitly defines "intuition" as "designating the *immediateness* of any act or object of knowledge" (BL, 10),[45] and the condition for such immediacy would be the collapse of all material objects into the spiritual truths they represent. "The highest perfection of natural philosophy would consist in the perfect spiritualization of all the laws of nature into laws of intuition and intellect. The phenomena (the material) must wholly disappear, and the laws alone (the formal) must remain" (BL, 12). We find here what M. H. Abrams and others have called the "apocalyptic" strain in romantic thought: the desire for a dramatic revelation of the truth that stands behind this world of appearances.[46] We might add that the violence in such apocalyptic fantasies often indicates an unacknowledged fear that no such truth exists and that the materialists will go unpunished for claiming the world apparent to the senses is the whole of reality.

However he chose to define reality, the Victorian writer lived in a world in which the real was not immediately available to him.[47] The Victorian's hold on reality was threatened on two fronts. Empiricists and scientists seemed determined to remove nature from the human, but culture was slipping from grasp as well. Victorian literature carries on the romantic protest against the banishment of mind from a mechanistic universe. The materialism of enlightenment science (in both its crudest forms and in the sophisticated skepticism of Hume) divorces mind from nature. Carlyle's identification of "this age of ours" as "the Mechanical Age"[48] initiates his protest against the use of the name *reality* only to designate the tangible and against the belief that nature functions according to its own laws without taking human knowledge or desires into account.

The Victorians have traditionally been distinguished from their romantic predecessors on the basis of their attitude toward nature. The romantics found

45. Bruns describes Coleridge's model of poetic knowledge as "an act or moment of 'intuitive knowledge,' in which 'reality' is encountered *mediately,* but with all the force and energy of an 'immediate presence' " (55). The poetic word "is to mediate between mind and world, not simply to correlate one to the other but to fabricate an *immediate* relationship between the two" (55). Coleridge maintains the category of "intuition" to explain the possibility of such an extraordinary relationship between knower and known.

46. Abrams, *Natural Supernaturalism,* pp. 37–46.

47. W. David Shaw's recent work on the epistemological bases of Victorian poetry approaches the subject from a perspective very similar to mine and has helped shape the view of Victorian literature presented in this book. See "Victorian Poetry and Repression: The Use and Abuse of Masks," *ELH* 46 (1979): 468–94; "The Optical Metaphor: Victorian Poetics and the Theory of Knowledge," *Victorian Studies* 23 (1979–1980): 293–324; and "Browning and Pre-Raphaelite Medievalism: Educated versus Innocent Seeing," *Browning Institute Studies* 8 (1980): 57–72.

48. "Signs of the Times," in *The Works of Thomas Carlyle* (New York: Charles Scribner's Sons, n.d.), Centenary Edition, 27:59.

in nature those symbols that granted access to spiritual principles that could be used to combat the age's materialism. But the Victorians ceded nature to the scientists and worked to find an alternative in culture.[49] While limited, this distinction seems valid to me. Mill's essay on "Nature" presents as an "undeniable fact, that the order of nature, in so far as unmodified by man, is such as no being, whose attributes are justice and benevolence, would have made, with the intention that his rational creatures should follow it as an example."[50] From this Mill draws the only conclusion that still makes religion possible: "If Nature and Man are both the works of a Being of perfect goodness, that Being intended Nature as a scheme to be amended, not imitated, by Man" (N, 391). Mill has no doubts about the superiority of man's "artificial works" (N, 381) to a nature Tennyson described as "red in tooth and claw."[51] Mill's unsentimental approach to nature is not shared by all the writers of the period, but the Victorians undoubtedly found it difficult to continue the romantics' faith in nature's goodness.[52] Of the writers I discuss in this book, Rossetti and Ruskin are most committed to finding in nature a transcendent principle that answers the needs of imagination. I will consider Rossetti's failure to find any spiritual message in the landscapes bequeathed by romanticism, and Ruskin's movement from praising nature in his early work to envisioning the ideal society in his later work.

This standard differentiation of the Victorians from the romantics, however, does not take into account the extent to which the reality of culture is also a problem for writers in the nineteenth century. Carlyle is the first Victorian because he is interested in cultural forms and reform, rather than natural inspiration, and because he raises the problem of culture as it will appear throughout the period—in the work of, among others, Ruskin, George Eliot, Browning, and Arnold. The Victorian writers I discuss want culture to rest upon a transcendent basis similar to the eternal principle the romantics found in nature. Carlyle is always vague about the exact nature of that principle, but Ruskin will call it "life" in *Unto This Last*, Arnold "the best that has been thought" in *Culture and Anarchy*, and George Eliot will identify it as "humanist sympathy." But culture proves no safe haven from the battle with the materialists. The utilitarians and the political economists stand for a

49. Raymond Williams, *Culture and Society, 1780–1950* (London: Chatto & Windus, 1958), remains the fullest treatment of the Victorian attempt to elevate "culture" into a value that would be recognized by all.

50. "Nature," in *Collected Works of John Stuart Mill*, 10:383. Subsequent references are given parenthetically in the text, with this essay abbreviated N.

51. "In Memoriam," sec. 56, line 15, in *The Poems of Tennyson*, ed. Christopher Ricks (London: Longmans, Green & Co., 1969).

52. The introduction to *Nature and the Victorian Imagination*, ed. U. C. Knoepflmacher and G. B. Tennyson (Berkeley: University of California Press, 1977), pp. xvii–xxiii, offers a good overview of the bases of the view that the Victorians could not continue the romantics' faith in nature.

view of culture that denies the more traditional humanist values associated with the major writers, and the apparent triumph of the materialist side in the England of the 1830s and 1840s calls forth the polemics of Carlyle. The relevance of mind and imagination to a culture that claims to pay heed only to "facts" (as Dickens portrays the materialists in *Hard Times)* must be proved.

This attempt to introduce principles of value into culture is further complicated by the new sensitivity to cultural change. Much has been written about the "discovery of time" in the nineteenth century.[53] Carlyle and Ruskin as historians, and George Eliot as a historical novelist, continually demonstrate that the human order of any given historical period is quite different from that of another era. To a writer searching for a reality that proves itself real by being true for all minds at all times, the new historical consciousness detracts from the reality of culture. The forms men create only reveal specific impulses of specific moments and not some truth beyond human desires and imaginings. The Victorians, of course, do not all respond in the same way to the transience of cultures, but all the writers I discuss view culture's subjection to the vagaries of history as a threat to its reality. For the Victorian writer, then, the gaps between the finite mind and eternal truths, between the changes men experience in history and an unchanging principle that is valid for all men, and between a desiring, active imagination and a mechanistic universe all threatened the ability of men to partake in reality. The Victorians both sought out mediators to overcome these gaps and resented mediation as a sign of their distance from what they desired.

Language serves as the primary means of mediation to which the writers I discuss appeal. The word is obviously a human product, yet it serves to designate objects in the world, and thus can be seen as standing between mind and world, as the site of their encounter. The Victorians, however, are nowhere more fully the sons of Locke than in their mistrusting language's ability to function smoothly. The fact of the word's difference from the thing suggests a new gap—that between language and reality—that might serve to increase mind's distance from the world instead of lessening it. Language appears as an essentially human and cultural product, the result of the active processes of thought and imagination. Far from passively reflecting a reality that exists independently of the speaker, language allows men to spin out visions generated from within, thus emphasizing human isolation from the real. The word serves to displace and even replace the thing, putting a human artifact (the representative) where the real, nonhuman thing (the represented) was. Rather than granting access to a reality that is already seen as hard to grasp, language

53. See Stephen Toulmin and June Goodfield, *The Discovery of Time* (New York: Harper & Row, 1965); Jerome H. Buckley, *The Triumph of Time* (Cambridge: Harvard University Press, 1966); and Peter Allan Dale, *The Victorian Critic and the Idea of History* (Cambridge: Harvard University Press, 1977).

might only increase the inability to break through human constructions to an apprehension of the real. Representation, for the Victorians as for Locke, offers a way to solve some of the problems raised by considering how mind knows reality, but it also introduces other problems of its own.

From the empiricist tradition, the Victorians get their passivity in the face of the real, their desire for a public knowledge based on shared perceptions of things to be seen by all, and their abiding suspicion of language. Except for Yeats (who is included by way of contrast), all the writers I discuss exhibit a distrust of language very similar to Locke's. Words have a tendency to drift away from a strict correspondence to the real. Carried away by fancy, by figurative language, or by the internal logic of his linguistic constructions, a man can lose sight of reality, can forget that his words do not accurately reflect the true state of affairs. Like Locke, the Victorian writers often call language to account, working to ensure its strict responsibility to the referent. A deep uneasiness with fiction (language with no existing referent) pervades the period.

The word's difference from the thing means that all approaches to reality through language are mediated. Victorian realism must come to terms with and explain the necessity of indirection. The Victorians follow both Locke and the romantics in trying to evade, or at least minimize, the reliance on mediation. Time and again these writers present images (usually based on "sight" or "insight") of direct perception that they feel are more desirable than representation (either by natural symbols or by words) as ways to apprehend the real. I have grouped these images of direct perception within the category of "revelation," and, as the title of this book indicates, my readings of the texts discussed focus on the writers' alternating between "representation" (indirection) and "revelation" (direct apprehension) as ways to discover the real. How does reality appear to the human knower: through mediate symbols or by direct revelation? And how can the writer, given his reliance on language, make the reality he perceives appear to his readers?

Even though all the Victorians at one time or another protest against the necessity of indirection, they all also manage (with the exception, perhaps, of Rossetti) to make a virtue of necessity. The readings I offer reveal a pattern quite familiar to students of English literature, that of the happy fall. A major theme of this study is the benefits the Victorians discover in an indirection they usually adopt only reluctantly. In fact, the Victorians, more than either the empiricists or the romantics, are inclined to forgo revelation altogether in favor of representation—a tendency, I think, attributable to the Victorian interest in cultural solutions. Where Locke and the romantics were more likely to envision the knower as an isolated individual looking at a natural object (despite thinking that that knower would see very different things), the Victorians were more apt to locate the knower in a community and to think of him as perceiving culturally produced objects. Culture is preeminently the field of mediation, and the pressure of cultural mediations on the individual's understanding of himself and the world is for Carlyle, Arnold, George Eliot, Dickens, and Browning a way to ensure harmonious communities. Romanticism seemed dangerous to the Victorians insofar as the romantics disavowed allegiance to communal standards of what is real and abandoned the passive, recording imagination described by Locke. Romanticism appeared to offer an image of subjectivism gone wild, the mind constructing a private world divorced from all ties to reality.[54]

But romanticism is a positive force in Victorian literature insofar as it offers methods for making indirection a happy necessity. When the "true" reality is a spiritual realm or emotional verities not apparent to the senses, a dependence on indirection is inevitable. The Victorian writers, even George Eliot, adopt the romantic insistence that reality is more than material facts. The romantics had emphasized the vatic powers of the poet and shown how the words of poetry could reveal a hidden, nonempirical reality. Adopting a similar goal, Victorian writers make use of certain fundamental romantic strategies.

Merging empiricist and romantic attitudes, the Victorian writers attempt to reveal reality through language. Their words call forth a reality in order to make it manifest. The individual knower must acknowledge the prior existence of that reality and its transcendence of all personal desires or constructs. To use a term from Edward Said that I will use throughout this study, reality in Victorian literature "molests" the more limited worlds created by the self.[55] The arrival on the stage of that molesting reality is often violent, always dramatic. From Carlyle to Yeats we find an apocalyptic tendency (often associated with romantic irony) in Victorian literature, a hope that the hidden thing will appear and that its appearance will overwhelm all epistemological doubts and all the temporary representatives that served in its absence. Language is placed at the service of the real; when the real itself is made apparent, language will dissolve.

But much more common than the apocalyptic vision of works like

54. In his essay "Coleridge," Mill characterizes the dispute between empiricism and romanticism as between a reliance on "sensation, and the mind's consciousness of its own acts, [as] the sole materials of our knowledge" and the belief in the power of "direct intuition, to perceive things, and recognise truths, not cognizable by our senses" (125–26). Mill goes on to state quite fully the objection that romantic theories would allow "a strong enough party . . . [to] set up the immediate perceptions of *their* reason, that is to say, any reigning prejudice, as a truth independent of experience; a truth not only requiring no proof, but to be believed in opposition to all that appears proof to the mere understanding" (127). As with his views on nature, Mill represents one extreme of Victorian thought, but his misgivings about romantic subjectivism are shared by writers more willing to be sympathetic to romantic attitudes.

55. See *Beginnings: Intention and Method* (New York: Basic Books, 1975), chap. 4. I discuss Said's use of the term *molestation* more fully in chap. 2.

"Childe Roland to the Dark Tower Came" is the Victorian recognition of and frustration with reality's reticence. Their obsessive need to identify the real indicates their inability to locate it with certainty. They live their daily lives with representatives, with words, not with the thing itself. We find here their habitual impatience with indirection and their continual attempts to break through to a more direct apprehension of the real. But the Victorians also discover the benefits of indirection, of this strategy imposed on them by the limitations of their situation. The need for indirection places these writers on the defensive, since they feel that pointing out reality should be easy. (After all, reality should not be that hard to find.) But their full experience of the torturous byways of indirection guarantees their status as artists, whether their medium is nonfictional prose, the novel, or poetry.

My individual studies of the seven writers considered in this book discuss how each writer defines reality and works to ensure mind's and language's link to that reality. Although I explicate certain "doctrines" that can be found in these writers—for example, Carlyle's notion of "symbol" or Ruskin's strictures on appropriate style—I usually take the doctrines for granted and work to show why the author adopts them, how consistently he is able to maintain them, and the ways in which they shape his text(s). My aim is not to reconstruct the writer's thought, but to examine its aesthetic implications and how it constitutes specific literary works. My premise is that the tensions, impossibilities, and contradictions within the writer's ideas are what make their artistic expression necessary. In other words, I read the author's doctrines as an indication of his desires, and see those desires as determining the shape of his art. By studying the Victorian search for reality and the Victorian mistrust of literary form and literary language, I hope to show what kind of art results when writers feel a deep uneasiness with the adequacy of their chosen medium.

My debt to the work of the so-called "post-structuralists," particularly that of Jacques Derrida and Michel Foucault, is obvious throughout this study. The antimonies of sight and language, presence and absence, direction and indirection, word and thing that govern many of my interpretations are drawn from the work of Derrida, while the attempt to present an era as sharing a set of common concerns and assumptions that shape individual texts finds its inspiration in Foucault's notions of "episteme" and "archaeology."[56] But my readers will also quickly discover that my discussions set themselves against much of the literary criticism carried on in Derrida's name. "Deconstruction," especially as practiced in this country, has most often followed one of two

---

56. *Of Grammatology*, trans. Gayatri Chakravorty Spivak (Baltimore: Johns Hopkins University Press, 1976), is the work by Derrida that most completely addresses the issues I pursue in this study, although I will find occasion to refer to some of his essays as well. Foucault's *The Order of Things*, as I have already stated, offers a general interpretation of the nineteenth century that has greatly influenced my work.

paths: either the deconstructed text is shown to display a set of contradictory and ultimately self-negating goals, or the studied author is shown (in a way similar to Freud's habitual claim that "the poets" anticipated the discoveries of psychoanalysis) to have already self-consciously deconstructed his or her own work.[57] In either case, the process of deconstruction indicates how the text's ostensible purposes are undermined.

In reference to the particular topic of this book, Derrida's work, if we stress its nihilistic character, can be read as asserting that mediation is both inevitable and intolerable. What the deconstructionist does is point out again and again how authors have tried to achieve an immediacy that is simply not possible, while admitting that such attempts will continue to be made because the desire for immediacy will never be eradicated. (The influence of Nietzsche on this version of deconstruction is obvious.) My way of approaching the issue will, I hope, be seen as significantly different. First, as I have already suggested, I do not think the writers I discuss were unaware of the inevitability of mediation, no matter how strongly they would have preferred immediate knowledge. Secondly, I argue that these writers do not find mediation or the difference between the word and the thing to be an unmitigated disaster, against which they must endlessly and ineffectually rage. Rather, they struggle to understand the implications of indirection's necessity and to construct within the world of difference an order that, as completely as possible, satisfies desire. If Derrida, Foucault, and their followers have provided the major topics of this study, the spirit, even more than the content, of Paul Ricoeur's work might be called its guiding genius. Ricoeur's determination to ground meaning in the context of the human "project" is founded on the rejection of the kind of formalism that loses the ability to understand why men wrote or did something in a particular way at a particular time.[58]

Each of the chapters that follow, with the exception of the final chapter on Yeats, can be read separately as a discussion of its individual subject. However, read as a whole this book demonstrates the prevalence of certain attitudes throughout the Victorian period and indicates the full range of issues

57. J. Hillis Miller's essay on *Middlemarch*, "Narrative and History," *ELH* 41 (1974): 455–73, can be taken as a good example of the approach that discovers an author has already deconstructed his own work, while Paul de Man's work, in *Blindness and Insight* and *Allegories of Reading* (New Haven: Yale University Press, 1979), offers examples of interpretations that reveal contradictions of which the author was not aware, although some authors are shown to be more aware than others.

58. My comment here refers to Ricoeur's essay "The Model of the Text: Meaningful Action Considered as a Text," in *Interpretive Social Science: A Reader*, ed. Paul Rabinow and William M. Sullivan (Berkeley: University of California Press, 1979), pp. 73–102. This essay and "Structure, Word, Event" in *The Philosophy of Paul Ricoeur*, ed. Charles E. Regan and David Stewart (Boston: Beacon Press, 1978), pp. 109–19, offer a good introduction to Ricoeur's work and the ways in which he situates himself in opposition to the structuralists and post-structuralists.

involved in trying to place literature at the service of reality. The chapters have been arranged in such a way as to develop the topic. In the final chapter, I use Yeats's work to consider the differences between "modernism" and Victorian literature, while also indicating the continuities between the two.

I begin with Rossetti because his work presents us with the Victorian predicament at its most acute. Deprived of the romantic ability to find meaning in nature, Rossetti tries various desperate remedies to overcome his isolation from any reality beyond his subjective states of mind. In Carlyle, we find the most important Victorian attempt to refashion the romantic heritage, as well as a definition of symbolic language that influences almost all the major writers who follow. Yet Carlyle reveals a fundamental impatience with the very symbolic processes he has gone to such trouble to describe, and his ambivalence about indirection also influences subsequent writers. Ruskin's analysis of the symbol and of mediation, which I consider next, shares certain common features with Carlyle's, although Ruskin has more sympathy for the material world and for empirical perception than Carlyle. Ruskin is much more able than Carlyle to find some advantages in mediation, a feature he shares with the next three writers—Dickens, George Eliot, and Browning—whom I discuss.

Dickens and George Eliot discover, in the process of writing the autobiographical novels *David Copperfield* and *The Mill on the Floss,* the ways imagination influences perception, and elevate this discovery into the constitutive principle of their art. Both novelists are almost completely uninterested in nature, working instead to create a community around imagination, a community that would serve the "real" needs of its members. Browning uses his art to create a community with shared perceptions, but his poetry also emphasizes the radical incompleteness of the human in relation to a more spiritual reality that lies beyond our grasp. Browning's Platonism returns us to the concerns of Coleridge, while his distinctive use of irony provides a strategy of representation more indebted to Carlyle than to the English romantics. Where Dickens and George Eliot are able to endorse a culture that is built on humanly constructed images of the real, Browning is more troubled by such a culture's lack of a legitimizing transcendent principle. Finally, my discussion of Yeats considers how he strives to develop the poetic word as an end in itself, stressing its human content as opposed to placing it at the service of a transcendent reality. However, Yeats cannot turn his back on reality completely since it still provides the pressure, albeit negative, that determines the shape of his art. The transfiguration of Rossetti's despair into Yeats's defiance indicates to what extent Yeats is the last Victorian as well as the first modern.

2

D. G. Rossetti's
Search for the Real

The work of a minor poet, the legend goes, offers us a better insight into the character of an age than the poetry of the transcendent genius. I have my doubts, but do wish to begin here with a study of Dante Gabriel Rossetti's work because I think it presents the basic situation the artists I discuss faced. Rossetti is overwhelmed by the gap between self and world, is frightened (although, at times, attracted) by the possibility that art as a product of mind is totally divorced from reality, and tries desperately to insure that art can serve as a means for adequate knowledge of the real. Trying to work from what can be recognized as basically a romantic notion of the symbol, Rossetti's poetry offers, finally, no fruitful solution for the difficulties it raises. But the extent of his perplexity and the depth of his anxiety do indicate the age's worst fears. All the other writers I discuss manage, as I suggest in my introduction, to develop ways in which art, albeit indirectly, can serve mind's need to apprehend and understand reality. Rossetti's work only suggests the intensity of that need, with the complementary desire for some saving revelation. But Rossetti cannot work out a way for that revelation to occur within art itself and waits in vain for some transcendent force beyond mind and art to carry him outside of himself.

In his *Autobiography,* Yeats claims that Rossetti, "though his dull brother did once persuade him that he was agnostic," was a "devout Christian."[1] This description is wildly inaccurate, yet suggests the central quest in Rossetti's poetry. Rossetti accepts the traditional Christian notion that man confronts a created world that contains within it certain universal meanings. The artist's task is to uncover those meanings and to present them to an audience, a task that involves a certain amount of interpretation of the real. Rossetti's problem is that he cannot get reality to speak to him; its meanings continually elude him, so that his poetry is unable to present the real fashioned in such a way as to make its true meaning evident. His poetry keeps falling away from the real and the universal to present the individual poet's search for meaning or his merely personal experiences and emotions.

This failure to find a poetic subject that satisfies him as being "true" to reality, and significant for a large number of people, might be attributed to Rossetti's lack of faith or even his lack of talent, but his struggles also indicate

1. *The Autobiography of William Butler Yeats* (New York: Macmillan, 1953), pp. 188–89.

the predicament of the Victorian poets, who found that the resources of romantic poetry no longer served their needs. The result is a poetry (which includes some excellent poems) constructed out of a recognition of its own failure, a poetry that continually undermines its own validity in face of the reality it has failed to express. Despite all his efforts, reality keeps its meanings hidden from Rossetti.[2]

In an early sonnet, "St. Luke the Painter" (later incorporated into *The House of Life*[3]), Rossetti outlines a sacramental aesthetic he clearly means to be an ideal, even if his own work seldom achieves the presented goal. Art should "rend the mist / Of devious symbols," finding in "sky-breadth and field-silence" the way to the Creator. Accepting the priestly role of the artist, Rossetti aligns himself with this art that sees its task as making apparent the meaning of experience. That the "symbols" offered to men in the world are "devious" seems a particularly Victorian conviction (Carlyle, Ruskin, and Browning reach a similar conclusion), and points to the possibility of misinterpretation while emphasizing the need for the gifted artist who leads understanding down the right path.

Rossetti's aesthetic here is recognizably romantic. The natural world is symbolic of realities beyond it, and art becomes the privileged space where the meaning behind appearances is revealed. Yet Rossetti also uses this aesthetic pronouncement to distance himself from romantic subjectivism. Lamenting the fact that modern art "has turned in vain / To soulless self-reflections of man's skill," he piously hopes that art will return to that time when it was "God's priest." The reality romantic poetry presented too often seemed personal and insubstantial, even if the romantics, as fervently as Rossetti himself, wanted to make the truth apparent to all. Like so many other Victorians, Rossetti looked back to the middle ages, in his case with a special emphasis on the poetry of Dante, to find a world in which the meaning of sensible appearances seemed readily available.[4] In this light, Victorian medievalism appears as a perspective from which to ratify the romantic conviction that the natural world represents a spiritual reality denied by eighteenth-century materialism, while also allowing the repudiation of the "modern" self-absorption of much romantic poetry.

2. The words *mystery* and *secret* recur throughout Rossetti's poetry, revealing the poet's belief that some truth or meaning exists, but is being kept from him. I won't be discussing the appearances of these words specifically, although they do appear in many of the passages I quote and discuss.

3. All references to the poetry are from *The Works of Dante Gabriel Rossetti*, ed. William Rossetti (London: Ellis, 1911). I have given the line numbers in parentheses for passages taken from "Jenny" but simply the title of the poem for all other passages. Sonnets from *The House of Life* are identified by title and number. "St. Luke the Painter" is the first of three sonnets (74–76) entitled "Old and New Art."

4. Joan Rees, *The Poetry of Dante Gabriel Rossetti* (Cambridge: Cambridge University Press, 1981), has, among recent critics of Rossetti, devoted the most attention to "the influence of Dante and Dante's contemporaries on Rossetti" (127).

This sacramental aesthetic presumes that the thing is never merely its appearance. There is always something, usually more important than surface appearance and often the "key" to the thing's true meaning, that exists beyond or behind or beneath what is present to the senses. Rossetti assumes we live in a world of representatives. While the artist will present the surfaces, he will also always be searching for some significance that escapes mere physical examination. The whole function of art for the Pre-Raphaelites was to present the natural thing so that the spiritual truth it represented was apparent. William Rossetti characterized "the intimate intertexture of a spiritual sense with a material form" as "one of the influences which guided the Pre-Raphaelite movement."[5] Holman Hunt would certainly have agreed with this statement as well as with the aesthetic of "St. Luke the Painter." Hunt thought the advantage of faithfulness to nature in pictorial representation was that such accuracy would make the symbolic import of the thing more apparent.[6] (I will discuss the basis of this Pre-Raphaelite theory in Ruskin's work, as well as the peculiar difficulties it raises, in my fourth chapter.)

Rossetti's allegiance to this theory that the physical thing always carries a symbolic meaning is, I will argue here, the very foundation of his art. But this foundation tortures rather than sustains him. Rossetti's painting testifies to his delight in physical beauty, even when uninformed by any evident spirituality, while his poetry shocked his contemporaries because it was "fleshly."[7] Yet it is a mistake (the opposite of Yeats's) to use such evidence as indicating Rossetti's worldliness. We have abundant evidence, both in the poetry and from the events of his life, that Rossetti felt guilty about his ability to become so fascinated with the sensual, and I will argue that the rock his poetry founders on is his continual attempt to pass from the sensual to the spiritual. Finally, delight in what is given to the senses is unacceptable to

5. Quoted from John Dixon Hunt, *The Pre-Raphaelite Imagination, 1848–1900* (London: Routledge and Kegan Paul, 1968), p. 129.

6. See Carol Christ, *The Finer Optic* (New Haven: Yale University Press, 1975), pp. 56–62; Herbert Sussman, *Fact into Figure: Typology in Carlyle, Ruskin and the Pre-Raphaelite Brotherhood* (Columbus: Ohio State University Press, 1979), chaps. 4–6; and Martin Meisel, " 'Half-Sick of Shadows': The Aesthetic Dialogue in Pre-Raphaelite Painting," in *Nature and the Victorian Imagination*, pp. 309–40. Meisel's comment on the relative status accorded to art and nature by the PRB fits the understanding of Rossetti I put forward here: "the assumption that seemed to argue the subordination of Art to Nature also implied the *inadequacy* of Art when set in light of Nature, and more broadly in the perspectives of life and truth" (310). George P. Landow, " 'Life Touching lips with Immortality': Rossetti's Typological Structures," *Studies in Romanticism* 17 (1978): 247–65, discusses Rossetti's poetry in relation to a typology of the sort espoused by Hunt. Landow argues that "Rossetti continually searches for analogous secular moments in life and art which could give human existence the same kind of meaning and essential coherence that types furnish for sacred history" (249), and (for the most part) concludes that the poet's search is not very successful.

7. Robert Buchanan's famous attack on Rossetti, "The Fleshly School of Poetry: Mr. D. G. Rossetti," is reprinted, along with Rossetti's reply, in *Pre-Raphaelite Writing: An Anthology*, ed. Derek Sanford (Totowa, N.J.: Rowman and Littlefield, 1973), pp. 37–45.

Rossetti unless a larger symbolic truth can be attached to such appearances. Conversely, dreams and imaginings that cannot be attached to a real existing thing separate from himself are also unacceptable, dismissed as mere phantoms of a wayward mind.

The inability to locate a thing's meaning simply in its appearance, the need for an artist to represent the thing so that its spiritual significance is manifest, gives art an active role. Artistic representation is, in its guiding of interpretation, better than a simple naive perception of the natural thing. But the acknowledgment that truth and meaning exist prior to the poet, already informing the things he sees, also introduces a passive element into the aesthetic introduced in "St. Luke the Painter." Luke is honored because he "first taught Art to fold her hands and pray," and the poet's hope is that art will learn to "pray again." The mystery of the world is such that the poet must pray that its hidden significance will be revealed.

Our resistance to Yeats's characterization of Rossetti as a Christian is based on Rossetti's having abandoned, after the early poems and paintings, specifically Christian themes or any adherence to Christian dogma. But Yeats's comment is true to Rossetti's retention, throughout his career, of his conviction in significances beyond sense and the need for "prayerful" poems. The problem is how to gain access to those hidden meanings. Hunt's belief that attention to the thing's physical details will bring an understanding of its spiritual significance is derived, of course, from Ruskin, but works only in the context of religious faith, a point borne out by Ruskin's career after that faith was weakened. Rossetti, as we shall see, lacks Hunt's faith, and his art is based on trying to develop satisfactory means (other than faith) of access to the spiritual. Long after his art has been stripped of any Christian trappings, the poem as prayer remains one of Rossetti's stocks in trade. In early, Christian poems like "Ave" the prayerful poet asks for an answer from the "voice" of God, but in later, more secular, poems the plea is generalized to the request that things will speak their significance to the questing poet.

> What thing unto mine ear
> Wouldst thou convey,—what secret thing,
> O wandering water ever whispering?
> Surely thy speech will be of her.
> Thou water, O thou whispering wanderer,
> What message dost thou bring?

"The Stream's Secret" (from which this stanza is taken) presents Rossetti at his most listless. The poet's passive stance is broken only by the voicing of his plea, but even that action is languidly performed, and continually announces its imminent end. Speaking the poem is an action that describes its own desire to become inactive. The poet hopes his own words will spur the stream to talk, to divulge its secret. He waits anxiously for his own voice to be replaced by the stream's. But in vain. "Still silent? Can no art / Of Love's then move thy pity? Nay . . ." The stream holds on to its secret, and the discouraged poet stops speaking in order to cry, adding his tears to the stream's "cold water." The poem is hardly Rossetti at his best or most attractive, but it points to the listless despair that generated the charges of "morbidity" to which he was subjected. The poet, immersed in Dante and the romantics, goes to nature to find an intimation (a symbol) of the larger significances that give experience meaning, and only finds dead material things that resist his prayer, remain silent, and refuse incorporation into art. Rossetti's poems often take as their explicit subject that exile from reality, from participation in a universe of meanings beyond the self, that afflicts the Victorian period as a whole.

"The Trees of the Garden" (Sonnet 89 of *The House of Life*) provides another example of Rossetti's attempt to get the world to speak. First, he addresses the dead and wants to know "is it all a show," the vague "it" presumably standing for everything that exists in this lower world. The inability to receive an answer to this question suggests the existence of an indifferent, removed power, "some inexorable supremacy / Which ever, as man strains his blind surmise / From depth to ominous depth, looks past his eyes, / Sphinx-faced with unabashed augury." All of man's "surmise" brings no response, and the dead are no help, only directing the poet to "rather question Earth's self." But nature yields no message either, leaving the poet facing those "ominous depths" with no clue to what they hold.

Rossetti's failure can be characterized as his never discovering an adequate symbolic process by which to enliven the world of material appearances. "The Woodspurge" is a famous example of how nature is dead for Rossetti in a way it was not for Dante or for the romantics.[8] The woodspurge's "cup of three" reminds the reader of the Christian synthesis that did unite the individual man to the world around him, but the poem's point is that this union has broken down. The speaker of the poem remains totally isolated in his grief, just as the woodspurge's particularity remains inviolate despite the speaker's investigation of it. The poem might almost be read as a repudiation of the Ruskinian aesthetic adopted by Hunt. The poet has gone to nature and looked with care at the particular thing, and the result is neither an awakening of faith nor a

8. Jerome J. McGann, "Rossetti's Significant Details," in *Pre-Raphaelitism: A Collection of Critical Essays,* ed. James Sambrook (Chicago: University of Chicago Press, 1974), pp. 230–42, uses "The Woodspurge" as one example of his thesis that "Rossetti does not want us to symbolize" (233), that in his poetry he deliberately divests objects of meanings beyond themselves so that the reader is "restored to a kind of innocence" (233) of immediate response. Obviously, McGann's understanding of Rossetti directly contradicts my own, since I would read the resistance of natural objects to symbolic interpretation in Rossetti's poetry as an indication of the poet's desire to find such meanings, a desire that is, in many cases, not satisfied. For another discussion of this particular poem and the "resistance" of details to interpretation, see Christ, *The Finer Optic,* pp. 40–44.

feeling of greater participation in some unity that includes both poet and flower. The Coleridgean experience of the natural symbol's "partaking" in the whole of which it is the "representative" eludes Rossetti. The physical thing is just the physical thing; its appearance offers no entrance into any other realm of meaning—or at least the poet holds no interpretive key that affords him entrance into that other realm.

Rossetti, of course, is a painter as well as a poet, a producer of images as well as a questioner of nature's appearances. Holman Hunt's faith illuminates the natural world for him, and the typological images of Hunt's paintings derive from that faith. But Rossetti initiates the less integrated, more ethereal, style that, mostly through the work of Edward Burne-Jones and his imitators, eventually became known as *the* Pre-Raphaelite style. Rossetti as painter produces certain appearances, but feels compelled to assign some greater significance to them. The strain of trying to bridge the gap between physical surfaces and spiritual meanings resonates throughout Rossetti's paintings.

The early religious paintings—*Ecce Ancilla Domini (The Annunciation)* and *The Quest of the Holy Grail,* for example—achieve their spiritual significance through the presentation of the physically attenuated figures that become the hallmark of the later work of Burne-Jones, Simeon Solomon, John Melhuish Strudwick, and Evelyn de Morgan. The Virgin of *Ecce Ancilla Domini* appears to be perched on a sick bed, only minimally connected to this world, with hollowed eyes unfocused on her immediate surroundings, which are only sketchily rendered. The spiritual, in these religious paintings, only connects to the physical world in the most tenuous fashion, emphasizing its transcendence by its distance and difference. Rossetti here produces allegorical figures by denying them any particular earthly identity, just as in *The House of Life* he peoples his sonnets with personified abstractions called Love, Sorrow, Joy, and so on. These figures are not concrete particulars whose typological (or figural) meaning the artist uncovers through close observation, but visitors from another realm altogether. They are manifestations, by way of revelation, of the hidden meanings and explanatory voices Rossetti often invokes in his poems.

But not all of Rossetti's paintings offer such spiritualized images. Increasingly, as his career progresses, he presents images of women that dwell quite openly on their earthly (even earthy) physical beauty. *Beata Beatrix,* with his wife Lizzie Siddal as Beatrice, provides an early example of this alternative style. The title suggests the desire to offer once again an allegorical understanding of the figure, but this is no otherworldly image. Subsequently, Rossetti painted a number of portraits of Jane Morris that are recognizably similar to *Beata Beatrix.* Not only is the figure unmistakably of this world, but the paintings' titles always strive either to offer an allegorical significance or reveal the figure's source in legend or literature. Simple physical beauty does not provide sufficient justification for artistic presentation. Only when painting his other favorite model of his later years, Fanny Cornforth, can Rossetti abandon all hope for a wider significance and just present the earthbound reality. (*Bocca Baciata, Woman Combing Her Hair,* and *Woman with a Fan* are some examples.) Yet Fanny surely represents Lilith, the devil woman of legend whose story and image haunts Rossetti throughout these years. To give himself over to Fanny would mean to accept that only the physical world, uncharged with higher meanings, exists. And *The House of Life* serves to resist such a conclusion. Love for Janey Morris, if not love for Fanny, can intimate the existence of spiritual truths.

The painting *Found,* which Rossetti struggled to finish for over twenty years, sums up the dilemma that both plagues and spurs on his efforts in paint and verse. The fallen woman, when found by a figure I would liken to the artist, can be saved from a life solely of this world, can be restored to her full significance as a spiritual being. But Rossetti cannot quite imagine how the artist can become the stalwart savior of the painting. (The failure to reclaim the fallen woman provides the subject for "Jenny," the companion poem for *Found.)* What does the artist have to offer? By what means can he effect this transformation? Burne-Jones's allegorical rendering of the Pygmalion legend represents Rossetti's essential position. The earthly can only be infused with the spiritual by a touch from above. The human artist can perceive, even re-create, earthly appearances, but the vital breath of spirituality must come from a nonhuman source. In the allegory, the sculptor, in the first of four scenes painted by Burne-Jones, muses on the lovely statue (just out of our sight) that he has created. "The heart aspires," the painting's title tells us, to enliven this piece of stone. In the second scene, "the hand refrains" as the sculptor resists the temptation to retouch his work, acknowledging that no effort of his could possibly give the statue what it lacks. Only with the visit of the goddess in the third scene ("the godhead fires") can Galatea come to life. And Burne-Jones makes it clear that spiritual elevation, not earthly lust, is the issue here by portraying Pygmalion kneeling at the feet of his new mistress, with the caption "the soul attains." The passive artist who knows his limits, the allegory suggests, may merit that divine assistance he needs to charge the physical appearances of his work with the spirituality to which he aspires. But the artist must know his limits and have patience.

What seems to come easily enough to Burne-Jones's Pygmalion, who lives in an idealized world already quite removed from a harsher Victorian reality, always causes Rossetti great anguish. Both "Jenny" and "The Portrait" are early poems in which Rossetti contemplates his art's inability to capture the full vitality of the realities it represents. In "Jenny" not the natural world (as in "The Woodspurge") but another person faces the speaker of the poem as the alien reality he cannot get to speak. The speaker stops several times to inquire of the sleeping prostitute: "Whose person or whose purse may be / The lodestar of your reverie?" (20–21), and "I wonder what you're thinking of" (58). Jenny, asleep, is unable to answer, so the speaker supplies the answers himself, telling us what he imagines Jenny's thoughts to be.

Nothing could more distinguish Rossetti from the romanticism of Wordsworth than this failure to find a voice beyond himself, either in the encounter with nature or with another person. The speaker of the poem is a scholar or writer who has hidden away from the world in his "room . . . full of books" (22–23). On this night he has escaped from his study to confront "life" and cull a lesson from the confrontation, such as Wordsworth does in his meeting with the leech gatherer.[9] But Rossetti's speaker, far from gaining new insights from this encounter, spends the night only with his own thoughts, almost as if he had never left his study. His habit of prolonged self-involved meditation is so ingrown that Jenny herself only plays the same role as a book to him. "You know not what a book you seem, / Half-read by lightning in a dream!" (51–52). Of course, the leech gatherer is only a pretext for Wordsworth's intensely personal meditation as well, but the difference is that Wordsworth believes his encounter with someone different from himself has been the source of his new "resolution." But the speaker in Rossetti's poem, as the metaphor of the book shows, never comes into contact with Jenny's reality apart from himself. She remains dreamlike, just another manifestation of his thoughts. The book metaphor also suggests that Jenny is totally within culture, unlike the leech gatherer who represents a more "natural" way of life, distanced from the culture that brings poets to "despondency and madness." Culture, at least as represented by Jenny and the speaker's books, has no more to offer Rossetti than nature. The prostitute is recognized as a living reality who offers the possibility of thoughts and insights not of the poet's own devising, but the speaker cannot break through to that reality. He fails to overcome the space between his thoughts and the world.

The futility of his thoughts, their emptiness and unreality, overcomes the speaker at various points in the poem: ". . . my Thought runs on like this / With wasteful whims more than enough" (56–57); "Let the thoughts pass, an empty cloud!" (155). The reality of Jenny is in front of the speaker, but he is painfully aware that the "truth" of whom she is has escaped him.

> Come, come, what use in thoughts like this?
> Poor little Jenny, good to kiss,—
> You'd not believe by what strange roads
> Thought travels, when your beauty goads
> A man tonight to think of toads!
> Jenny, wake up . . . Why there's the dawn! (298–302)

9. See "Resolution and Independence," in *William Wordsworth: The Poems,* ed. John O. Hayden (New Haven: Yale University Press, 1981), pp. 551–56.

"Thought," traveling by "strange roads," strays from the real, merely taking what presents itself to the senses as the starting point for its own constructions. Everything seems to return the speaker to the prison of self, rather than affording a transcendence of self in a higher communion with the real. The absence of sexual union in the poem points toward the absence of any corresponding spiritual union. Many of the sexual puns that would describe the situation also adequately describe the speaker's failure to effect a union between thought and reality, self and other. The romantic marriage of mind and world becomes, in this poem, the absolutely sterile meeting between the speaker and a prostitute; the speaker fails to penetrate the incomprehensible otherness of this thinking being whose thoughts remain completely unknown to him. That Rossetti himself was at least dimly aware of the parallels between the physical and epistemological planes in the poem is suggested by its ending.

> And must I mock you to the last,
> Ashamed of my own shame,—aghast
> Because some thoughts not born amiss
> Rose at a poor fair face like this?
> Well, of such thoughts so much I know:
> In my life, as in hers, they show,
> By a far gleam which I may near,
> A dark path I can strive to clear. (383–90)

This passage is difficult because the reference of "thoughts" is ambiguous. I will offer two readings. I do not want to choose between the two because each illuminates certain important features of Rossetti's poetry. I also think both readings make coherent sense of the poem as a whole. The first possibility is that the thought that "shames" the speaker is lust, and he mocks Jenny because she has fostered that emotion in him. Much of the poem has focused, in no flattering terms, on "man's changeless sum of lust" (228–29). The last lines suggest, then, that the speaker has formed a new resolution (in Wordsworthian fashion) as a result of his meeting with Jenny. The experience of lust has intimated to him (the "far gleam") the existence of love, a state that he might attain by "clearing" the "dark path" of his base desires. (The path is also dark because the speaker is still ignorant and inexperienced.) The speaker leaves Jenny to go seek love. We might call this the "Wordsworthian" or "optimistic" reading, since it finds in this last stanza a revelation that can guide future action. Although union with this particular woman is impossible, the speaker has recognized that physical love is an analogue of spiritual love, and that through physical love he can move toward the realm of spiritual love. In other words, he has found a path that allows him the passage from the material to the spiritual that he seeks. Love can be the solution to the radical split between the speaker and Jenny. Their union has been sterile because it involved no love. In love two bodies and two minds actually do interpenetrate, and the prison of self can be escaped. The dead world can be brought to life by love, and much of Rossetti's poetry explores both how physical love can symbolize or can lead to spiritual love, and how love serves to connect self to the world.

This "optimistic" reading must be qualified, however, since the poem, as I have suggested, does not exhibit a Wordsworthian confidence that any substantial contact with the other has been made. If we take "thoughts" (385) to refer to the meditations on Jenny contained in the poem, a more ironic understanding of the poem's ending follows. The speaker's "shame" is his chagrined awareness that, characteristically, his night with the prostitute was spent in "thought," not in bed. He recovers his self-pride by asserting his difference from Jenny, an assertion cemented by his placing the coins in her hair. "Thoughtless" Jenny belongs to one realm, the speaker to another. The physical is separated completely from the thoughtful, and the speaker leaves Jenny and her physical world behind to retreat into the realm of pure thought at the end of the poem. The poem evidences a strong disgust with the bestial in man, and so the final choice of purity by the speaker, even if that choice is read as (at least in part) a defensive reaction to his inability to escape his thoughts and participate in Jenny's world, is not a total surprise.

I think the reader's ironic understanding of the speaker's limits is deliberately set up by Rossetti, but the tensions explored by the poem are Rossetti's as well as the protagonist's. While at times able to find the physical an analogue of the spiritual, at other times Rossetti can only see the physical and the spiritual as complete opposites. The speaker's attitude toward Jenny, with its strange mixture of sympathy and contempt, combined with a tender farewell that nevertheless emphasizes that Jenny and the speaker occupy two very different worlds, points to Rossetti's own confusions over the exact relation of thought to life, the spiritual to the material. He longs for the correspondences between world and mind found by the romantics. But those correspondences elude him, and he finds himself often forced to choose between the world constructed by thought or the world offered to the senses. And he is not consistent in his choosing. In a poem like "The Blessed Damozel" physical earthly love strikes the reader as far more appealing than the spiritual love enjoyed by the blessed in heaven, even though the poet strives to make earthly love a means by which to pass on to spiritual love. In other cases, Rossetti anticipates modern aestheticism in finding the world constructed by imagination far superior to the dull world of material fact. However, Rossetti is rarely able to affirm one or the other completely while maintaining a clear conscience. He believes in a reality that exists independently of thought, and which is also stronger than thought. The material world cannot be ignored because it should serve as our access to that reality. If Rossetti's difficulty in finding adequate symbols in nature distinguishes him from the romantics, his uneasiness with residence in the halls built by imagination reminds us he is no modern. The images offered by memory and dreams are not a satisfactory consolation when he feels himself to have lost contact with that greater reality that transcends mind.

Poem after poem places the speaker in a position of readiness from which he strains to perceive the message he is persuaded the world must hold. In "Love-Lily" the speaker's "life grows faint to hear" the approach of a "spirit" who "on my mouth his finger lays" and "shows" the silenced poet the "Eden of Love." "The Sea-Limits" is another listening poem, in which "secret continuance sublime" is identified as the sea's song. The poem ends with the poet's exhorting his readers to listen not only to the sea but also to a shell "which echo[es] . . . the whole sea's speech." When he emphasizes listening to the world, Rossetti's conception of poetry can be likened to this shell. In "choral consonancy" (Sonnet 55), poetry and the poet's voice should "echo" the voice of the world, not introducing personal or solipsistic reveries, but the meaning of a world all men live in.[10] The word *echo* appears in many Rossetti poems, and often carries the same weight the metaphor of the Aeolian harp carried for Coleridge. (Examples include "Plighted Promise," "Fareweel to the Glen," "A Day of Love" [Sonnet 16], "Stillborn Love" [Sonnet 55], and "The Cloud Confines.") The echo suggests a perfect harmony, a faithful reproduction of something given to the poet and not created by him. On the negative side, the echo is secondary and also weaker than the original sound. But if the poet simply echoes truths intimated by nature he escapes the guilt of a megalomaniac creation in thought of his own world and his own truths. Like all the writers I discuss, Rossetti is determined to find meaning in the world given to him, not in a world created by his imagination. But "the pass is difficult" through which the poet must move in order to have his questions about the significance of things answered and thus escape the "bitterness of things occult."[11] The secret of life's meanings is withheld from the poet.

Rossetti also typifies the writers I discuss in allowing his sense of thought's isolation from the real to afflict his estimate of art's truth and worth. Far from being an "aestheticist" in the sense that he wishes art to have no relation to life,[12] Rossetti continually laments art's failed attempt to embody the real. His poetry points the way toward modern "aestheticism" only insofar

10. Yeats, in various poems, takes up this image of the shell and transforms it into an image of solipsism, of a failure to make contact with the real, as if commenting on the nature of Pre-Raphaelite poetry. See my discussion of this image in Chapter 8.

11. The lines quoted are from the sonnet written for the painting "Our Lady of the Rocks" by Leonardo da Vinci. Florence Saunders Boos, *The Poetry of Dante G. Rossetti* (The Hague: Mouton, 1976), pp. 224–28, offers a detailed reading of this interesting poem.

12. José Ortega y Gasset, *The Dehumanization of Art* (Princeton: Princeton University Press, 1968), offers one classic statement of the "aestheticist" position, with its insistence that art and life should remain absolutely distinct from one another. For Ortega, the "new art . . . abhors nothing so much as blurred borderlines. To insist on neat distinctions is a symptom of mental honesty. Life is one thing, art is another—thus the young set think or at least feel —let us keep the two apart" (31).

as it contemplates art's inability to reach beyond itself and be reality itself. But Rossetti hardly celebrates this inability, and the difficult task he would have art assume is the presentation of reality's meaning. In "Jenny," the speaker tries to imagine how Jenny's "true nature" might be portrayed by the artist. The speaker considers how "Raffael" or "Leonardo" would have painted the prostitute. The beautiful women painted by these masters showed to "men's souls" what "God can do" (238–40), but the artist who would portray Jenny must show a beautiful face that reveals the evil man has done while still showing that God cherishes the fallen woman. The speaker concludes that a successful portrait of Jenny could not be painted, for reasons that seem archetypally Victorian: religious doubts, the prudery of the audience, and despair over the "culture" of his contemporaries. How could the artist portray God's love for the sinner when he has "no sign" that such love exists? "All dark. No sign on earth / What measure of God's rest endows / The many mansions of his house" (250–52). This failure to see a way to paint Jenny is followed by the lament: "If but a woman's heart might see / Such erring heart unerringly / For once! But that can never be" (250–52). The flat despair of the second sentence falls limply after the soaring hope of the first. Even where reality could be made to speak by the artist, the cherished respectability of the Victorian audience would insure that the revealed meaning would never be heeded. The artist cannot penetrate to the significance of the real because the evil done by society overwhelms any image of God's goodness; but even if that vision was granted to him, society's hypocrisy would prevent him from finding a sympathetic audience. (Thus Rossetti is deprived of the great consolation that accompanies the criticisms of contemporary society found in Dickens and George Eliot: a faith in the ability of art to create a community that shares certain judgments and values.)

Our understanding of the relation of art to the real is complicated when, continuing his complaint that no Victorian audience would allow itself to contemplate the reality of Jenny, the speaker describes the prostitute as "a rose shut in a book / In which pure women may not look, / For its base pages claim control / To crush the flower within the soul" (253–56). This passage, on one level, links Victorian prudery to the horror of Jenny's existence. (In another passage, the speaker imagines Jenny's inevitably miserable end when she becomes old and/or diseased.) Society condemns Jenny to her particular life and death by turning its face on her just as surely as the book crushes the rose, and yet this same society is hypocritical enough to claim that the book which would present Jenny faithfully will corrupt "pure" women, will crush the "flower" within their souls.[13]

13. Rossetti's claim that Jenny cannot find a place within "a book in which pure women may . . . look" reads like an anticipation of the "fleshly poet" controversy. Before publishing his *Poems* of 1870, Rossetti, fearing an attack like Buchanan's and having already had Ruskin

More interesting from my point of view is how, on another level, this passage develops the relationship between art and life, with art being understood as a product of mental processes divorced from the real. The metaphor of the rose that is killed when it is pressed into the book suggests that the artist kills reality when he transforms it into art. Hasn't the poet himself taken the "rose" Jenny and shut her in his book? Making Jenny the subject of a poem is an extension of the process by which the speaker has attributed all his own thoughts to the sleeping prostitute. The translation of the real into art substitutes art for the real just as the speaker has substituted his own thoughts for Jenny's. Everything—God's silence, society's fragmentation and prudery, the speaker's attribution of his own thoughts to Jenny, and the poet's imposition of form and interpretation—conspires to leave life's secrets inviolate and to identify art as merely the domain of personal reveries. Art turns in upon itself as the mind's own play. The active poet, it seems, does not "rend the mist of devious symbols" but only offers "soulless self-reflections."

Both poems entitled "The Portrait" consider how the artist, through his art, appropriates reality and the meanings it reveals.[14] The sonnet (Sonnet 10) ends by triumphing in this ownership of the real by the artist: "Let all men note / That in all years (O Love, thy gift is this!) / They that would look on her must come to me." The form the portrait painter has given to his love is the form in which she will exist for all men from this point on. The earlier poem of the same title is more troubled by the hubris implied by the artist setting up his art as the sole point of access to a particular reality. The poem opens by establishing that where art is, reality is no longer: "This is her picture as she was." The poet laments that "only this [the portrait], of love's whole prize, / Remains." The painting is so lifelike that the poet can cry "'Tis she!" but he quickly qualifies this ecstasy: "though of herself, alas! / Less than her shadow on the grass / Or than her image in the stream." Art faithfully represents the real, but art is only representative, not the represented, and when the desire is for the represented, art will not satisfy that desire.

Furthermore, art's ability to represent is limited. The portrait is what remains of the poet-painter's love, but those remains are incomplete since the painting has not succeeded in capturing "what is secret and unknown, / Below the earth, above the skies." Not only does the loved one's life elude the artist's attempt to capture it, but the portrait also fails to convey some "mystery" about the loved one which "takes counsel with my [the speaker's] soul alone."

refuse to forward "Jenny" to the *Cornhill Magazine* for consideration, was afraid readers and reviewers would find a long poem about a prostitute offensive. See James Paul Seigel, " 'Jenny': The Divided Sensibility of a Young and Thoughtful Man of the World," *Studies in English Literature* 9 (1969): 677–80.

14. The longer poem entitled "The Portrait" is one of Rossetti's earliest poems, written in 1847, but revised before inclusion in the volume of poems published in 1870.

The material image is not the living woman and is not able to represent some essential spiritual truth about her. Where the portrait is our only access to the reality of the woman it represents, we are confronting a diminished image.

It might seem a long way from the "living woman" of this poem to the "dead, thoughtless" prostitute of "Jenny." But I think these two ways of characterizing the other for Rossetti are linked. Jenny is dead insofar as the artist must enliven her to make her suitable material for poetry. The speaker has interpreted her, created an image of her in his thoughts, tried to imagine her reality. But, in doing all this, he wonders if he has crushed the "rose" of the actual Jenny. The appeal to a "mystery" that escapes or transcends the painted image of the woman in "The Portrait" is another way to address the fear that the woman present in art is only the artist's re-creation of the real in terms of his art. To claim that something is not conveyed by the painting is to claim that something exists beyond art. Even if it means belittling his art, Rossetti needs to assert the existence of a reality that is other than the artist and the representative images he fashions.

In fact, "The Portrait" implies that life and art are inimical, that the living thing is never art, that art only holds images of the dead. The poem narrates how the two lovers first exchanged vows of love. The "next day" after this first union the poet-painter remembers his ecstasy and decides he "must make them all [his] own / And paint this picture." He begins the task immediately.

> And as I wrought, while all above
> And all around was fragrant air,
> In the sick burthen of my love
> It seemed each sun-thrilled blossom there
> Beat like a heart among the leaves.
> O heart that never beats nor heaves,
> In that one darkness lying still,
> What now to thee my love's great will
> Or the fine web the sunshine weaves?

The speaker's feeling that all nature is alive as he paints is juxtaposed with the fact of the loved one's death. The "sick burthen" of his love is that avaricious need to make the previous day's perfection all his own by freezing it in a painting. The cause of the woman's death is never given, but it seems as if the poet-painter's attempt to capture her in a particular moment makes it fitting that he has been forced to exchange her for the portrait with which he is left. Reality, the poem implies, always exceeds its representation in art, and the attempt to reduce the real to a representation kills the real. (We find in Browning a very similar conviction about the relation of a limiting art to an excessive reality.) The substitution of the representative for the thing itself suggests that where art is, reality is not. And since (in this pre-Wildean era) for Rossetti reality comes first, and art then tries to represent it, the belated work of art supplants the reality that was its origin. Convinced that representatives are inadequate, yet marooned in a world that he understands to represent a hidden spiritual truth, Rossetti is condemned to his unhappy search for some kind of access to the truth that will reveal its totality to him.

The last four stanzas of "The Portrait" show that Rossetti thinks art and life are mutually exclusive, but in this case he hesitates between which he would choose if forced to do so. We find here one clue to Rossetti's lack of faith, his inability to find in the world presented to him satisfactory symbolic meanings. Rossetti has none of the Wordsworthian assurance that nature is benign; instead, Rossetti half suspects that mind, working on its own, can imagine a better world than the one it is given. He is Victorian enough to resist this suspicion, but it partly determines his failure to offer images of the apocalyptic marriage found in romantic poetry. In Rossetti, the marriage embrace is almost always associated with death, which suggests that the self can only achieve union at the cost of abandoning its most cherished desires. Rossetti's passive side wishes to make that surrender, but his resistance to surrender, his desire to retain art as a separate realm of human desires asserted in the face of a nonhuman reality, is developed in Yeats into a strikingly different understanding of art's value.

In "The Portrait," reality is associated with "day" and "light," art with "darkness" and "night." Reality is the world of present objects we must see in the light of the day; art exists in a nighttime realm populated by the images of dream and memory which arise to fill the void of darkness. Only in art can the speaker retain his memory of that once perfect love: "For now doth daylight disavow / Those days,—nought left to see or hear. / Only in solemn whispers now / At night-time these things reach mine ear." Reality here is reduced to the world of perceived sensations in which only what is present to the senses right now has any existence. The poet, tied to the reality of the lover he remembers, must escape this limited vision. Art, existing in the realm of dream and memory, remains a repository for contents that the harsh light of material reality "disavows." The speaker, preferring nighttime, "delay[s] [his] sleep till dawn" (an ominous foreshadowing of Rossetti's later troubles with insomnia). But he cannot live entirely in the night world; the dawn is inevitable: "And as I stood there suddenly, / All wan with traversing the night, / Upon the desolate verge of light / Yearned loud the iron-bosomed sea." Implacable ("iron-bosomed") and desolate, reality returns, usurping the speaker's reveries and memories, reintroducing him into the harsh world in which his loved one is dead and he is alone.

The better world the poet establishes in his art, the more satisfying realm of night in which desires are fulfilled in dream and imagination, must yield to the cold world of day where the reality principle rules. Art, for Rossetti, is not substantial enough to hold its own against this harsh reality; only an even greater spiritual reality could overcome the cruelty of material reality, and the poem ends with the hope that death will reveal that spiritual reality to the speaker. But Rossetti also fears that the spiritual reality does not exist at all. The very fact that he is led to ask the question of meaning and finds no answer makes him suspect that reality is unalterably antithetical to human desires, and this suspicion encourages the retreat to an artistic world full of significances. This dialectic, between an ideal world of art and a reality whose very nature gives birth to that ideal world (because of the need to imagine something better than reality) *and* denies that ideal world's validity, pervades Rossetti's poetry.

Edward Said discusses nineteenth-century literature in terms of an oscillation between "authority" and "molestation."[15] Writers of the period are searching for an "authority" beyond self to justify their own artistic visions, and are concerned about the hubristic "author" who sets himself up as a creator of a world. Said finds in the period's novels a number of characters who try to create worlds out of themselves and who are finally "molested" by a reality that is larger than their individual visions. (Examples are Lydgate in *Middlemarch* and Ahab in *Moby Dick.)* These characters embody self-assertive urges in the writers themselves, but the nineteenth-century writer finally works to assure that his vision, as distinct from that of his characters, is "authorized" by the very nature of things; in other words, the author, in the end, aligns himself with the forces that "molest" the characters. Said's discussion suggests one reason for the Victorian author's desire to discover the real, and I will consider the moment of molestation in many of the texts discussed in this book. Rossetti displays a continual need to molest his more extravagant desires, to the point of aligning himself with the prime agent of molestation: death.

Rossetti's acceptance that there exists a reality independent of self and its desires, and that art should depict that reality, necessitated his submission to "the bitterness of things occult." Reality continually evades his efforts to understand it and to include it in his art, but also undermines the personal as merely "subjective" and dreamlike. In *The House of Life,* individual experiences of intense moments of personal emotion are always perceived as stolen from a larger reality that inevitably returns to claim its property, leaving the artist once again isolated and denied participation in the real.

The poet's goal in *The House of Life* is to ground personal experience in reality by finding in emotion and the loved woman symbols of general truths about Life, Love, Hope, and those other personified abstractions that occupy these sonnets alongside the detailed descriptions of individual things and events. Of *The House of Life* Rossetti wrote: "To speak in the first person is

15. See Edward Said, *Beginnings: Intention and Method* (New York: Basic Books, 1975), chap. 4.

often to speak most vividly; but these emotional poems are in no sense 'occasional.' The 'life' involved is life representative, as associated with love and death, with aspiration and foreboding, or with ideal art and beauty. Whether the recorded moment exist in the region of fact or of thought is a question indifferent to the Muse, so long only as her touch can quicken it."[16] With Buchanan's attack on Rossetti's poetry for merely wallowing in the sensual and the particular in mind, the temptation is to read this statement of purpose as defensive, as the poet's attempt to justify the personal nature and self-involvement of his art by claiming general significance for it.

To call the statement defensive, however, does not necessarily mean it is insincere. To infuse the here and now with deeper meaning necessarily involves tying present experiences and appearances with larger issues of "life." The tyranny of daylight, of what is given to the senses, can only be overcome if, in Coleridge's words, "poetry as poetry is essentially *ideal,* that it avoids and excludes all accident; that its apparent individualities of rank, character, or occupation must be representative."[17] Rossetti's poetic goals are quite similar to Coleridge's here, even though he was well aware (and was so before Buchanan's attack) that his poetry often has trouble effecting this desired movement from the particular to the general.

The poems themselves address this last problem directly. The importance of love for Rossetti lies in its seeming to elevate personal experience into the realm of the archetypal. The loved woman embodies all life and all truth. In "Heart's Hope" (Sonnet 5) the poet tells us that "one loving heart" can "signify" to "all hearts all things," that the present spring can represent "other Springs gone by." The poet dedicates himself to the task of symbolizing absent things and meanings in these given particulars; the woman serves as the symbol for which the poet has been searching. The way in which the symbol works is left vague; we only learn that there exist moments of "instantaneous penetrating sense," a description reminiscent of romantic appeals to extraordinary moments of "intuition." Dawn, birth, and spring imagery dominate this sonnet, as similar imagery does in many of Rossetti's happier love poems when he feels that love is granting him an insight into and union with a world beyond himself. Perceiving the loved one, the meaning of things dawns on the poet; he is born into a new world that now makes sense to him. And this insight validates his art. The sonnet begins by asking "what word's power" will allow the poet to realize and embody his newfound knowledge in his art. Love can give his art a confidence, a contact with reality, it has never before enjoyed. However, "Heart's Hope," it should be noted, is set almost entirely in the

16. Quoted from Oswald Doughty, *A Victorian Romantic: Dante Gabriel Rossetti* (London: Oxford University Press, 1960), p. 379.
17. *Biographia Literaria,* chap. 22.

subjunctive mood, and stands as a statement of the poet's project and hopes, not of what he has already accomplished.

There is no need to deny that love (be it for Lizzie Siddal, Janey Morris, or any other woman) granted Rossetti both a feeling of being at home in a world in which the bitterness of hidden meanings was, at least temporarily, assuaged, and the artistic power to give coherent form to experience. No other activity, pursuit, or sensation afforded Rossetti such a satisfying contact with the world beyond self. But the success of much of the love poetry need not blind us to the problems the poet encounters in trying to make his love experiences "signify all things."[18] The woman in the poems is often a shadowy figure, and she is seldom given any lines to speak even though the poet hears all reality speaking through her. At other times, the woman becomes a mystery herself, rather than a transparency through which all things are revealed, and the poet is reduced to contemplating a reality that excludes him, that he cannot know. Of "True Woman" (Sonnet 56) he writes: "How strange a thing to be what Man can know / But as a sacred secret! Heaven's own screen / Hides her soul's purest depth and loveliest glow."

More than any individual poem, however, the structure of the entire sequence of *The House of Life* reveals Rossetti's uneasiness with the immersion in personal experience. The poems move from the personal to the impersonal, from happy moments with the loved one to memories of her and meditations on the general significance of love after her death.[19] Most readers will agree that the sonnets of Part 1, "Youth and Change," are better than those of Part 2, "Change and Fate," but what is interesting is that Rossetti feels compelled to relinquish his celebration of an individual love experience to write the more general poems of the second part. Rossetti is uneasy with the personal unless he can attach general significance to it (hence his susceptibility to Buchanan's criticisms), and so designs his sonnet sequence to move from the particular to the general.

The title of the first part—"Youth and Change"—also suggests that the pride and self-confidence of youth, which finds in itself and its love all that is necessary to make a world, is undermined by the passage of time. The harsh

18. The fullest description of love's place in Rossetti's poetry is Stephen Spector's excellent essay "Love, Unity and Desire in the Poetry of Dante Gabriel Rossetti," *ELH* 38 (1971): 432–48. Spector sees love as one expression of Rossetti's overwhelming need "to bridge the gap between the subjective and objective worlds" (432), but concludes that love does not afford such unity and that Rossetti's poems are about the "desire for unity," not the "experience of unity" (443).

19. There have been a number of studies of the structure of *The House of Life* over the past fifteen years. The most important for my purposes, and the ones from which I have drawn the quick outline given here, are Robert D. Hume's "Inorganic Structure in *The House of Life*," *Papers in Literature and Language* 5 (1969): 282–95, and Houston A. Baker, "The Poet's Progress: Rossetti's *The House of Life*," *Victorian Poetry* 8 (1970): 1–14. *Victorian Poetry* will be abbreviated as *VP* in subsequent notes.

realities of change and death break in to show the youth that something exists beyond him. The beauty of a poem like "Silent Noon" (Sonnet 19) depends not only on its evocation of a perfect moment, but also on its suggestion of the moment's fragility. The lovers have succeeded in escaping, for a brief instant (while the sun stops overhead), a reality that is indifferent to their needs.[20] *The House of Life* as a whole sequence denies that we can rest in the particular or the moment, pleasant as such resting may be. Reality always crashes in and returns us to a less satisfactory, but more real, world.

Rossetti's celebration of the intense moment must be understood within the basic pattern of his striving in all his poetry to connect particulars to more general significances. After the moment is isolated, the poet always works to reincorporate that moment into the general continuity of time. The momentary, almost mystical, flash of "instantaneous penetrating sense" in Rossetti's poetry acts, along with love (and, as we shall see shortly, death), as the means by which the self penetrates otherness. Such moments of union, of sudden understanding of meanings that have eluded the poet, occur throughout romantic and postromantic literature, with famous examples being Wordsworth's "spots of time," Joyce's "epiphanies," and Pound's "images." Rossetti's sonnet on the sonnet presents his formulation of this familiar idea: "A Sonnet is a moment's monument,— / Memorial from the Soul's eternity / To one dead deathless hour." The moment is both "dead" and "deathless" because it is past, lost forever, and yet the significances it offers, taken from the "eternal" realm which is the "soul's" domain, are timeless and always true. Art can "memorialize" these significances. Here, then, seems to be the solution to the bitterness of things occult. Moments of revelation illuminate the true meaning of things in the world, and art can record these momentary insights.[21]

Twentieth-century readers are familiar with the consequences of an aesthetics of the moment. Inevitably, emphasis on the moment leads to a discontinuity between moments of revelation and the uninformative daily life of "habit" and "oblivion" (to use Proust's terms). Often enough, the aesthetic of the moment also leads to a celebration of art's superiority to life, since art

20. Spector, "Love, Unity, and Desire," pp. 445–46, offers a fine evaluation of these moments of escape in Rossetti's love poems and how they generally combine light and dark, suggesting that the peace of escape is also a retreat from the world toward death.

21. John Dixon Hunt, "A Moment's Monument: Reflections on Pre-Raphaelite Vision in Poetry and Painting," in Sambrook, *Pre-Raphaelitism: A Collection of Critical Essays*, pp. 243–64, offers a full account of the adherence to an aesthetics of the moment by the various writers and artists associated with the Pre-Raphaelite movement. I, of course, want to qualify Hunt's identification of that aesthetic as *the* aesthetic of the PRB by indicating the moment's existence for Rossetti in tension with a temporality that, although not revelatory, cannot be ignored. George P. Landow, " 'Life Touching lips with Immortality'" (see esp. pp. 258–61), takes essentially the same position on this issue as I do here. For another view of the moment's place in Rossetti's poetry, see Stanley M. Holberg, "Rossetti and the Trance," *VP* 8 (1970): 299–314.

affords us these glorious instants of insight, and then preserves them. Certainly some of Rossetti's sonnets find in the moment the only pleasures that make life worth living. In "Severed Selves" (Sonnet 40) the lovers look forward to the hour of reunion, "an hour how slow to come, how quickly past,— / Which blooms and fades, and only leaves at last / Faint as shed flowers, the attenuated dream." In this poem, life itself becomes a dream when compared to the intensity of passion's hour. Rossetti is close at times to Pater's advocation of concentrated moments of intense feeling, and to identifying those moments as the most real things we ever encounter, and the resultant acceptance of art, which provides and preserves those moments, as more real than life.

But Rossetti remains on the Victorian side of Pater, and it is the tension between art and life, along with the conviction that life is more real than art, that determines the nature of Rossetti's poetry. Where the moment of feeling and insight is an end in itself for Pater, and that moment turns life into art for Proust, the moment exists in Rossetti as an exception, a wonderful but somewhat unreal escape from the reality of ordinary life, with its boredom, its pain, its changes over time, and its separation of the individual from higher meanings. And the moment's very isolation from the reality of the everyday leads Rossetti to try to reincorporate it back into the larger framework of life. A poet whose experience of radical discontinuities generates in him a desire for continuity, Rossetti will be satisfied only when the particular touches on the general, the personal is a fit subject for the public, art expresses and clarifies the nature of the real, and the moment of revelation or union takes its place in the sequence of interrelated moments called time. Whenever the particular, the personal, art, and the moment cannot be linked to these larger frameworks, Rossetti suspects that the small entities do not partake of the real, are only figments of the imagination.

Various poems in *The House of Life* reveal either this attempt to connect the moment to time in its entirety or the sense that the moment is unreal and thus unable to sustain itself. In "Love and Hope" (Sonnet 43) the poet is thankful to have salvaged "one hour at least" from "many a withered year," an hour of full love. But the sonnet's sestet stresses the hour's unreality, its existing only if the lovers willfully avoid asking what most concerns them: does love endure? The moment is only granted when the lovers can avoid wondering how long it will last; even to admit that questioning the moment's length is forbidden is to recall "how brief the whole/of joy, which its own hours annihilate" (Sonnet 45). Poems like "Hoarded Joy" (Sonnet 82) and "The Love-Moon" (Sonnet 37) show how Rossetti habitually qualifies the moment by reinserting it in a full temporal sequence. The latter poem seems especially close to Rossetti's world view, since it touches on a sensitive topic: the relation of his past love to his present one.

"When that dead face, borrowed in the furthest years,
    Which once was all the life years held for thee,
    Can now scarce bid the tides of memory
Cast on thy soul a little spray of tears,—
How canst thou gaze into these eyes of hers
    Whom now thy heart delights in, and not see
    Within each orb Love's philtred euphrasy
Make them of buried troth remembrances?"

"Nay, pitiful Love, nay, loving Pity! Well
    Thou knowest that in these twain I have confess'd
Two very voices of thy summoning bell.
    Nay, Master, shall not Death make manifest
In these the culminant changes which approve
The love-moon that much light my soul to Love?"

In this sonnet, Rossetti is addressed by one of those voices beyond the self he so often seeks. But the voice only speaks to accuse the poet of hiding himself in the present, and of having lost all reverence for the past and for love. The present love lacks substance, especially since the ability to forget a past love entirely and lose oneself in the new lover suggests a certain levity on the poet's part. Only something that lasts is truly real, and the poet's need to take refuge in a physically present lover as opposed to the memory of his absent dead lover indicates a lack of spirituality on his part. The poet's reply to the accusing voice weights the moment (of present love) by placing it back into an understood progress: the movement of his "soul to Love." Both his lovers are signs, "voices of [the] summoning bell," that guide the movement of the soul. The poet's defense is also a plea. Don't I get any sign while here in the physical realm? The taking of the second love does not contradict his first love since both, in this sublunary world, connect him to his "Master." "Changes" in this realm, including "Death," all serve to "make manifest" the existence of transcending love. The poet claims to value the moment only because it can guide him to the eternal. All moments, even his present "delight," are subject to death, and are only valuable insofar as they aid the soul's progress through a series of moments to an eventual goal outside earthly time.

The quest for meaning is as intense in *The House of Life* as elsewhere in Rossetti's poetry: "shall my sense pierce love—the last relay / And ultimate outpost of eternity?" (Sonnet 34). The threat of a physical realm that carries no meaning beyond itself is embodied in Lilith, "subtly of herself contemplative" (Sonnet 78), while the poet "vainly" attempts to probe "the unyielding caves of some deep treasure-trove" (Sonnet 54). His sleepless nights introduce him to a "thicket hung with masks of mockery" (Sonnet 39), beyond which he cannot penetrate. The listless Rossetti is in evidence as well. His "lost hours" of "idleness" are evidenced by his inability to "know, for longing, that which [he] should do" (Sonnet 69).

More and more, as the sonnet sequence moves toward its end, Rossetti almost masochistically yields himself to a reality that overwhelms his aspirations. The poet who has been unable to get reality to speak when he pleads for it to do so discovers a voice for reality in its acting to deny him the things he wants. Passivity becomes submission as Rossetti recognizes reality in this resistance to his desires. The "Willowwood Sonnets" (49–52) begin with the poet sitting with "Love" by a well, listening for the "certain secret thing" Love has to tell. Turning Love's lute playing into the "passionate voice" of his dead beloved, the poet is granted a vision of the lady in the well's water. Now that the poet is absorbed in this vision, Love begins to sing and the poet becomes aware "of a dumb throng / That stood aloof, one form by every tree, / All mournful forms, for each was I or she, / The shades of those our days that had no tongue." Longing for reunion with his first love, for repossession of a happy past, the poet learns that the visions of memory only bring pain since they image forth a world that will never be real, which will always stand aloof. When the poet finally hears Love's song in the third sonnet, the message is a despairing one. "Your last hope lost, who so in vain invite / Your lips to that their unforgotten food." Love's advice is to forget the past since memory only causes the poet to wander helplessly through the wood. With the end of Love's song, the face in the well falls "back drowned," and the poet is alone once more. The intensity of his personal memories and desires cannot sustain a vision in the face of the brute facts of change and death. He has been granted the moment of revelation he seeks, but what he has learned is that reality does not serve the human desire for permanence. The force of desire is too weak to stand up against the strength of reality.

It seems odd, perhaps, that when Rossetti uncharacteristically succeeds in getting a voice outside the self to speak, the message is so often dismal. The poet has begged life, reality, to reveal itself and its deepest meanings to him, and on the few occasions his request bears fruit, the lesson is that life's laws and man's hopes inevitably conflict. "Death-In-Love" (Sonnet 48) might appear an extreme case (given its probable origin in one of the most traumatic events of Rossetti's life) but, in fact, it stands as one of the very few poems in which the poet does receive a message from the beyond.[22]

> There came an image in Life's retinue
> That had Love's wings and bore his gonfalon:
> Fair was the web, and nobly wrought thereon,

---

22. I have discussed in detail "The Love-Moon" and the Willowwood sonnets, which also include a transcendent voice. Only five other poems in *The House of Life* introduce such a voice: "Love's Bauble" (22), "The Morrow's Message" (38), "Love's Fatality" (54), "Love's Last Gift" (59), and "The Sun's Shame" (93). Of these, only "Love's Bauble" and "Love's Last Gift" could be considered "positive."

O soul-sequestered face, thy form and hue!
Bewildering sounds, such as Spring wakens to,
   Shook in its folds; and through my heart its power
   Sped trackless as the immemorable hour
When birth's dark portal groaned and all was new.

But a veiled woman appeared, and she caught
   The banner round its staff, to furl and cling,—
   Then plucked a feather from the bearer's wing,
And held it to his lips that stirred it not,
   And said to me, "Behold there is no breath:
I and this Love are one, and I am Death."

In the octave, the "image" from "Life's retinue" possesses the poet utter-ly, granting him a "power" that he likens to being present at the mysterious origin of all life, the primal Spring. That origin, that making of reality that will serve as the basis of all future constructs, is an "immemorable hour," its fundamental reality seemingly guaranteed by its transcending any incorpora-tion into human memory or speech. Thus, even when granted an insight into reality, and even a partaking in it, far beyond what he has enjoyed before, the poet can only distinguish "bewildering sounds." As in Browning, such direct apprehension of life's mysteries strains the poet's ability to represent his vision.

In the sestet, the full consequences of this revelation become apparent. Even to have penetrated this far into "Life's retinue" is to have gone beyond the limits of the human as Rossetti conceives it. Direct contact (as opposed to indirect contact through symbols) with the other world pulls the poet from life toward death. We might be tempted to read "death" metaphorically here. The poet could be saying that the union with another in love, which results in the birth of new life (a child, his poetry), also involves a death to self that makes the new life possible. "Death," here, tied as it is to birth, might even take on its Elizabethan, sexual meaning, with the "power" that possesses the poet being the power of sexual passion. But the brutal and bare statement "Behold, there is no breath" denies all metaphorical readings. The creative union the poet has hoped to find in love, a union beyond self with the real, is declared to be identical with death. "I and this Love are one, and I am Death." Denied any experience of union in life, Rossetti comes to believe that the only possibility of union lies in death. The "joyous" romantic marriage becomes in Rossetti the *Liebestod* characteristic of the darker side of romanti-cism.

Such a reading would be preposterous if it were not for the evidence of the poems. We must remember that the sonnets were written over a number of years, and not all take such a despairing outlook. But a poem like "Mi-chelangelo's Kiss" (Sonnet 94) states clearly Rossetti's sporadic conviction that no satisfactory union will be experienced in this life: "even thus the Soul, / Touching at length some sorely-chastened goal, / Earns oftenest but a little." After such disappointment, hope comes to rest in the next life: "What holds for her Death's garner? And for thee?" At times, Rossetti welcomes reality's bitterest message—the necessity of death with its annihilation of all hopes for this life—because at least this action to end life proves that the reality he seeks is out there. Determined to prove reality exists and is meaningful, even if its meanings elude him, Rossetti can find in the forces that thwart his ordinary desires a confirmation that something exists beyond the self.

Rossetti's need to yield his own desires, his imaginative art, in the face of reality explains the presence of death, even the worship of and wish for it, found in many of his poems. Death represents that violent apocalyptic moment when the frustrating obstacles to understanding will be dissolved and all will be revealed. One part of the poet identifies with the transcendent force that will sweep all before it. In "The Monochord" (Sonnet 79) he considers how "Life's self," imagined as the "sky's vast vault or ocean's sound," "draws my life from me," pulling his small self back into a larger, universal self. And the poet's ambiguous response to this dissolution is expressed by his experiencing "regenerate rapture" at the very moment he perceives "the devious coverts of dismay." In death, the poet's isolation, his sojourn in what one poem calls the "cloud's confines," will end, and he will participate in the reality he never quite penetrated during his lifetime. With death will come complete knowledge of the meaning of things occult. " 'Strange to think by the way, / Whatever there is to know, / That shall we know one day' " ("The Cloud Confines"). In "The Portrait" that demystifying death is imagined as a birth into union and knowledge.

> How shall my soul stand rapt and awed,
> When, by the new birth borne abroad
> Throughout the music of the suns,
> It enters in her soul at once
> And knows the silence there for God!

A longing for death because it will rectify the painful ignorance of life would seem proof enough of a poet's failure to fashion, through his art, some satisfactory means by which experience can be made to yield its significance. But Rossetti's failure is both more complete—and more poignant. He cannot even affirm death wholeheartedly, because he does not know for certain that it will satisfy the desire for union. Along with the poems that call on death as the solution are those poems that wonder if death, too, might cheat his hopes. "Cloud and Wind" (Sonnet 44) contemplates the awful possibility that death only reveals "that all is vain / And that Hope sows what Love shall never reap." Death might only be a "sleep" which "ne'er notes" the very things the poet hoped to witness. Ignorant even here, Rossetti is forced back to prayer, pleading "That when the peace is garnered in from strife, / The work re-trieved, the will regenerate, / This soul may see thy face, O Lord of death!" (Sonnet 66).

3

Carlyle's Characteristics

"In fact, unity, agreement is always silent, or soft-voiced; it is only discord that loudly proclaims itself."

Pathetic, even ludicrous, sounds this blustering, long-winded prophet's repeated call for silence. "Well might the Ancients make Silence a god; for it is the element of all godhood, infinitude, or transcendental greatness" (Ch, 28:16).[1] "Let us honour the great Empire of *Silence,* once more! The boundless treasury which we do *not* jingle in our pockets, or count up and present before men! It is perhaps, of all things, the usefulest for each of us to do, in these loud times" (H, 5:101). The wordy praise of silence takes its place as but one of many confusions and contradictions in Carlyle's work. Born three years after Shelley and the same year as Keats, influenced by the German romantics who stand behind so much of Coleridge's work, Carlyle is by virtue of time and reading a romantic. Yet accidents of temperament, development, and provincialism not only delayed his career's start, but also rendered his work distinctively different from that of the English romantics. Still recognizably in the romantic tradition, Carlyle's ideas depart strongly enough from those of his predecessors to become the founding tenets of Victorianism. Most significant for my purposes is the deep mistrust of language and of fiction that contrasts with his strong claims for the power of the poetic word. Of the writers considered in this book, Ruskin, Dickens, George Eliot, and Browning were all directly influenced by Carlyle, while Dante Rossetti and the Pre-Raphaelite Brotherhood were influenced indirectly by way of Ruskin. Only Yeats stands apart, by virtue of his lack of interest in the nonpoetic.

Focusing on the essay entitled "Characteristics" and on *Sartor Resartus,*

---

1. All passages from Carlyle's works (except those from *Sartor Resartus)* are taken from the Centenary Edition of *The Works of Thomas Carlyle* (New York: Charles Scribner's Sons, 1900), 30 vols., with references given parenthetically in the text. In addition to giving volume and page numbers, I also identify the title of the work cited by the following abbreviations: "Characteristics", Ch; *Sartor Resartus,* SR; *On Heroes and Hero-Worship,* H; and *Past and Present,* P. Thus, my epigraph, which comes from "Characteristics," would be cited (Ch, 28:1–2). Passages from *Sartor* are from *Sartor Resartus,* ed. Charles F. Harrold (Indianapolis: Odyssey Press, 1937), with page numbers given in the text. Passages from the letters are from *The Collected Letters of Thomas and Jane Welsh Carlyle,* ed. Charles R. Sanders and K. J. Fielding (Durham: Duke University Press, 1970), abbreviated CL in the text.

I will emphasize Carlyle's ambivalence toward the poetic word as something that is a recognized necessity and yet is unreal in itself. Carlyle oscillates between his strong desire for direct, unmediated, and intuitive knowledge of the real and his understanding that such revelation is impossible. Almost everything he says can be placed into two categories: praise of the immediate and intuitive, or the outlining of strategies made necessary by the inevitability of indirect apprehension and expression. George Levine has written that the recognition that "certain things could only be said by indirection" was common to all the Victorians.[2] Carlyle is crucial to this study because, unlike Rossetti, he does not simply bemoan his failure to experience the intuitive knowledge the romantics claimed was possible. In response to this failure, Carlyle offers an elaborate theory of the symbol, a theory that justifies the necessity of indirection and explains how knowledge through representatives is achieved. That theory of the symbol, akin to Coleridge's but with significant differences, influences almost all Victorian thought about the nature of poetic language. At the same time, Carlyle resists the very indirection he presents as inevitable, so that he becomes a source for the allegiance of later writers to models of immediate perception and knowledge.

In "Characteristics" Carlyle's desire for direct participation in the real produces the compelling, yet odd, notion of unconsciousness that structures the essay. "The healthy know not of their health" (Ch, 28:1); to be unconscious means to be healthy, to be "whole" (Ch, 28:2). Carlyle avoids the Freudian paradox of "unconscious knowledge," but just barely. He seeks a primordial "mystic Union" (Ch, 28:12) between man and nature, man and God, for which the terms *participation* or *possession* seem to offer the best expression. Strictly speaking, there is no knowledge, no consciousness, of this union, although Carlyle breaks the silence in which that union should remain inviolate by identifying this alignment of human with divine will as "freedom" (Ch, 28:8).

To be conscious is to be separate. To identify the human already indicates its difference from the divine will, with this application of distinct names breaking the "silence" of "unity." Wholeness and participation stop when the thinker steps back and identifies himself and the object as two distinct things. Carlyle, of course, is well aware that his own practice is self-contradictory, that his praise of unconsciousness is conducted using the tools afforded by consciousness. But the deeper contradiction depends on whether divisive consciousness is inevitable or not. On this issue Carlyle wavers. His attack on consciousness follows the romantic disdain for "divisive Reason" and even shares a distant kinship with Blake's version of the Fall. And, like Blake, Carlyle acts (at least some of the time) as if the Fall was not inevitable and

2. *The Boundaries of Fiction: Carlyle, Macaulay, Newman* (Princeton: Princeton University Press, 1968), p. 20.

is not irreversible. "The beginning of Inquiry is Disease: all Science, if we consider well, as it must have originated in the feeling of something being wrong, so it is and continues to be but Division, Dismemberment, and partial healing of the wrong. Thus, as was of old written, the Tree of Knowledge springs from a root of evil, and bears fruits of good and evil" (Ch, 28:2–3). The fall into knowledge is the beginning of disease, even though Carlyle adds that the tree of knowledge, rooted in evil, does manage to bear (unspecified) good fruit along with the bad.

Carlyle recognizes that language is the primary agent of consciousness, and thus is led to denigrate the word.

> The virtue of Patriotism has already sunk from its pristine all-transcendent condition, before it has received a name. So long as the Commonwealth continues rightly athletic, it cares not to dabble in anatomy. Why teach obedience to the Sovereign; why so much as admire it, or separately recognise it, while a divine idea of Obedience perennially inspires all Men? Loyalty, like Patriotism, of which it is a form, was not praised till it had begun to decline. . . . For if the mystic significance of the State, let this be what it may, dwells vitally in every heart, encircles every life as with a second higher life, how should it stand self-questioning? It must rush outward, and express itself by work. Besides, if perfect, it is there as by necessity, and does not excite inquiry; it is also by nature infinite, has no limits; therefore can be circumscribed by no conditions and definitions; cannot be reasoned of; except *musically,* or in the language of Poetry, cannot yet so much as be spoken of. (CH, 28:14)

When we are conscious of something we name it. And this act of naming, as the term *definition* tells us, is an act of setting limits, which Carlyle deplores. Unconsciousness is whole, with its "vital force" (Ch, 28:5) pervading and uniting all things, but consciousness divides, giving each thing its distinct name. The fall into consciousness and knowledge is the fall into language. Against these divisive words, Carlyle will praise silence, action, and, at times, a special type of language called poetry. The man who partakes of the truth finds no need to speak of it, and he acts out of his participation, spontaneously and unreflectively. Words only mark a thing's absence. Insofar as the thing is present, no word is needed. "Already, to the popular judgement, he who talks much about Virtue in the abstract, begins to be suspect; it is shrewdly guessed that where there is a great preaching, there will be little almsgiving. Or again, on a wider scale, we can remark that ages of Heroism are not ages of Moral Philosophy; Virtue, when it can be philosophized of, has become aware of itself, is sickly and beginning to decline" (Ch, 28:8).

Awareness is the product of distance, of difference, of loss. At the heart of the word lies the empty space of the negative, resulting from the word's acting to set out the distance between the speaker and the thing named. We name the thing we wish to call to mind because it is not immediately here. Carlyle sees the very need for the word as proof that the thing is no longer possessed, as a reminder that the desired unity is not achieved.

The word is always a dialectical product, a meeting place for subject and object that contains within itself that negativity characteristic of all dialectical products. On the deepest level Carlyle remains a purist. His Calvinist heritage overcomes his acquired philosophical sophistication.[3] His most passionate metaphors envision purification by fire or exclusion; his most passionate desires are for single, unmixed conditions.[4] His fundamental world view remains stubbornly Manichean, separating the chosen from the damned, the creative from the mechanical, the natural from the artificial, the healthy from the sick, and so on.[5] The list of pairings could be endless, since Carlyle's habitual approach to a topic is to divide possible attitudes toward it into an approved stance and a reprehensible one. What complicates any such reading of his work, however, is that a dialectical view is almost always superimposed over the purist ideal, especially in the early writings. The outright condemnations of consciousness, of language, of the artificial, and of speculation are mixed in with another line of thought that grudgingly admits the inevitability of these impurities and explains their possible usefulness.

Carlyle's desire for the "pure unmixed life" of unconsciousness (Ch, 28:16) is so strong that he has trouble admitting the Fall was necessary and irreversible, not to mention trying to present it as fortunate. In all his work Carlyle will, at some point, accept the fact that we live a postlapsarian existence, but he will also always talk as if such were not an inescapable destiny. In "Characteristics" he claims that each man, in his youth, "stood as in the centre of Nature, giving and receiving in harmony with it all" (Ch, 28:2). This

3. To claim that Carlyle remains a Calvinist underneath all his acquired German ideas is the oldest cliche of Carlyle criticism, but nonetheless true. Froude is one of the primary sources for this view. See James Anthony Froude, *Thomas Carlyle: A History of the First Forty Years of His Life, 1795–1835* (New York: Charles Scribner's Sons, 1882), vol. 1, chap. 1, pp. 1–18.

4. For example, Carlyle asks if this era's self-consciousness is "the effort of Nature, exerting her medicative force to cast-out foreign impediments, and once more become One, become whole?" (Ch, 28:32). I will discuss a passage containing metaphors of purification by fire at the end of this chapter.

5. Again, to speak of Carlyle's essentially dualistic vision is to repeat one of the fundamental tenets of Carlyle criticism. For a good summary of the polarities of Carlyle's thought and their influence on how and what he writes, see George Levine, "The Use and Abuse of Carlylese," in *The Art of Victorian Prose,* ed. George Levine and William Madden (New York: Oxford University Press, 1968), pp. 101–26. G. B. Tennyson, *Sartor Called Resartus* (Princeton: Princeton University Press, 1965), argues that "the conflict between dualism and monism in Carlyle is more apparent than real" (151). Tennyson stresses how Carlyle manipulates his contrasts to "demonstrate an underlying inexpressible unity in all phenomena" (151). I am also interested in Carlyle's attempts to forge "unmixed wholes" (Ch, 28:16), but find that the "habitual dualism of his writings" (Tennyson, 151) often works against the stated goal of making all one. Carlyle's urge to overcome a dualistic vision is, of course, another indication of his continuity with the romantic tradition.

Wordsworthian image is used to suggest the possibility of that unconscious, healthy harmony the essay as a whole presents as the ideal human condition. Earlier, happier eras in history are also presented to the reader as proofs that Carlyle's ideals can in fact be lived by men. The golden age is not just an Edenic myth, but also a historical fact. Carlyle stands at the beginning of Victorian medievalism, and, of the writers I discuss, only Dickens never resorts to a historical myth of an ideal past. Republican Rome, rather than feudal Europe, represents the ideal in "Characteristics." "Society was what we can call *whole,* in both senses of the word. The individual man was in himself a whole, or complete union; and could combine with his fellows as the living member of a greater whole. For all men, through their life, were animated by one great Idea; thus all efforts pointed one way, everywhere there was *wholeness*" (Ch, 28:15).

Carlyle's goal is to restore such wholeness, as some of his pronouncements at the end of the essay make clear. He hails "a new revelation" (Ch, 28:40) that is working slowly so that "the Certain come to light, and again lie visible on the surface" (Ch, 28:40). (Note the visual imagery characteristic of passages about revelation.) "Remarkable it is, truly, how everywhere the eternal fact begins again to be recognised, that there is a Godlike in human affairs" (Ch, 28:42); ". . . and from the bosom of Eternity there shine for us celestial guiding stars" (Ch, 28:43). All these passages suggest that the truths that for now lie hidden beyond sight can be perceived and acted upon. At present, perhaps, "the Divinity has withdrawn from the Earth" (Ch, 28:30), but Carlyle offers hope of his return so that all men might again recognize the same "great governing idea." We should note that, in spite of appealing to the romantic image of the child's union with nature, Carlyle's vision of an unfallen world is primarily cultural, expressed as a society that inspires a perfect unity of purpose in all its citizens.

Yet how are these "eternal facts," upon which the perfect society rests, to be apprehended? Carlyle tries to have it both ways. At times he describes the truth as a "mystery" that lies too deep for human knowledge or words; at other times he insists that the facts are there for all to see. This contradiction finds expression in the oxymoronic phrase Carlyle borrows from Goethe: "the open secret."[6] When stressing the "openness" as distinct from the "secret," Carlyle almost always uses imagery of sight.[7] The poet or hero is defined at various times as one who looks "direct[ly] into the heart of things, and *sees*

6. Charles Frederick Harrold, *Carlyle and German Thought: 1819–1834* (New Haven: Yale University Press, 1934), pp. 117–20, discusses fully Carlyle's sources for the expression "the open secret" and the difficulties Carlyle overlooks by resorting to this paradox.

7. Carlyle's habitual use of light-dark imagery and metaphors of sight has been noted by various critics. The fullest accounts can be found in Tennyson, *Sartor Called Resartus,* pp. 195–200, and in John Holloway, *The Victorian Sage* (New York: W. W. Norton, 1965), pp. 33–41.

the truth of them" (H, 5:68). Carlyle simply sidesteps the epistemological problems here by resorting to paradox or to a romantic notion of the poet as inspired seer; what is crucial to note is his impatience with indirection and his reliance on direct apprehension of fact when he needs, at crucial moments, to identify the real.

At his most confident (and, we might add, his most obnoxious) Carlyle allows himself to proclaim the "eternal facts" against which he judges contemporary society and finds it wanting. *Past and Present,* in which Carlyle brings his society before the "court of fact," offers the most examples. "Can you any more continue to lead a Working World unregimented, anarchic? I answer, and the Heavens and Earth are now answering, No" (P, 10:273). "The mandate of God to His creature man is: Work" (P, 10:275). The comedy of Carlyle's need to make his own favorite doctrines the word of some higher power should not blind us to what is at stake here. Like Rossetti, Carlyle wants to align himself with some truth beyond the self. And, like Rossetti, although with a greater confidence in his ultimate success in probing the "mystery" of reality, Carlyle develops a series of complicated strategies to grant him access to the real.

The necessity for these strategies remains a recurrent problem for Carlyle's critics. In the first place, despite all the talk about mysteries that frustrate efforts at expression, when Carlyle does make one of his pronouncements, the banality of the truth he presents discredits the winding paths he took to reach it. Stated baldly, these truths are seldom very distant from quite traditional Christian morality. Furthermore, since he is willing to present revealed truths in order to ground his social prescriptions and moral precepts, why does Carlyle continue to insist the world is a mystery whose secret can only be fathomed through elaborate indirections? I agree with G. B. Tennyson that Carlyle ultimately "subordinates form to meaning," that his goal as a writer always rests in communicating his message.[8] But, if such is the case, why do we find such formal and stylistic extravagance in works that present fairly straightforward meanings? The only possible answer is that Carlyle, at least some of the time, required those extravagances to reach the truths he presents. Direct revelation is only available to him intermittently; he finds it necessary to develop other means of access to the real.

Victorian doubt, with its consequent weakening of moral authority, offers one explanation for Carlyle's inability to rely exclusively on direct revelation. Carlyle's career demonstrates that such doubt was often not cen-

8. Tennyson, *Sartor Called Resartus,* p. 92, discusses "Carlyle's subordination of form to meaning." The point is a valid one: Carlyle has little interest in words themselves; his primary focus is always on the meaning the words convey. Yet what strikes the reader of *Sartor Resartus* most forcefully is the oddity of the form and the extravagances of the style. Such was John Sterling's reaction in 1835, and surely still is ours. For Sterling's letter to Carlyle, see *Sartor Resartus,* pp. 307–16.

tered on the nature of the truth but on what contemporaries would recognize as acceptable evidence of that truth. In the later works (*On Heroes and Hero-Worship, Past and Present,* and *Latter-Day Pamphlets*), a confidence in the authority of his own voice (gained, of course, by his finally winning recognition and acclaim in the 1830s) allows Carlyle to assert boldly positions he is much more reticent about proclaiming in the earlier works. The earlier works show a much stronger effort to "earn" their truths, to have eternal principles grow (we might say "organically") out of the interaction of the writer with his age ("Signs of the Times," "Characteristics"), with literature (review essays, essays on the German romantics, Burns, Boswell, and others), or in the dynamics of the work itself (*Sartor Resartus*). In other words, the earlier works are less expository, more elaborate in the rhetorical means used to draw forth the truth and the reader's consent to it. John Holloway has argued that Carlyle's writing works to persuade not by logic but by emotion and by appeals to the imagination. He enacts his ideas by dramatizing them, often relying on metaphorical associations.[9] Of course, the later works still employ these techniques, but they also substitute assertion for them with a frequency not found in the earlier works. Not that such assertions mean that all doubt is gone. Victorian doubt manifests itself not in explicitly questioning traditional Christian truths (which most Victorians felt were indispensable to the maintenance of society), but in trying to find new grounds that justified the ratification of those truths. If Carlyle's end point is close to banality, how he gets there reveals his uneasiness with the formulas, and modern critics have, inevitably, been more interested in those works in which he arrives at his "philosophy" through a variety of linguistic and metaphorical manipulations rather than by willful assertion.

Carlyle's doubt is the other side of the myth of a golden past. The present age stands condemned because it cannot believe unquestioningly as the wholesome society of the past did. "That this is the age of Metaphysics, in the proper, or sceptical Inquisitory sense ... we regard as our indubitable misfortune" (Ch, 28:27). "This is specially the misery which has fallen on man in our Era. Belief, Faith has well-nigh vanished from the world" (Ch, 28:29). The "mysterious" nature of reality, its being hidden from direct perception, becomes particularly troublesome in an age when faith does not guide knowledge. Ruskin, Browning, George Eliot, and countless other Victorians will echo Carlyle's view of the age, a time when Christians, uncertain of their faith, were unable to combat the ethical monstrosities of the political economists. Only a reorganization of society around a recognition of certain realities now ignored would satisfy these writers.

Carlyle's condemnation of the age as faithless also introduces the consciousness of historical change, including his own sense of living in an un-

9. See *The Victorian Sage,* chap. 1.

blessed time. The "Divinity has withdrawn" (Ch, 28:30) at this point in time, Carlyle informs us, a declaration that would seem to shift blame from the individual who has doubts to the distinctive characteristics of the age. Carlyle's position here approaches historical determinism; not only can the individual not be expected to possess a faith the age itself does not possess, but the age's own faithlessness is determined by the peculiar feature (the withdrawal of God) that defines it as a distinct historical period.

As we might expect, Carlyle does not rigidly adhere to such an historical determinism. We have already seen that he has argued that individuals in any age can experience the harmonious union with nature that he advocates, and that he hopes his work can overcome the present age's faithlessness. And he also collapses all historical differences in the other direction as well, portraying all human existence as lived in the faithless condition characteristic of life after the Fall. Even in an essay as short as "Characteristics" these contradictions appear without Carlyle's (apparent) awareness. Shortly before describing the perfection of Rome, Carlyle applies his notion of unconsciousness to moral behavior. The ideal moral stance is an alignment of the will with God's commands, resulting in a silent and complete obedience. But Carlyle adds: "This, true enough, is an ideal, impossible state of being; yet ever the goal towards which our actual state of being strives; which it is the more perfect the nearest it can approach" (Ch, 28:8). Later we get this viewpoint elevated into a maxim: "Perfection of Practice, like completeness of Opinion, is always approaching, never arrived; Truth, in the words of Schiller, *immer wird, nie ist;* never *is,* always *is a-being*" (Ch, 28:38). That "dualism of Soul and Body" that is "itself a symptom of disease" early in the essay is not an historical, but a universal, condition some twenty pages later: "Everywhere there is Dualism, Equipoise; a perpetual Contradiction dwells in us" (Ch, 28:27).

In this second version, the fall into knowledge, into consciousness, defines the human condition, so that unconsciousness, total harmony with and participation in the truth, is an ideal condition never achieved in history. In the world after the Fall, knowledge is always partial, is always afflicted by its sense of distance from that reality it longs to know. The epistemological problems that plagued the Victorians become, from this perspective, part of the universal human condition. While praising unconsciousness, Carlyle recognizes that man's very being is consciousness. Speech and speculation are precisely what define the sort of animal man is. "In the perfect state, all Thought were but the picture and inspiring symbol of Action; Philosophy, except as Poetry and Religion, would have no being. And yet how, in this imperfect state, can it be avoided, can it be dispensed with? Man stands as in the centre of Nature; his fraction of Time encircled by Eternity, his handbreath of Space encircled by Infinitude: how shall he forbear asking himself, What am I; and Whence; and Whither?" (Ch, 28:25).

I want to turn now to Carlyle's understanding of the best way to live in this "imperfect state," an understanding that deeply influenced the Victorians. But the reader is asked to recall Carlyle's ambivalence throughout the ensuing discussion. Carlyle devotes a great deal of attention to this effort to mitigate the consequences of the Fall, but the basic protest against the fact of the Fall and the refusal to accept its irreversibility is ever present as well. We should also recognize that the Fall for Carlyle, while moral, is also fundamentally epistemological, a fact that reveals Carlyle's allegiance to the neo-Platonism characteristic of romanticism. The Fall is measured by man's distance from the spiritual reality with which he longs to be united, so that a strategy to allow a more complete apprehension of that reality is the offered remedy.

Carlyle's strategies for dealing with our fallen condition are generally dialectical. Kenneth Burke has identified the dialectic with irony, because in dialectical thought every assertion is always immediately qualified by confrontation with its opposite. In the dialectic no entity or viewpoint is absolute, but is subordinated to the grand design of the dialectic as a whole.[10] The dialectic, of course, is also apocalyptic, since the particular event is transformed once we grasp its significance in the whole scheme. Romantic irony becomes the characteristic stance of the dialectical outlook of the German romantics who influenced Carlyle's use of the dialectic.[11]

Carlyle's most sustained effort in dialectical thought is, of course, *Sartor Resartus*. Given Carlyle's tendency, throughout his career, to declare direct perception of divine fact possible and to announce these facts in his own voice, the restraint of *Sartor Resartus* is both remarkable and admirable. In fact, Carlyle's strict adherence to dialectical logic produces the key distinction between his theory of the symbol and Coleridge's. The complexity of *Sartor Resartus,* its idiosyncratic and fundamentally ironic form, and, yes, its excesses, reflect the difficulties accruing from the author's concerted effort to give the negative its due. While the antiintellectualism and mistrust of language (in favor of action and fact) found in Carlyle's other works greatly influenced many Victorian writers, his more subtle examination of symbols in *Sartor Resartus* also found a receptive audience. He explores the limits and ambigui-

10. Kenneth Burke, *A Grammar of Motives* (Berkeley: University of California Press, 1965), pp. 511–17.
11. The annihilation of the particular to allow an indeterminate but overwhelming truth to stand forth is usually called "romantic irony" in order to distinguish it from more limited forms of irony in which the meaning implied by the ironic statement or structure can be reconstructed and determined. For a discussion of this distinction between two types of irony and an application of it to Carlyle, see Janice L. Haney, " 'Shadow-Hunting': Romantic Irony, *Sartor Resartus* and Victorian Romanticism," *Studies in Romanticism* 17 (1978): 307–33; Anne K. Mellor, *English Romantic Irony* (Cambridge: Harvard University Press, 1980), pp. 109–34; and Peter Allan Dale, "*Sartor Resartus* and the Inverse Sublime: The Art of Humorous Deconstruction," in *Allegory, Myth, and Symbol,* ed. Morton W. Bloomfield (Cambridge: Harvard University Press, 1981), pp. 293–312.

ties of the symbol, examining the use of material forms to represent non-material realities. He remains faithful throughout the book to the symbol's indirection, to its silences, to its lack of clarity, resisting (for the most part) the temptation to denigrate the word for frustrating the desire for uncloudy, unmixed truths.

The symbol, as defined in *Sartor Resartus,* is a dialectical product, consisting of the material and the immaterial, the articulate and the silent. (This definition is crucial for any discussion of Victorian literature and I will find many occasions to refer back to it.) "In a Symbol there is concealment and yet revelation: here therefore, by Silence and by Speech acting together, comes a double significance. And if both the Speech itself be high, and the Silence fit and noble, how expressive will their union be" (SR, 219). "In the Symbol . . . the Infinite is made to blend itself with the Finite, to stand visible, and as it were, attainable there" (SR, 220). The symbol conceals as well as reveals; its silence is a reticence, an indication of what is lost in the translation of the represented into the symbol that represents it. A difference between represented and representative resides in the symbol as a negativity, a silence, a concealment.

This emphasis on the symbol's inbuilt silence differentiates the Carlylean symbol from the Coleridgean one. For both writers, the symbol provides access to the real (which is understood as spiritual), but Carlyle is more insistent that the symbol is not the real itself. Coleridge's symbol reveals reality by virtue of being a participant in it. (See my discussion of Coleridge's views in the Introduction.) In Carlyle's schema, reality is much more radically absent; the symbol exists in a separate, mediate realm that indicates the absent reality as much by "silence" as by "speech," as much by "concealment" as by "revelation." In other words, Carlyle makes the relation of worldly appearances to spiritual reality more distant than Coleridge does. Consequently, Carlyle finds the passage from appearance to reality more difficult than the romantics did, and Carlyle reveres and enjoys nature much less than the romantics. The apocalyptic impulse to pierce appearances, "the shows of things" to use one of Carlyle's favorite phrases, dominates his relation to this material world since he understands its primary function to be its symbolic indication of a truth quite distinct from its physical presence.

Here is the central explanation for that "double vision" critics find in *Sartor Resartus.* [12] The "double significance" of the symbol is both what it signifies and its limits. The symbol is the material thing that brings the immaterial to mind, but its difference from the immaterial must always be remembered. A reliance on symbols is explained by the assertion that reality is ineffable, a position Browning will also take. The reality worthy to serve as poetry's subject is complex and multifaceted, never to be fully com-

12. See Tennyson, *Sartor Called Resartus,* p. 277.

prehended in any sign, as opposed to those "mechanical" truths that are the subject of scientific treatises and utilitarian tracts. Carlyle's theory of the symbol is consistent with his identification of reality as a "mystery" and his insistence that the most important realities are not accessible to the forms of representation, logic, and evidence that prevail in a materialistic understanding of the world. The "organic" cannot be reduced to a sign without losing its vitality, so the symbol's reticence protects the life of complex organic reality even while serving to indicate its existence. The Carlylean symbol mitigates the danger of the word's displacing the thing it represents by carrying within it the insistence that the represented far exceeds this representative. His theory guarantees the insignificance of the symbol in the face of the reality symbolized.

The frustrating consequence of the symbol's reticence is the necessity to always approach the real by roundabout methods. We might suspect this insistence on the need for indirection is only an attempt to wriggle out from under the materialist's request to *see* these "eternal facts" the poets keep flapping about. But we need not doubt that Carlyle also experienced the difficulty of finding words that expressed adequately what he was struggling to say. "Alas, the *thing* I want to do is precisely the thing I cannot do. My mind would so fain deliver itself adequately of that 'Divine Idea of the World'; and only in quite *in* adequate approximations is such deliverance possible" (CL, 7:6).

The symbol's inadequacy also serves as the basis for Carlyle's stress on history and historical change.[13] Since all material facts only approximate the truth about the world, there must be a series of approximations, each striving to represent more fully—or, at least, in a new way—the truth. The very basis of change lies in imperfection. But we should not overestimate Carlyle's historicism. His radical distinction between the symbol and the thing it symbolizes allows him to maintain belief in a reality that transcends change. Material forms change in time, but the underlying spiritual foundations remain always the same. A more radical historicism would argue that reality itself is different in different eras, but for Carlyle reality (which is spiritual) does not change, only modes of representation (which are material) do. "Thus in all Poetry, Worship, Art, Society, as one form passes into another, nothing is lost; it is but the superficial, as it were the *body* only, that grows obsolete and dies; under the mortal body lies a *soul* which is immortal; which anew incarnates itself in fairer revelation" (Ch, 28:39). Just as Carlyle's mistrust of words recurs throughout Victorian literature, so his attempt to avoid the relativistic consequences of historicism is repeated by a number of writers. The Victorian search for the real is often a search for that truth that resists the ravages of time. In

13. Critical discussions of Carlyle's theory of history abound. I have found Peter Allan Dale's *The Victorian Critic and the Idea of History*, chap. 1, especially helpful and interesting.

fact, the mistrust of words is motivated in part by the recognition that they change and thus cannot satisfy the desire for an unwavering truth. Carlyle willingly lowers the symbol into the world of flux, but fully intends to hold reality out of that sublunar realm. We should note, in passing, that Carlyle can only maintain this distinction between changing representations and a changeless reality if he assumes an ability to perceive the difference between representative and represented. The problem here is the same one encountered by Locke: if all we perceive are our ideas, then how do we even know that there are things that cause those ideas and are distinct from them? Only Carlyle's assumption that he knows the nature of reality apart from the ways it is represented in symbols allows him to escape a complete historical relativism and to identify the difference between the symbol and reality. His theory of the symbol, which is a theory of mediation, depends, then, on an assumption of some revealed, immediate knowledge.

But, even though Carlyle's historicism is hardly radical, submitting the symbol to change presents him with enough problems, ones written into the very form of *Sartor Resartus.* The unwelcome truth of indirection, of the symbol's inadequacy and its temporal status, is taught by Teufelsdröckh (sometimes directly, sometimes indirectly), while the Editor expresses the normal man's exasperation at the obstructions that frustrate the desire for direct knowledge. "Singular Teufelsdröckh, would thou hadst told thy singular story in plain words" (SR, 18). The reader gets the truth about Teufelsdröckh and the clothes philosophy indirectly, by way of various detours and through the mediation of the Editor. The book seems to serve Carlyle as an exercise in humility and patience, an exercise he also imposes on the reader. He has forced himself to take in the German message, despite all his impatience with German methods and even his lingering intolerance of the message itself.

Impatience and exasperation are certainly appropriate responses to *Sartor Resartus,* and its achievement rests on its not relinquishing either side of its understanding of the symbol as concealment and revelation. The extent of the concealment cannot fail, at times, to disconcert. "For my own part, these considerations, of our Clothes-thatch, and how, reaching inwards even to our heart of hearts, it tailorises and demoralises us, fill me with a certain horror at myself and mankind" (SR, 57). The symbol will be hated for its distortions, for the way it shapes our lives so completely in spite of its inaccuracies. "For it is true what Goethe teaches, and every day I feel it truer: 'The first *word* we utter we begin to *err*' " (CL, 7:20). But when he most fully accepts the necessity of indirection, Carlyle can insist that nothing at all would be known if not presented to thought or to others by way of the symbol. "If Clothes, in these times, 'so tailorise and demoralise us,' they have no redeeming value; can they be altered to serve better; must they of necessity be thrown to the dogs?" (SR, 59). Clothes cannot be abandoned because they are the only access to certain truths. Clothes may falsify what we believe to be naked reality, but they serve as the only way to represent it. "Must not the Imagination weave Garments, visible Bodies, wherein the else invisible creations and inspirations of our Reason are, like Spirits, revealed?" (SR, 73). Where reality is invisible, the symbol is necessary even though the limits of its accuracy have been acknowledged. The naked truth, because immaterial, can not be apprehended, it can only appear in the material symbol. Yet something is lost in the truth's translation into the "visible Body" that represents it. When he manages to resist the paradox of an eloquent silence, Carlyle can endorse the necessity of words even while admitting their distortion.

The defense against distortion is irony. If all clothes, all symbols, are inadequate representations, then irony functions to indicate any particular symbol's inadequacy. Irony is humility, the admission of incompleteness, of the symbol's not being the thing itself. The ironic undermining of any particular perspective is found in George Eliot and Browning as well as in Carlyle, with both Eliot and Browning also reproducing Carlyle's attempt to suggest a global perspective beyond irony that would encompass all particular representations. Irony serves to remind the reader that any given topic is not *the* topic, the real.

Carlyle's irony tends toward annihilation; these clothes must be dissolved in favor of the spiritual reality they are meant to convey. Lurking behind Carlyle's habitual irony is the mystic's masochism, the desire to abolish the self in the face of the overwhelming truth of God. Protesting continually that his formulas are only approximations, and that others' formulas are equally inadequate, Carlyle points us toward the more violent apocalypse (revelation) when all things human will be destroyed and the divine will stand forward in its full glory. By aligning himself, at times, with the apocalyptic, "molesting" forces, Carlyle can overcome some of the limits of the human. He can see the futility of merely human actions and strategies.[14] However, the price paid for this continual irony is an almost total loss of concreteness.[15] The particular things of this world are of little interest to Carlyle. They are only important insofar as they function to illustrate the divine or Victorian man's reprehensible distance from the divine. Thus, Carlyle can read the "signs of the times," yet refuse to attach any importance to particular political issues of the day such

14. For two excellent discussions of Carlyle's refusal to recognize any political action as potentially effective see Philip Rosenberg, *The Seventh Hero: Thomas Carlyle and the Theory of Radical Activism* (Cambridge: Harvard University Press, 1974), chap. 2, and Patrick Brantlinger, *The Spirit of Reform: British Literature and Politics, 1832–1867* (Cambridge: Harvard University Press, 1977), chap. 3.

15. See *The Boundaries of Fiction*, pp. 38–41. Levine argues, I think convincingly, that the piling up of instances, examples, and metaphors in Carlyle leads not to a density of texture in his work, but to an overriding sense that all particular things are roughly equivalent, only meaningful insofar as they act as symbols and serve to reveal what is essentially a monochromatic truth.

as the Reform Bill or repeal of the Corn Laws. He cannot believe political action one way or the other will significantly alter the essential structure of human life, a structure determined by our distance from the monolithic eternal truth that all human appearances strive to embody. Only a complete restructuring of society, a complete change of heart, offers the kind of reform he seeks.

Words and symbols are inevitably inadequate for Carlyle because they are material, while what they try to represent is spiritual. "Language is called the Garment of Thought: however, it should rather be, Language is the Flesh-Garment, the Body of Thought" (SR, 73). Carlyle's style, of which this sentence is a good example, demonstrates how fundamentally material language is for him. The persistent capitalization of nouns turns categories like *thought* and *body* into objects, which then can be moved around on various sides of the verb *to be*. For all the doctrinal stress on action in his work, Carlyle's sentences generally feature very weak verbs, with the emphasis falling on the manipulation of stressed nouns. He uses *to be* for purposes of definition; the shifting about of nouns lands them in new categories that alter their meaning for the reader.[16] Examples abound. Looking at the three paragraphs on page 15 of "Characteristics" reveals that Carlyle has capitalized the abstract nouns of Society, the Perfect, Religion, Opinion, Action, and "the one great Idea." Out of sixteen sentences in these three paragraphs, thirteen have some form of *to be*. The continual struggle to make words point beyond themselves manifests itself in a constant redefinition of terms so that they might function better.

Totally accurate symbols will never be achieved in the fallen world that makes the recourse to symbols necessary, and in at least one place Carlyle finds reason to be thankful for this limitation. While living in a world of approximations, man can maintain his separate existence, a theme Ruskin will develop more fully. Once the full truth is known and man is united with it, time and life will end. "Could you ever establish a Theory of the Universe that were entire, unimprovable, and which needed only to be got by heart; man then were spiritually defunct, the Species we now name Man had ceased to exist. But the gods, kinder to us than we are to ourselves, have forbidden such suicidal acts" (Ch, 28:38). Here Carlyle finds comfort in the fact that ignorance is assured; the Fall is fortunate because the ignorance it imposes establishes the very possibility of our existence. But even here, Carlyle's fundamental desire to reverse the Fall comes through. Man as described by Carlyle will continually thirst for that knowledge which, if achieved, could only destroy him; "the

---

16. Holloway, *The Victorian Sage,* chap. 1; Levine, "The Use and Abuse of Carlylese"; and Mark Roberts, "Carlyle and the Rhetoric of Unreason," *Essays in Criticism* 18 (1968): 397–419, offer a thoughtful discussion of Carlyle's style. In *Sartor Called Resartus* (320), Tennyson illustrates Carlyle's fondness for definition by listing fifteen different definitions of man found in *Sartor.* Holloway describes Carlyle's definitions as being presented in such a way that Carlyle can claim "to discover the true meaning" of the word, "not to prescribe his own" (44).

gods, kinder to us than we are to ourselves," guarantee that this inappropriate desire is never satisfied. Carlyle's theory of history, then, can be read as an assurance of the continued inaccuracy of representation, which means that history and the species will continue. Obviously, this perspective, while still ironic in its qualification of every single representation, works against the apocalyptic desire to do away finally with representations and live in the presence of the real. The absence of apocalyptic and ironic impulses in Ruskin results, in part, from his allegiance to the material human existence that ignorance allows us to maintain.

Even if we are unlikely to escape our material condition in the near future, Carlyle still insists that man's true concern must be the spiritual. This insistence, of course, is Carlyle's response to the various technicians, political economists, utilitarians, and early capitalists who seemed so clearly to believe that, and act as if, the world is governed by material impulses alone. While Carlyle's own brand of earnestness and antiintellectualism could make him denounce philosophy (as he does in "Characteristics") and fiction,[17] such denunciations did not much bother his followers in the literary world. Clearly Carlyle was on the literary side in the battle shaping up between (what we would call today) the technocrats and the humanists. The new materialists had little patience with literature and the values it represented, and used its fictive nature to discredit its viewpoints. Carlyle, of course, shared some of the puritanism that lay behind the technocrats' (who were almost all Dissenters) contempt for literature. His various denunciations of fiction also stem from a distaste for the frivolous and a mistrust of the indirect, but more centrally he was simply trying to insure that literature grapple fully with moral issues. Until Pater, all the major Victorians accepted Carlyle's position on this matter. Fiction, if used at all, must be justified by its referring to recognizable social and moral issues. The "facts" to which fiction must be faithful (in the Carlylean formula) need not be historical facts in the strictest sense, but could be the moral and spiritual "facts" that Carlyle was continually struggling to prove were more real than the facts of the materialists. Admittedly, Carlyle at times let his double use of the word *fact* (to designate "real" events and entities in the world and to indicate spiritual realities) confuse him, and so he talks as if no fiction were admissible because it is not related to fact. When, in

17. Much critical attention has been devoted to Carlyle's statements against fiction. A. Abbot Ikeler in *Puritan Temper and Transcendental Faith* (Columbus: Ohio State University Press, 1972) offers the fullest documentation of Carlyle's statements against fiction, demonstrating beyond a doubt that Carlyle had contradictory things to say on the subject from the beginning of his career to the end. Ikeler, however, depends entirely on the split between Carlyle's Calvinism and his love of the Germans to explain the contradiction. Levine's discussion in *The Boundaries of Fiction* is more fruitful since it focuses on the advantages that accrue to the writer when he uses fictional forms; yet Levine remains aware that Carlyle's avowed trust in "facts" and facts alone makes fiction suspect to him. From my perspective here, Carlyle's ambivalence toward fiction is part and parcel of his ambivalence toward indirection. Why, we can expect him to ask impatiently at times, must we write known falsehoods in order to say something true?

"Biography," Carlyle has his fictional persona Gottfried Sauerteig write, "Fiction, while the feigner of it knows that his feigning, partakes, more than we suspect, of the nature of *lying;* and ever has an, in some degree, unsatisfactory character" (27:31), he not only blatantly contradicts his own practice in the essay, but has lost sight of the distinction between historical fact and eternal facts that is usually so crucial to him. Carlyle should (as he does at times) recognize that historical facts, like fictional creations, must be looked *through* since their substantial existence is of little importance compared to their serving as material manifestations of the divine. Fiction actually might be preferable to history since fiction does not tempt us to focus on this sublunar realm, but indicates immediately that the things presented have no value in and of themselves. In this vein, Carlyle can write to Mill in 1834: "I approve greatly of your purpose to discard Cant and Falsehood of all kinds: yet there is a kind of Fiction, which is not Falsehood, and has more effect in addressing men than many a Radical is aware of" (CL, 7:71). Only slightly perturbed by Carlyle's strictures against fiction, the writers who came after him valued his adamant rejection of materialism. In England, unlike France, "realism" in nineteenth-century literature almost always rested on the assertion that the true reality is spiritual and that literature's task is to be faithful to emotional and spiritual values. (Even George Eliot, the "realist" with the closest ties to the positivists, eventually came to stress emotional and spiritual realities over material and environmental ones.) "Realism" is a defensive term, one that insists on the reality of precisely those entities the opposition refuses to credit as real. Carlyle is one of the founders and most radical proponents of this Victorian realism. Where Dickens will suggest that both "fact" and "fancy" exist and that literature functions to make certain that "fancy" is not overlooked,[18] Carlyle insists that the material world is but a "show" and that only the spiritual is real.

Claiming the spiritual is the real leaves Carlyle with serious epistemological problems. How are we "to look through the Shows of things into Things themselves" (SR, 205)? "Everywhere do the Shows of things oppress him, withstand him, threaten him with fearfullest destruction: only by victoriously penetrating into Things themselves can he find peace and a stronghold" (SR, 206). Such insight becomes possible only when Clothes are made *"transparent"* (SR, 67). If only the material sign had no body, no existence of its own, and served exclusively to indicate the existence of the true and the real behind it. With this desire, Carlyle's resistance to the symbol's "concealment" rears its head once more.

The ideal situation would involve a medium of expression that dissolved

18. Dickens's willingness to accept "steam engines" along with fancy is indicated in a letter written to a critic of *Hard Times* in 1854: "I often say to Mr. Gradgrind that there is reason ... in all he does—but that he overdoes it. Perhaps by dint of his going his way and my going mine, we shall meet at last at some halfway house, where there are flowers on the carpet, and a little standing room for Queen Mab's chariot among the Steam Engines." Quoted from Michael Goldberg, *Carlyle and Dickens* (Athens: University of Georgia Press, 1972), p. 29.

itself after allowing the truth to be perceived, a desire echoed by Browning in the metaphor of the ring at the beginning of *The Ring and the Book.* Carlyle describes this desired medium as "a beam of perfect white light, rendering all things visible, but itself unseen, even because it was of that perfect whiteness, and no irregular obstruction had yet broken it into colours" (Ch, 28:2). The difference between the word in the text and the real thing the writer wants to present causes a strain felt by all "realisms," and realistic writers strive, in various ways, to minimize that difference. The modernist abandonment of realism is founded on a heightened awareness of and insistence upon the very difference the realistic writer tries to minimize. Since words and things are distinct entities, the modern writer decides that literature should simply focus on the enclosed system of language without expecting words to refer to anything outside of themselves.[19] When forced to choose, Carlyle's purism makes him want the thing itself, not its representative, but modern purism has tended to choose the word itself, uncontaminated by any connection to the world of things. For Yeats, "words alone are certain good," a conclusion no Victorian writer would reach. The difficulties suffered by the Victorian writers in their quest to insure the word's ability to represent the real in spite of that word's difference from reality forms a large part of my subject in this study; and the extent of those difficulties makes the modernist decision to sever completely the tie between word and world more understandable.

Carlyle never confuses words and things; he never attempts to make them equivalent. His concern is that the word must be able to represent the real in spite of its difference from it, and the ideal of a dissolving medium expresses the hope that the word will disappear once it has succeeded in making the designated thing appear.[20] His theory of the symbol is meant to explain the process by which material things serve to make the spiritual known. Knowledge through symbols is difficult and partial; it is the knowledge available to fallen man. But Carlyle also allows himself other kinds of knowledge

19. See Gerald Bruns, *Modern Poetry and the Idea of Language,* for an extended description of the "hermetic tradition" that isolates literature from the world. Perhaps the most vocal contemporary champion of this tradition is William Gass. See, for example, the essays collected in *The World Within the Word* (New York: Alfred A. Knopf, 1978).

20. The ideal of a disappearing word fits the definition of prose offered by Paul Valery. Prose, says Valery, is language that "vanishes once it has *arrived."* Once "understood," the words of prose melt away and are "entirely and definitely replaced by the meaning." Valery typifies a particular modern stance when he emphatically differentiates poetry from prose. Poetry insures that, if the reader does move through the words toward their meaning, "the living pendulum is brought back, at each line, to its verbal and musical starting point." In poetry, our focus should be on the words, not what they denote. See "Remarks on Poetry," in *The Art of Poetry,* vol. 7 of *The Collected Works of Paul Valery* (New York: Pantheon Books, 1958), esp. pp. 206–12. Although Carlyle is hardly consistent on the subject, he would certainly at times define poetry in a way directly contrary to Valery's definition. Poetry would be the form of language in which words, since most perfectly suited to their meaning, would be *most* transparent, would least get in the way of our perceiving the things they indicate. Hence the distinction between the poetic word and "hearsays and formulas" in *Heroes and Hero-Worship.*

not available through symbolic mediation. When Carlyle claims such knowledge can be gained, he works within the Christian tradition of direct revelation.

Even in *Sartor Resartus,* in which Carlyle is most stringent in his reliance on symbolic mediation, revealed knowledge plays a crucial role. The Incarnation, God's revelation of himself to men in history, stands as the basis of all knowledge. Christ is the epitome of all symbols (SR, 224), just as he is the type of all heroes (H, 5:11). All other symbols and heroes function as manifestations of the infinite because the Incarnation has revealed to men how the material is permeated by the divine. Thus, in his own way, Carlyle repeats the Coleridgean argument that a priori knowledge is required in order to grasp more mediated truths. And, like Coleridge, Carlyle appeals to revelation to ground lesser truths as well. "For the God-given mandate, *Work thou in Welldoing,* lies mysteriously written, in Promethean Prophetic Characters, in our hearts" (SR, 183). If the truth is so directly given to us (the word *mysterious* does not belie the directness of the revelation here), why all the agony about how to read symbols and how to avoid being misled by their necessary inadequacy?

The agony stems from the fact that men certainly do not act as if that "mandate" were written in their hearts. Clearly, some men do misread the signs given by the divine, and even, it would seem, misinterpret direct revelation. Such misconduct might simply be the result of willful disobedience. Men know the command, but refuse to follow it, a position Carlyle assumes predominantly in *Past and Present* and *Latter-Day Pamphlets.* But in *Sartor Resartus* Carlyle adopts a more Platonic position: if men knew the good they would love and honor it. But divine truth couches itself in difficult symbols and thus some men are simply ignorant of what is required of them. (Also, Carlyle argues in *Sartor* that the symbols themselves are in the process of being changed, so that his contemporaries live in an era when basic truths might very well appear in unfamiliar forms or even remain unarticulated for want of an appropriate symbol.)

This possibility of ignorance serves to introduce the need for a special group of men who can interpret the world for its inhabitants. The name—*philosopher, poet, hero*—given to these men by Carlyle differs from passage to passage, but their role is most accurately described by a word he uses less often: *prophet.* " 'The Philosopher,' says the wisest of this age, 'must station himself in the middle;' how true! The Philosopher is he to whom the Highest has descended, and the Lowest has mounted up; who is the equal and kindly brother of all" (SR, 67). The philosopher, like the symbol itself, stands in the middle because he partakes of both the spiritual and the material. When not bypassing the epistemological problems involved in moving from the material to the spiritual, Carlyle recognizes the crucial function of the middle in any dialectical scheme. When he turns away from words and contemplation to action, Carlyle still places the hero in the middle, "a Man actually sent down from the skies with a God's-message for us" (H, 5:43). I delay a full discussion of mediation for the next chapter; right now I want to consider Carlyle's presentation of poetic language as a particularly potent form of symbolic mediation and the poet as a seer who can lead more ignorant mortals to the truth.

For all his mistrust of words and of fiction, Carlyle is also heir to the romantic tradition and its belief in a poetic symbol that can pierce through the phenomenal world to the truth at the heart of things. Carlyle, like Coleridge, differentiates absolutely between the enervating language of everyday speech and "poetry." Thus, in *Heroes and Hero-Worship* Carlyle can explain modern man's failure to see nature clearly as the result of its being "veiled under names and formulas" (H, 5:7). "Hardened round us, encasing wholly every notion we form, is a wrappage of traditions, hearsays, mere *words*" (H, 5:8). Words distance us from things. Yet, barely three pages later, we are told that the great man's "word is the wise healing word which all can believe in" (H, 5:13). Carlyle expands this last notion into his theory of "articulation." The poet and genius say what "all men were not far from saying, were longing to say" (H, 5:21). It is not all names that veil things, that prevent direct and correct participation by shaping our expectations, but only false names. A true language is possible, a language to which Carlyle ascribes great power. "Poetry itself is no other, if thou consider it, than a right *Naming*" (SR, 88).

A. Dwight Culler offers one description of this distinction between poetic and ordinary language as it was understood in Carlyle's time. "Two different conceptions of language can . . . be found . . . throughout the nineteenth century. On the one hand, . . . words were the poor husks of reality, abstract denotative counters. On the other hand, there was still alive something of the older conception of language as a magical instrument, a means of incantation or ritual, which gave one power over reality or revealed its true nature. By this view words were proper names, containing the ontological secret of a thing."[21] When Carlyle adopts this romantic belief in the magic of words he abandons his dialectical understanding of the symbol as both revelation and concealment. Instead, he uses the concept of a "right Naming" to make an absolute distinction between the false word ("cant" and "sham" in Carlylese) and the true words of literature. To name the thing aright becomes poetry's sacred task. The same holds true for religion, which must foster a "living . . . Word." "Church-Clothes are, in our vocabulary, the Forms, the *Vestures,* under which men have at various periods embodied and represented for themselves the Religious Principle; that is to say, invested the Divine Idea of the World with a sensible and practically active Body, so that it might dwell among them as a living and life-giving Word" (SR, 214).

21. *The Poetry of Tennyson* (New Haven: Yale University Press, 1977), p. 4.

Carlyle grants this living Word (clearly based on the beginning of the fourth gospel) incredible powers. Accurate naming is not just a passive recognition of what is really there, but serves to allow perception to take place. Until the thing is named, is given a representative form, it does not exist for men. The poet, in using the right words, makes the world appear. The very possibility of perception depends on the poet's creation of those "representative forms" that allow the "Divine Idea of the World" to become "sensible." "The Tailor," Carlyle concludes, "is not only a Man, but something of a Creator or Divinity" (SR, 289). " 'Who but the Poet first made Gods for men; brought them down to us; and raised us up to them' " (SR, 290). Few claims for poetry could be more insistent on its absolute necessity and importance. Carlyle is completely within the romantic tradition as exemplified by Coleridge and Shelley when he makes these pronouncements; all our most valuable knowledge comes from the poets. Yet this is the same writer who is suspicious of fiction because it does not stick strictly to the facts.

Carlyle hedges on the source of the poet's power. In "Characteristics" he is content to refer to "inspiration" and to locate the vision's source in an "unconscious" union with the divine. In *Sartor Resartus,* as we might expect, he offers two possibilities, one direct and one indirect. Either the poet works through mediate forms like everyone else, but simply succeeds in phrasing the appropriate representative expressions for his age, or the poet is a privileged seer who penetrates "the shows of things" to perceive divine truth. By the time he writes *Heroes and Hero-Worship,* Carlyle rarely relies on indirection as the means of knowledge, except for the unenlightened masses. The hero perceives directly where most men perceive mediately, which explains the special and unique value of the hero's words. "While others walk in formulas and hearsays, contented enough to dwell there, this man could not screen himself in formulas; he was alone with his soul and the reality of things. . . . The word of such a man is a Voice direct from Nature's own Heart" (H, 5:54). Parts of *Sartor Resartus,* especially the definition of symbol, attempt to explain how all men can only know indirectly, but Carlyle's strong predilection to argue by way of contrasted opposites leads him to set up, especially in the later works, an absolute distinction between those who know indirectly and those who know directly. The latter are obviously in a better position to perceive the truth of things, and their possession of the truth justifies the contention that more ordinary men should "worship" them. Theories of intuition often are forced to consider why the vital processes of intuition are not practiced by all, which can lead to elitism. Carlyle, of course, has often been viewed as promulgating a particularly vicious form of such elitism.

The return to a belief that direct knowledge is possible makes Carlyle once again forsake the dialectical for the pure. His radical claims for the power of poetry can not be reconciled with his dialectical definition of the symbol as containing both revelation and concealment. Instead he takes these two qualities and makes them diametrically opposed. Once he begins talking of "true words direct from Nature's own heart" Carlyle immediately warns us against cant. "As a Priest, or Interpreter of the Holy, is the noblest and highest of all men, so is a Sham-priest . . . the falsest and basest." We must watch out for those forms which are "mere hollow Shapes, or Masks, under which no living Figure or Spirit any longer dwells" (SR, 216). The false formulas and hearsays are everywhere, and Carlyle wants to make sure we do not mistake them for the true poetic word.

The falling away from dialectic to purity represents a failure to confront fully the inevitability and the consequences of ambiguity. Carlyle is crucial to an understanding of this book's topic because he does offer a theory that admits and tries to explain the experience of language's frustrating limitations, its necessary distance from and even concealment of the thing represented. His theory of the symbol, more fully than those associated with the English romantics, takes account of the fact of "difference," and my general contention is that the Victorians as a group were more self-conscious about (even if often greatly troubled by) the difference between symbol and the symbolized than the romantics were.[22] But we must also recognize that Carlyle tries over and over to evade recognizing the inevitable distance between word and thing, between the knower and what is known. Both his recognition of difference and his attitudes toward it recur throughout the work of the Victorian period.

Carlyle's way of phrasing the fact of ambiguity reveals why the notion is so fearful to him. "There is a Devil dwells in Man, as well as a Divinity; and too often the bow is but pocketed by the former" (SR, 239). The Victorians were plagued by fears resembling Descartes's paranoid fantasy of a world governed by an "evil genius." (Recall Rossetti's image of "some inexorable supremacy / Which ever . . . looks past [man], / Sphinx-faced with unabashed augury.") The dependence on the divine to assure that human conclusions about the nature of the world are correct (as in Descartes and Locke) leads to horrible uncertainty when combined with a Calvinist belief in the Devil and in man's degenerate nature. That Carlyle felt fully the pains of this uncertainty, generated by the world's ambiguous duality, is made clear in a letter to John Stuart Mill. "I have a general feeling growing of late years that 'I am all in the wrong';—and, by the Devil's malice, shall always have it, for we live in a Dualistic world." After this statement of doubt, Carlyle characteristically quickly reasserts his faith: "Strange how in ourselves, as in

22. I do not want to attach any value to such self-consciousness, but simply want to state, as a matter of literary history, that the "question of the real" is of greater moment to the Victorians than it was to the romantics. Attention to that question includes a heightened awareness of the difficulties involved in claiming that the words on a page represent things in the world. My use of the word *difference* is derived from the work of Jacques Derrida, especially the essay "Differance," in *Speech and Phenomena* (Evanston: Northwestern University Press, 1973), pp. 129–60.

all earthly things, a little nucleus of Truth and Good rolls itself on in a huge comet-like environment of Error and Delusion; and yet at length in some degree the Error and Delusion evaporate and vanish (as Nonentities, mere Negations) and the fraction of Good is *found* to be a reality" (CL, 6:438). By denying reality to the Devil and to evil Carlyle can reassure himself that the good will triumph—but only to "some degree." Underneath such optimism there is always the old Calvinist fatalism that sees no way toward bettering sinful man. "Not so easily can the old Adam, lodged in us by birth, be dispossessed" (SR, 183).

Of more consequence to the history of literature is Carlyle's latent recognition that ambiguity, with its undermining of the claims to full and accurate knowledge, blurs the distinction between reality and fiction. Surely the Victorian preoccupation with identifying reality and representing it faithfully stems from a new uncertainty about where and what reality is. Again, only in *Sartor Resartus,* with its fairly consistent refusal to retreat into purism, does Carlyle follow this dim track. Reality is hidden so deeply beneath the "shows of things" that it remains obscure and mysterious to all who search for it. The interpreter acts on what hints he finds, but given the similarity between true signs and false signs or, more accurately, the mixture of the true and the false in every sign, he can only present tentative conclusions about what is real. *Sartor Resartus* is, like *An Essay Concerning Human Understanding,* a book about the rather severe limits of human knowledge. As Peter Dale writes: "In an important sense, *Sartor* is not a mythus of belief but a testimony to the difficulty of knowing when one is confronted with a genuine religious myth and when with a mere phantasm of subjective 'poetic' imagination."[23] The possibility of error is ever present, and even if what the interpreter says is substantially correct, the forms of his expression must contain some concealment. These difficulties make the task of uncovering the real all the more urgent, but the real and the fictional will often be impossible to distinguish from one another. (This impossibility makes falling back on divine guidance —it's not, finally, the Devil's world—necessary.) The peculiar form of *Sartor Resartus* serves as an illustration of these difficulties.

These issues are addressed most fully when the Editor "gives utterance to a painful suspicion" that the "Autobiographical documents" are forgeries (SR, 202). The Editor outlines various reasons for his suspicions, and an interpretation of why Teufelsdröckh may have wanted to play such a trick, only to conclude: "We say not with certainty; and indeed, so strange is the Professor, can never say. If our suspicion be wholly unfounded, let his own questionable ways, not our necessary circumspectness, bear the blame" (SR, 204).

Raising this question of the documents' facticity, and then refusing to

---

23. Dale, *The Victorian Critic and the Idea of History,* p. 74.

answer it, serves three purposes. First, of course, it lets the reader know that *Sartor Resartus* is fictional insofar as its incidents and characters go.[24] Secondly, on a more theoretical level, the episode underlines the point that all material things are fictions, are to be understood as possible signs of the real, but not the real itself. The importance of the biographical "facts" lies not in their facticity, but in their heuristic possibilities. Such facts should interest only for the insight they offer; the material "shows of things" are important not on their own account, but for what they can indicate about the spiritual. Hence, Carlyle's irony, while comic and close to brutal at times, is also profoundly earnest, since it serves the fundamental epistemological purpose of moving us from the material to the spiritual. Finally, even after we grant the irrelevance of the distinction between fact and fiction when applied to material things, there remains the question of whether any given interpretation of the signs is correct. In this particular instance, the Editor's inability to say with certainty if these biographical documents are factual or not suggests that all interpretations, as the work of men, partake of uncertainty. We have no infallible criteria, while in this world, that allows us to distinguish, without a doubt, the true from the false. If we live entirely in a world of signs, of mediate representations, then we must accept that such uncertainty is our lot.

A final consideration of "Characteristics" will offer one more chance to consider how Carlyle can both present uncertainty as inevitable *and* insist that it can be overcome. Truth and falsehood, knowledge and ignorance, good and evil are, Carlyle assures us in one passage, always mixed together in this human world. "Under all her [Nature's] works, chiefly under her noblest work, Life, lies a basis of Darkness, which she benignantly conceals; in Life, too, the roots and inward circulations which stretch down fearfully to regions of Death and Night, shall not hint of their existence, and only the fair stem with its leaves and flowers, shone on by the fair sun, shall disclose itself, and joyfully grow" (Ch, 28:4). The claim that darkness remains hidden is invalidated by Carlyle's own ability to know of its presence. But more important is the complexity of vision here, the insistence that "in our actual world . . . in all senses Light alternate[s] with Darkness" (Ch, 28:8).

If we trace Carlyle's metaphoric use of "light" and "dark" through the essay, his fundamental ambivalence manifests itself. The values assigned to light and dark keep fluctuating. Most often, darkness stands for evil, death, and ignorance, as it does in the passage just quoted, or in the following: "Thus Evil, what we call Evil, must ever exist while man exists; Evil, in the widest sense we can give it, is precisely the dark, disordered material out of which man's

24. Carlyle, obviously amused, attached (as an appendix) to the first English edition of *Sartor Resartus* an earnest, but rather baffled, American review of the book that finally reaches the conclusion that "no such persons as Professor Teufelsdröckh or Counsellor Heuschrecke ever existed." See *Sartor Resartus,* p. 320.

Freewill has to create an edifice of order and Good" (Ch, 28:28). Yet, when involved in his praise of unconsciousness, darkness can stand for the deepest reality, for those hidden truths of which consciousness knows nothing. "Unconsciousness belongs to pure unmixed life; Consciousness to a diseased mixture and conflict of life and death. . . . In the same sense, too, have Poets sung 'Hymns to the Night'; as if Night were nobler than Day; as if Day were but a small motley-coloured veil spread transiently over the infinite bosom of Night, and did but deform and hide from us its purely transparent eternal deeps" (Ch, 28:16). To follow this path would link Carlyle up with the darker side of romanticism and its descent into chaos, a path Carlyle most often avoids. Even in this case, we should note that his praise of the night is put forth rather timidly, hiding behind the "as if." Usually Carlyle's attempt to avoid "diseased mixtures" leads him to embrace the light, not darkness.

> Deep and sad is our feeling when we stand yet in the bodeful Night; equally deep, indestructible is our assurance that the Morning also will not fail. Nay, already, as we look round, streaks of a dayspring are in the east; it is dawning; when the time shall be fulfilled, it will be day. The progress of man towards higher and nobler developments of whatever is highest and noblest in him, lies not only prophesied to Faith, but now written to the eye of Observation, so that he who runs may read.
>
> One great step of progress, for example, we should say, in actual circumstances, was this same; the clear ascertainment that we are in progress. About the grand course of Providence, and his final Purposes with us, we can know nothing, or almost nothing: man begins in darkness, ends in darkness; mystery is everywhere around us and in us. (Ch, 28:37)

"Man begins in darkness, ends in darkness" but the dawn is coming and will not fail. So hostile to facile talk of progress by others, Carlyle cannot abide the consequences of his own position, so must introduce his own notion of progress.[25] We can know nothing—or "almost nothing" as he quickly qualifies it—about Providence's designs, but the "progress of man toward higher and nobler developments" has been "prophesied to Faith." And in the present fortunate time, we are not even solely dependent on direct revelation for our knowledge; the fact of progress is "written to the eye of Observation" as well. Revelation and direct perception remove Carlyle from the uncertainties of living in a world of ambiguous signs. The mixture of darkness and light, of revelation and concealment, is unbearable to Carlyle. He needs to proclaim

25. G. M. Young has called an "incapacity to follow any chain of reasoning which seems likely to result in an unpleasant conclusion" a characteristic trait of Victorian writers. See *Victorian England: Portrait of an Age* (London: Oxford University Press, 1960), p. 75. Young's formula is no doubt unnecessarily harsh; it is easier for us, a few generations later, to see the implicitly secular, radical, or unpleasant consequences of certain Victorian positions than it was at the time. Still, I think it is true that Victorian writers often turn away from the direction in which their own thoughts seem to be leading them.

truths that his theory of knowledge asserts must remain unknown, "mysteries" to which the human knower cannot penetrate.

> The fever of Skepticism must needs burn itself out, and burn out thereby the Impurities that caused it; then again will there be clearness, health. The principle of life, which now struggles painfully, in the outer, thin and barren domain of the Conscious or Mechanical, may then withdraw into its inner sanctuaries, its abysses of mystery and miracle; withdraw deeper than ever into that domain of the Unconscious. . . .
>
> Of our Modern Metaphysics, accordingly, may not this already be said, that if they have produced no Affirmation, they have destroyed much Negation? It is a disease expelling a disease; the fire of Doubt, as above hinted, consuming away the doubtful; that so the Certain come to light, and again lie visible on the surface. (Ch, 28:40)

Here all acceptance that human life is a mixed lot disappears. All impurities and doubts must be burned away. But the results of such purification are presented in two contradictory ways. "The principle of Life" will "withdraw" from "the outer, thin and barren domain" of consciousness to take up residence in the vital depths; or the "Certain" will "come to light, and again lie visible on the surface." We could say that the two are equivalent, since in both cases the vital stands alone, its dialectical opposite (whether presented as "consciousness" or "darkness") annihilated. But in another sense the confusion is absolute since Carlyle, when opting for purity, does not know which term of the dialectic he wants: night or day. He wants and needs both, but he also wants to have them without the frustrating obstructions that result from their mixture. He wants them pure.

4

"The Kindly Veil": Ruskin's Mysterious Clouds

John Ruskin's aesthetic theories rival Carlyle's in the influence they exerted on subsequent Victorian artists, and Ruskin had much to do with the adoption of explicitly "realistic" intentions by the Pre-Raphaelites and George Eliot, among others. Ruskin's thoughts on representation are sufficiently different from Carlyle's to warrant attention here. Unlike Carlyle, Ruskin respected and was influenced by the empiricist tradition, and his work provides a more balanced union of romantic and Lockean elements than those found in the older writer. Ruskin also focuses more sharply on the mediating function played by the symbol and by the artist who employs it. Ruskin's nonironic temperament leads him to respect the symbol's individual existence and to find a rationale for mediation in place of Carlyle's apocalyptic annihilation of particulars. But the Ruskin who presented himself as the proponent of clear sight always evidenced an impatience with mediation and indirection, a tendency that became both more pronounced and more desperate during the long decline into madness of Ruskin's later years.

Ruskin is a self-proclaimed realist. He insists that his famous prose descriptions of landscapes and of paintings are based on precise attention to the thing described, and he values equally precise depiction of natural objects in art. But no one, any longer, would call Ruskin a simple, or naive, realist—if by that term we mean that he believes human perception apprehends real objects in the world simply and directly. Simple realism, extended to art, preaches an exact translation into art of the perceived object. As various commentators have demonstrated, Ruskin believes that a more complicated process of selection and interpretation must take place before the artist succeeds in transforming natural objects into works of art or before the perceiving subject can grasp the full significance of either a natural object or a work of art.[1] Ruskin does not doubt the reality of perceptual data, but he does not

1. Among the critics who discuss the limits to Ruskin's realism, see especially Darrell Mansell, Jr., "Ruskin and George Eliot's 'Realism,'" *Criticism* 7 (1965): 203–16; Michael Sprinker, "Ruskin on the Imagination," *Studies in Romanticism* 18 (1979): 115–39; George P. Landow, *The Aesthetic and Critical Theories of John Ruskin* (Princeton: Princeton University Press, 1971); George P. Landow, "Ruskin, Holman Hunt, and Going to Nature to See for Oneself," in *Studies in Ruskin,* ed. Robert Rhodes and Del Ivan Janik (Athens: Ohio University Press, 1982), pp. 60–84; and David Sonstroem, "Prophet and Peripatetic in *Modern Painters* III and IV," also in *Studies in Ruskin,* pp. 85–114. The most important recent defender of Ruskin as a straightforward realist is Patricia M. Ball in *The Science of Aspects* (London: Athalone Press,

believe that the thing's meaning can be equated with its material appearance. Significance cannot be simply perceived sensually; the mind, or imagination, must work on the objects presented to perception before they reveal their full meaning for men. The difference between meaning and appearance necessarily involves the recognition that the object's full reality is not immediately available to perception, but that difference also insures that meaning will not be reduced to solely material (perceptible) factors.

Of Ruskin's recent critics, Michael Sprinker has pushed hardest on the intervention of imagination in this perceptual process, arguing that Ruskin is led to adopt the distinction between "things as they are in themselves (noumena) and things as they are perceived and recorded by human consciousness (phenomena)."[2] Although Sprinker uses the Kantian terms here, we can recognize the basic Lockean distinction between *idea* and *thing,* where *idea* is equivalent to *phenomena* and *thing* to *noumena.* Because the mind works on the objects it perceives, we are only aware of those mental entities by which we represent to ourselves a world. Access to things in themselves is never possible. Since we cannot get beyond these mental images to the thing itself, it follows for Sprinker that all representations are "a fiction, a phantasm, a figural rendering of that which is always real but never experienced except as something phantasmagoric."[3]

I think we misunderstand Victorian realism if we attribute Sprinker's conclusion to Ruskin. The Victorians, Ruskin included, fought against the absolute separation of mind from world, and of imagination from reality, that a position like Sprinker's simply accepts. The Victorian writer was troubled by the gap between representations and reality; he might even dread that all representations are fictions, but that dread generates efforts to insure such is not the case rather than theoretical demonstrations of representation's fictional status. Ruskin struggles throughout his career to establish the accuracy and truth of representation. George Levine, resisting the modern reinterpretations that have imputed twentieth-century attacks on realism to nineteenth-century writers, puts the case well: "The Victorians, surely, did write with the awareness of the possibilities of indeterminate meaning and solipsism, but they wrote *against* the very indeterminancy they tended to reveal."[4]

My goal in this chapter is to consider the ways in which Ruskin displays, both by his theoretical statements and in his practice, how he understands the aesthetic sign's ability to represent the real. A radically dualistic account of representation like Sprinker's underestimates the cultural forces that promote

---

1971); but also see Elizabeth K. Helsinger, "Ruskin on Wordsworth: The Victorian Critic in Romantic Territory," *Studies in Romanticism* 17 (1978): 267–91.

2. Sprinker, "Ruskin on the Imagination," p. 123.

3. Ibid., p. 128.

4. Levine, *The Realistic Imagination,* p. 4.

the intelligibility of signs. The deconstructionists have often taken the "difference" between the representative and the represented as necessarily undermining the possibility of successful reference. The confusion here is between a picture theory of language and a representational theory. A picture theory calls for "natural" signs, ones that *resemble* the thing for which they stand. A representational theory does not require resemblance between signifier and signified, but only a conventionally assigned relation between them.[5] The signifier's failure to resemble the signified does not entail a necessary loss of intelligibility, and the use of the word *arbitrary* to describe the relation of signifier to signified suggests a tentativeness users of the system do not experience. Problems of intelligibility between two speakers of the same language rarely stem from the fact that linguistic signs carry no overt marking of their conventional significance, and certainly users of ordinary language do not take *arbitrary* to mean haphazard or unfixed. *Conventional* is not the same as *fictional*, especially since creating a system of signification lies beyond the power of the individual.[6] The "difference" between signifier and signified is not debilitating because the relation between the two is established for all speakers of the language.

When we move from intelligibility to truth, a nonpictorial theory of representation runs into more serious problems. How do we guarantee that this system of signs says something true about the nature of the world? Ruskin addresses himself at length to this issue. At times he does rely on a picture theory of language that demands a resemblance between world and human artifact (or sign). (His taking up these questions originally in relation to painting is largely responsible for his inclination to think that the sign must resemble what it represents.) But at other times, he holds to a more genuinely representational theory, one in which the differences between signifier and signified are acknowledged as well as the connection between them. A fully representational theory accepts that we do not have immediate access to things-in-themselves but also insists that we do obtain (accurate) knowledge of those things through the mediation of representatives.[7]

Ruskin's concern with the truth value of representation certainly increased over the years. In the first volumes of *Modern Painters* Ruskin generally relies on the typological tradition to code the ways in which natural objects

5. As I discuss in the introduction, Locke's representational theory involves a recognition of the arbitrariness of the sign. See *An Essay Concerning Human Understanding*, bk. 3, chap. 2, sec. 8, and J. L. Mackie, *Problems from Locke* (Oxford: Clarendon Press, 1976), pp. 38–58.

6. Ludwig Wittgenstein, in his arguments against the possibility of a "private language," has presented the fullest case for the contention that a language system's being man-made and arbitrary does not mean that any speaker could develop his own code for connecting a set of signs with a certain set of contents. See *Philosophical Investigations*, trans. G. E. M. Anscombe (New York: Macmillan, 1968), pp. 89–107.

7. See Mackie, *Problems from Locke*, pp. 41–42, where he argues that Locke's notion of representation necessarily involves mediation, "dealing with other things by way of ideas" (42).

represent spiritual truths; this code is, for Ruskin, barely historical since it is valid for all men in the Christian era. Similarly, the early Ruskin generally assumes that men all share a basic understanding of how words express meaning. It is only later in his career that Ruskin becomes interested in the fact that different eras develop different ways of understanding the meaning of things. He first stumbles onto this new perspective in his works on Venice, *The Stones of Venice,* and on architecture, *The Seven Lamps of Architecture.* The recognition that art changes from era to era leads Ruskin to the realization that different eras organize their knowledge about the world differently and, thus, have distinct modes of representation. In many of these later works, he turns to a consideration of Victorian England, questioning how the ways in which it understands itself and the world reflect its interests and prejudices. Once representations are viewed as changing from era to era the question of their truth value takes on a new urgency, and the later Ruskin finds it more difficult to accept patiently the necessity of gaining knowledge through representatives.

The key to Ruskin's thoughts on representation lies, I think, in his shifting attitudes toward mediation. While he constructs elaborate theories of the imagination, Ruskin has surprisingly little to say directly or theoretically about the representative itself. He talks a lot about signifieds—either as natural things to be represented by the artist or as spiritual truths to be symbolized. And he discusses at length the acts of mind or imagination by which a truly "artistic" or "moral" perception of signifieds might occur. But he rarely discusses the signifier, certainly not in the way Carlyle addresses himself to defining the symbol. This silence can be traced to several causes. Most crucial, I think, are the way natural things act as both signifieds and signifiers in Ruskin, and his uncertainty about the desirability of differences between signifiers and signified.

The symbol in Ruskin will be asked, as it is in Carlyle, to serve as "some embodiment and revelation of the Infinite" and will contain its share of "concealment" as well as "revelation."[8] The symbol stands between two realms, two speakers, and Ruskin understands its making communication between the two possible by virtue both of the distance it marks between them and the point of connection it affords. Ruskin rarely looks for a Carlylean silence born of total unity, but praises instead the possibility of infinite speech. When he considers the relation between God and man, the place of mediation is the clouds. By tracing through Ruskin's comments on clouds we can gain a full view of his attitudes toward representation through the mediation of a natural object.[9] I hope my presentation and discussion of various passages on

8. Thomas Carlyle, *Sartor Resartus,* pp. 219–20.
9. Most overviews of Ruskin's work note briefly the progression of his cloud imagery to the final "storm-cloud." The best summary, containing in brief several themes I discuss here, is found in John D. Rosenberg's *The Darkening Glass* (New York: Columbia University Press,

clouds will make it clear that they are continually associated in Ruskin's mind with the material clothing of spiritual truths and with "mystery." Ruskin's understanding of how natural things act as signs parallels his understanding of how words signify, and I will discuss his notions of representation as being fundamentally the same for things (as "types") and for words. The metaphor of clouds as mediating symbols gathers together and even organizes Ruskin's thoughts on the subject.

In his autobiography, *Praeterita,* Ruskin, between proofs and the printed text, decided to delete a confession to a characteristic weakness (his editors restore the confession in a note): "One great part of the pleasure, however, depended on an idiosyncrasy which extremely wise people do not share,—my love of all sorts of filigree and embroidery, from hoarfrost to high clouds."[10] Earlier in his career, Ruskin did not hesitate to confess this pleasure, or feel any need to apologize for it. In *Modern Painters IV* he writes: "Truly, the clouds seem to be getting much the worst of it; . . . having been myself long a cloud-worshipper, and passed many hours of life in the pursuit of them from crag to crag, I must consider what can possibly be submitted in their defence, and in Turner's" (6:75). Ruskin's readers hardly need this admission; clouds are a major topic of concern in *Modern Painters,* culminating, in the third volume, with the identification of modern painting with clouds. "If a general and characteristic name were needed for modern landscape art, none better could be invented than 'the service of clouds' " (5:318).

The importance of clouds is a subset of the importance of light in Ruskin's world, an importance it would be difficult to exaggerate. Light serves both as that which makes knowledge possible and as the final object of knowledge. Jay Fellows has described brilliantly Ruskin's reliance on sight as the primary source of knowledge, as well as the young Ruskin's obsessional fear that he was going blind.[11] The presence of light, necessary to sight, often determines Ruskin's moods; a famous case is the storm cloud, but various letters in *Fors Clavigera* as well as entries in the *Diaries* reveal the same connection.

1961), pp. 213–16. Recently, Raymond E. Fitch has written a study of Ruskin's whole career that heavily emphasizes Ruskin's desire for light and his relation to the clouds that stand between man and the sun (*The Poison Sky: Myth and Apocalypse in Ruskin* [Athens: Ohio University Press, 1982]). Fitch, I think, allows the final image of the storm cloud to dominate too completely his understanding of Ruskin's earlier work, with the result that *The Poison Sky* emphasizes Ruskin's apocalyptic impatience with indirection where I want to indicate the benefits Ruskin derives from living "in the cloud."

10. *The Works of John Ruskin,* Library Edition (London: George Allen, 1908), 35:157n. Subsequent references to Ruskin's works are from the Library Edition, with volume and page number given parenthetically in the text.

11. See *The Failing Distance: The Autobiographical Impulse in John Ruskin* (Baltimore: Johns Hopkins University Press, 1975), chap. 1.

Ruskin associates light (the sun) with God and truth. His authority for this identification is the Bible. He quotes "God is light, and in Him is no darkness at all" (4:128) and goes on to assert that "light . . . is a type of wisdom and truth" (4:130). Ruskin reasserts this basic symbolism throughout his career. He insists on "the practical connection between physical and spiritual light. . . . You cannot love the real sun, that is to say physical light and colour, rightly, unless you love the spiritual sun, that is to say justice and truth, rightly" (28:614). His love of light finds its complement in a hatred of darkness, identified as all that obscures truth. "In the deeper and final sense, a work of darkness is one that seeks concealment, and conceals facts; or even casts disdain and disgrace on facts" (28:540). And when, during the period of his "unconversion," he replaces belief in God with the "religion of humanity" (29:90), the identification of light with the most important object of knowledge is so ingrained that he announces, "Man is the sun of the world; more than the real sun" (7:262).

But visual knowledge, while primary, is not absolutely direct in Ruskin. Unmediated apprehension of the divine is neither possible nor desirable. Just as direct sunlight might cause blindness, so contemplation of the naked divine would be dangerous. Clouds are cherished as a necessary intermediary, a "kindly veil" between men and light.

> If we insist upon perfect intelligibility and complete declaration in every moral subject, we shall instantly fall into misery of unbelief. Our whole happiness and power of energetic action depend on our being able to breathe and live in the cloud; content to see it opening here and closing there; rejoicing to catch, through the thinnest films of it, glimpses of stable and substantial things; but yet perceiving a nobleness even in the concealment, and rejoicing that the kindly veil is spread where the untempered light might have scorched us, or the infinite clearness wearied. (6:89)

The cloud contains light, but is not light itself. Rather, it "clothes" (to use Carlyle's term) light so as to allow men to view it, but such viewing will not grant us "perfect intelligibility." The function of clouds is to call attention to light, "*luminous* cloud being the most difficult thing to do in art" (3:411–12n). Clouds mediate between the perceiver and the final object of perception. That final object, in much of Ruskin's work, is God. "In whatever is an object of life, in whatever may be infinitely and for itself desired, we may be sure there is something of the divine; for God will not make anything an object of life to His creatures which does not point to, or partake of, Himself" (4:46). Clouds indicate the existence and nature of something they are not themselves.

If clouds are mediators, painters and writers belong to "the cloud of witnesses in heaven and earth" (5:72; Hebrews 12:1). To the poor artist, Ruskin tells us, our request might well be: " 'Stand aside from between nature and me';

yet to the great imaginative painter—greater a million times in every faculty of soul than we—our word may wisely be, 'Come between this nature and me—this nature which is too great and too wonderful for me; temper it for me, interpret it to me; let me see with your eyes, and hear with your ears, and have help and strength from your great spirit' " (5:187). All the same motifs from the description of clouds reappear in this appeal to the great artist. It is a mistake to believe we can understand nature best when we perceive it directly; rather, when our vision is guided by the clouds that gather and organize the light, or by the painter who "tempers" and "interprets" natural beauty, we are granted the greatest insight. Ruskin, like Carlyle, believes that those selected for direct vision, the great artists, are few indeed. "Hundreds of people can talk for one who can think, but thousands can think for one who can see. To see clearly is poetry, prophecy, and religion,—all in one" (5:333). In *Modern Painters I* the prophet-seer Turner is placed among the clouds from where he sends down the message of God to men, ". . . sent as a prophet of God to reveal to men the mysteries of His universe, standing, like the great angel of the Apocalypse, clothed with a cloud . . ." (3:254).

Clouds and art are finally necessary because our access to the absent object, to the divine, is limited. Ruskin accepts this substitution of a mediator for the thing itself as a "mystery." The fact of clouds' existence, of the "*partial and variable mystery . . . caused by clouds,*" points Ruskin toward the existence of the "continual mystery caused . . . by the absolute infinity of things. WE NEVER SEE ANYTHING CLEARLY" (6:75). Mystery is raised to the status of an ultimate truth. As we shall see, this mystery is, in part, the mystery of representation itself. How can something stand for some other thing that it is not? How is the undeniable difference between represented and representative to be understood?

Before probing the mystery of representation further, we should first consider why Ruskin, the prophet of clear sight, should celebrate mystery at all.[12] The long passage from *Modern Painters IV* that I quoted above suggests two reasons: divine light is dangerous, and boring. The clouds protect us from a "scorching light," which reminds us that Ruskin's God is almost always the Old Testament God of judgment and vengeance.

More positively, Ruskin claims the cloud saves us from possible "weariness," a conclusion Carlyle, who did not share Ruskin's fervent love of the natural world, would never have reached. When considering how clouds conceal as well as reveal, Ruskin notes the aesthetic effect of mystery. The symbol's resistance to complete identification with its meaning allows its representation in art as a distinct thing. Ruskin needs to maintain the symbol's

---

12. In *The Last Romantics* (New York: Barnes and Noble, 1961), pp. 1–12, Graham Hough offers the fullest account of the traditional opinion that Ruskin taught the Victorians how to see.

integrity as a thing in nature while also ensuring that it can point us toward the meaning it symbolizes. It is "no little marvel" (3:396) to Ruskin that the old masters never realized the potential of clouds.

> These phenomena are as perpetual in all countries as they are beautiful, and afford by far the most effective and valuable means which the painter possesses, for modification of the forms of fixed objects. The upper clouds are distinct and comparatively opaque, they do not modify, but conceal; but, through the rain-cloud and its accessory phenomena, all that is beautiful may be made manifest, and all that is hurtful concealed; what is paltry, may be made to look vast, and what is ponderous, aerial; mystery may be obtained without obscurity, and decoration without disguise. (3:395–96)

Clouds grant us variety. Truth with a capital T is an unchanging unity. But in the world of the cloud, a world of mediators, we have truth with a small t, dark approximations of the ultimate Truth. Unable to produce the Word (identified with God Incarnate in the fourth gospel), the writer uses the endless possibilities offered by the words of human language.

Ruskin glories in this distance from the divine. Unlike Carlyle, he is not anxious to annihilate the things of this world in favor of the divine truth that lies behind them. Ruskin's prose depends not on irony, but on delighted play with the "infinite variety" this world offers. "The truths of nature are one eternal change—one infinite variety. . . . And out of this mass of various, yet agreeing beauty, it is by long attention only that the conception of the constant character—the ideal form—hinted at by all, yet assumed by none, is fixed upon by the imagination for its standard of truth" (3:145–46). In this fallen world we never perceive "ideal form"; it is an abstraction formed by thought, but never actually seen in experience. Difference is protected; we are sheltered from "weariness," given instead the "infinite variety" of this world. We find here one explanation for the lack of order, the endless digressions in Ruskin's works.[13] To avoid coming straight to the point is to continue speaking and living. The difference between the material and the spiritual realms is what allows each side to have a voice and a life. And, at least at the beginning of his career, Ruskin does not find this gap a threat. The mind can still form an idea of a "standard of truth" through a process of abstraction from its perceptions of a number of imperfect material approximations. (The process Ruskin has in mind is very similar to that by which Locke thought men formed "complex ideas.")[14]

No wonder, then, that Ruskin writes of modern painting, "The next thing that will strike us, after this love of clouds, is the love of liberty" (5:319). Love of clouds *is* love of liberty. It is delight in decoration, in variety, in

13. For an excellent discussion of digressions in Ruskin, see Fellows, *The Failing Distance*, pp. 92–96.
14. See John Locke, *An Essay Concerning Human Understanding*, bk. 2, chap. 12, sec. 1–2.

embroidery, in ornamentation. Similarly, Ruskin's praise of Gothic art in *The Stones of Venice* can be seen as a praise of imperfection and of the liberty that lowered standards afford the individual worker.[15] Man hidden from the direct sight of God is free to be man, to be different.

Our whole happiness, Ruskin tells us, depends on our comparative blindness.

> Knowledge is good, and light is good, yet man perished in seeking knowledge, and moths perish in seeking light; and if we, who are crushed before the moth, will not accept such mystery as is needful for us, we shall perish in like manner. But accepted in humbleness, it instantly becomes an element of pleasure; and I think that every rightly constituted mind ought to rejoice, not so much in knowing anything clearly, as in feeling that there is infinitely more which it cannot know. None but the proud or weak men would mourn over this, for we may always know more if we choose, by working on; but the pleasure is, I think, to humble people, in knowing that the journey is endless, the treasure inexhaustible,—watching the cloud still march before them with its summitless pillar, and being sure that, to the end of time and to the length of eternity, the mysteries of its infinity will still open farther and farther, their dimness being the sign and necessary adjunct of their inexhaustibleness. (6:90)

In the "mystery" of signs, the obscurity of our insights into the infinite, rests their glory. This is Ruskin's version of the "fortunate Fall." The division of man from the divine that the Fall institutes is only lamented by the "proud" or the "weak." "Accepted in humbleness," this condition "becomes an element of pleasure." Material things are symbols of their divine creator, but in their difference from the creator is established the space for human existence. Even more than Carlyle, Ruskin insists upon the "concealment" within the symbol. While romantic theorists of the symbol (most notably Coleridge), all too aware of the gap between the human and the divine, wish to emphasize the divine presence within the symbol given to perception, Ruskin wishes to emphasize the symbol itself, its physical presence and appearance, because for him the difference held within that symbol is just as important as its indication of God's existence.

Ruskin's theory of signs, his respect for both their "concealment" and their "revelation," opens up the vexed question of his "realism" and his relation to two influential, and usually opposed, theories of language: Locke's empirical position and Coleridge's description of the symbol. Roughly speaking, a Victorian writer could view language in two ways. He could follow Locke's suspicion of the word, especially of figurative words, a suspicion generated by the ever-present threat that the word will divorce perception and thought from

15. My comment on Ruskin's attitude toward imperfection is derived from remarks made by Robert Hewison in *John Ruskin: The Argument of the Eye* (London: Thames and Hudson, 1976), p. 135.

the actual world to carry them along the path of language's own internal logic. In this view, often identified with the eighteenth century as a whole, language frequently misleads by focusing attention on words themselves rather than on the objects words denote. Literary language is a particularly notorious offender in this respect. For the empiricist, words exist only to facilitate communication about objects, and strict attention to the word's referential sense is necessary to avoid confusion. Confusion can arise because there is no necessary link between things and words, only conventional ones. (We might add here that Locke's theory of language underestimates the rigidity of social conventions, with the result that Locke considers language seriously threatened by the tendency of individual speakers to attach private meanings, inaccessible to others, to the words they use.)

The alternative position open to the Victorians was the romantic theory of the symbol, most fully expressed by Coleridge. Here, the symbol (reached in the ecstatic moment when opposites unite) allows us, in a thrilling moment of instantaneous insight, to pierce the diversity of the phenomenal world and perceive the true unity that exists behind it. The romantic symbol is not just an arbitrary sign, but partakes of the very reality it indicates and serves as the unique instance (in this world) of a desired communion.

Ruskin tries to be faithful to both traditions, empiricist and romantic, since each offers him possibilities he needs to keep open. He does not manage to hold on to both without contradicting himself at times, but I do wish to indicate the basic synthesis he tries to forge and to suggest why this particular mixture appeals to him.

Ruskin's empiricism is most obvious in his insistence on clear perception. "Truth," for Ruskin, before it is religious or moral truth, is the propositional truth of the empiricist.

> The fact is, truth and beauty are entirely distinct, though often related, things. One is a property of statements, the other of objects. . . . Therefore, in things concerning art, the words true and false are only to be rightly used while the picture is considered as a statement of facts. The painter asserts that this which he has painted is the form of a dog, a man, or a tree. If it be *not* the form of a dog, a man, or a tree, the painter's statement is false; and, therefore, we justly speak of a false line, or false colour; not that any lines or colours can in themselves be false, but they become so when they convey a statement that they resemble something which they do *not* resemble. (5:55–56n)

Ruskin's view here coincides exactly with that associated with positivist theories of language from Locke to the early Wittgenstein. Truth is purely a function of language, and resides in the faithfulness of a statement to the "fact" of the matter. This position almost always assumes a simple faith in perception; we know the "facts" because we can see them, and now language's statements can be measured against those facts. The words or images of the statement (note that Ruskin is talking of a painting's "statement" in this case) should be transparent, not calling attention to their own existence or to their difference from the referent, but merely indicating the existence of that referent and certain facts about it.

Ruskin, unlike any romantic, is not afraid of quantifying "truth." "The quantity of truth is in proportion to the number of facts" (3:157), although quality returns immediately to balance the formula: "and its [truth's] value and instructiveness in proportion to their [the facts'] rarity" (3:157). Here Ruskin upholds that absolute realism most fully outlined in the preface to the second edition of *Modern Painters I.* Art should never mediate between the perceiver and the "real." (Obviously, the position I am about to outline contradicts Ruskin's other statements about our asking the great artist to stand between us and nature, and the insistence that "we never see anything clearly.") The "skill of the artist, and the perfection of his art, are never proved until both are forgotten. The artist has done nothing till he has concealed himself; the art is imperfect which is visible" (3:22). The religious basis for this self-effacement of the artist is a respect for divine creation. "Every alteration of the features of nature has its origin either in powerless indolence or blind audacity" (3:25).

Ruskin describes a passive imagination, very similar to the one traditionally associated with Locke, that can only recombine the elements given to it in perception, and not actively create new objects on its own.[16] And when Ruskin is preaching such an absolute realism, which he certainly does not do all the time, the ideal work of art displays its object as transparently as ideal positivist languages denote their objects. "The second great faculty is the Imaginative, which the mind exercises in a certain mode of regarding or combining the ideas it has received from external nature. . . . And the error respecting this faculty is, in considering that its function is one of falsehood, that its operation is to exhibit things as they are *not,* and that in so doing it mends the work of God" (4:36).

Ruskin's emphasis on visual perception usually follows this same line. Sight grants us immediate apprehension of the thing, without involving any action of the self, thus preventing any tampering with the pure reality of the perceived object. The "utter forgetfulness of self" (12:370) in looking at things insures vision's accuracy and offers a welcome release from the burdens of personality. "The whole technical power of painting depends on our recovery

16. For a discussion of the passive imagination in Ruskin and how this doctrine serves to differentiate him from the romantics, see Elizabeth Helsinger, "The Ruskin Renaissance," *Modern Philology* 73 (1975): 168–70.

of what may be called the *innocence of the eye*" (15:27n). Ruskin appeals both to notions of revelation (the meaning of the word *Apocalypse)* and to passivity when he explains how such vision generates the most realistic art works.

> All the great men *see* what they paint before they paint it,—see it in a perfectly passive manner,—cannot help seeing it if they would; whether in their mind's eye, or in bodily fact, does not matter; very often the mental vision is, I believe, in men of imagination, clearer than the bodily one; but vision it is, of one kind or another,—the whole scene, character, or incident passing before them as in second sight, whether they will or no, and requiring them to paint it as they see it; they not daring, under the might of its presence, to alter one jot or tittle of it as they write it down or paint it down; it being to them in its own kind and degree always a true vision or Apocalypse, and invariably accompanied in their hearts by a feeling correspondent to the words,—"Write the things *which thou hast seen,* and the things which *are.*" (5:114)

This praise for realistic painting carries over into a veneration for a simple, plain style in language. Ruskin equates painting and language. "Painting . . . is nothing but a noble and expressive language" (3:87), he writes, and throughout his career Ruskin uses examples from Turner, Scott, Dante, and Titian interchangeably when he wishes to make a point about art. The image in a painting, like the word in a sentence, should not be allowed to get in the way of *what* is to be expressed. Ruskin, like all the Victorian writers discussed in this book, proclaims the superiority of content over expression.

> It is not by the mode of representing or saying, but by what is represented and said, that the respective greatness of either the painter or the writer is to be finally determined. . . . It is not, however, always easy, either in painting or literature, to determine where the influence of language stops, and where that of thought begins. . . . But the highest thoughts are those which are least dependent on language, and the dignity of any composition, or praise to which it is entitled, are in exact proportion to its independency of language and expression. (3: 88–89)

Not a statement we would expect from one of the greatest prose stylists in the English language.

Not surprisingly, Ruskin's twists and turns in designating the relation between the aesthetic artifact and reality have the critics arguing over his connection to nineteenth-century realism. George Landow writes: "Despite the fact that both Ruskin and his editors carefully explained the purpose of his remarks about accurate representation of natural forms, one still encounters arguments that his program entailed a mimetic theory of painting or photographic 'realism.' "[17] Patricia M. Ball is one of those who willfully persists in

17. *The Aesthetic and Critical Theories of John Ruskin*, p. 24.

taking this view. "In the mission of proving Turner's truth to nature he [Ruskin] found a way of fulfilling his strong need to concentrate on sensory perception, and the study of the object. . . . To the end *Modern Painters* upholds the place of fact, especially natural fact, in art, and the duty of the artist to respect it totally."[18] Both critics, I think, are faithful to parts of Ruskin. The goal is to determine why Ruskin both desires complete accuracy and fears it, and how he reconciles his contradictory impulses, if he does.

We can begin by recognizing that Ruskin's "realism" is of two types, even though it is unclear whether he recognized the distinction between them. He does preach a materialistic realism at times, one that stresses accuracy in pictorial representation and the careful use of the most plain, most direct words. But he also upholds a tradition of realism that is much older: medieval scholastic realism. This older realism asserted the existence of absolute universals in the Platonic sense. These universal Forms or Ideas stood behind all objects in the material world; worldly objects are only approximations of these forms.[19] When Ruskin is concerned with proving the reality of and granting us access to these spiritual forms, he is closer to Carlyle and the romantics than to the empiricists.

Ruskin, like Carlyle, clearly wants to apply the word *real* to a set of nonmaterial values that will serve as the standards by which material objects are judged. In the "infinite variety" of nature, the "ideal form" is "hinted at by all, yet assumed by none" (3:145–46), but that "form" must be recognized as governing the shape and significance of the individual thing. "Beauty" and "truth" in this perspective would serve as value terms that designate the best relation of individual things to the nonmaterial standard. In other words, Ruskin believes that the objects present to sight, apart from their own material reality, are always signs, always point to a greater reality, a greater truth.[20] The outlines of his epistemological position are clear enough. Reality appears to men through the objects of this world. But how we are to look through those objects to the spiritual realm they should reveal remains a problem for Ruskin, as it was for Rossetti. Ruskin's nostalgia for the Middle Ages reflects his being denied the medieval assurance that men can easily and correctly interpret the significance of the visible world.

The way in which Ruskin describes how we grasp the truth and how

---

18. *The Science of Aspects,* p. 62.

19. *The Encyclopedia of Philosophy* (New York: Macmillan, 1967), 7:77, defines medieval realism as "the doctrine that universals have a real, objective existence."

20. Most commentators on Ruskin have linked his belief that material things convey spiritual truths to the Christian typological tradition. See George P. Landow, *The Aesthetic and Critical Theories of John Ruskin,* chap. 9, and Herbert Sussman's discussion of Ruskin in *Fact into Figure: Typology in Carlyle, Ruskin, and the Pre-Raphaelite Brotherhood.*

art should represent the object of knowledge can almost always be taken as an indication of his faith's strength at that moment. When he is most certain, Ruskin just tells us to observe nature carefully and its deeper meanings will be plainly revealed to us. (This is the position Holman Hunt adopted and that Rossetti refutes in "The Woodspurge.") When he is more doubtful, Ruskin is more likely to stress the need for mediators; art becomes useful not just because it presents the natural thing to us, but because the great artist organizes our perception of the thing to assure that we do not miss its spiritual significance. In both cases, since knowledge is not immediate, but through material appearances, Ruskin pleads with men to be *humble* in their assertion of knowledge, announces that the divine truth is a mystery men can never fully know, *and* suggests that men pay close attention to the visible objects that offer a clue to reality, to the nature of the invisible God. Thus, if we take nineteenth-century realism as "a commitment to describing real events and showing things as they actually exist,"[21] Ruskin is certainly a realist. But his motives for realism and his definition of the real are not those of Courbet or Zola. Ruskin's realism is a form of worship and a task; to see clearly the things of this world is the work at hand—work that, if well done, will grant some insight into that other reality hidden beyond the clouds.

Ruskin's attention to fact, his realism, does not resemble other nineteenth-century realisms precisely because the nature of signs—which other realisms take for granted—is *the* problem that drives Ruskin to take shelter in physical things. We may not know for certain what the thing means or how it can function as a sign, but we can at least be accurate about its physical appearance. But, for Ruskin as for most of the Victorians, mere interest in physical appearance can never justify the artistic rendering of an object. Our seeing is only moral if we are alive to the representative function of the thing, if we are searching for the deeper truths it reveals even while we are attentive to the facts of appearance. In the sections of *Modern Painters I* on the "Truth" of skies, clouds, and such things, Ruskin means these objects' physical *and* their typological truth. Thus, the old masters' failure to paint clouds accurately is a failure of observation and a failure in insight.

> But perhaps the most grievous failure of all, in the clouds of these painters, is the utter want of transparency. Not in her most ponderous and lightless masses will nature ever leave us without some evidence of transmitted sunshine; and she perpetually gives us passages in which the vapour becomes visible only by the sunshine which it arrests and holds within itself, not caught on its surfaces, but entangled in its mass,—floating fleeces, precious with the gold of heaven. . . . Nothing, on the contrary, can be more painfully and ponderously opaque than the clouds of the old masters. (3:380)

21. Raymond Williams, *Keywords* (New York: Oxford University Press, 1976), p. 216.

Ruskin jumps from the physical to the moral here; failing to portray the transparency of clouds implies a rejection of the "gold of heaven." It is within the sign, the significant things of the world, that the two realms—physical and moral, worldly and divine—are brought together.

Here, obviously, is where Ruskin joins up with the romantic tradition. When he sees art as necessary in order that the significance of the natural world might be revealed to men, he elevates the artist and the artistic symbol as much as any romantic enthusiast. The symbol offers the point of passage from one kind of truth to another. In Ruskin, then, the artistic symbol's mediation between men and natural things is deplored when seen as interfering with direct perception of the thing; but art's mediating role is viewed positively when Ruskin considers that the natural object in art represents not only physical appearance, but also indicates typological truth. Hence, Ruskin's practice tends to be more complex than the theoretical statements in which he generally manages to present only one side of this double vision of art. His prose, in particular his metaphors (like clouds), enacts that double vision his theories can never quite express.

How does the mediating word or image in Ruskin signify? He offers two answers: one a statement of faith, the other the trials of practice. The statement of faith simply asserts the truth of Evangelical typology. *Modern Painters II,* which Ruskin later called the most religious of his works (19:87), insists on "the inevitable stamp of God's image on what he creates" (4:143). The created object's beauty is the most clear indication of its divine origin. George Landow describes the logic of this faith. "In . . . beauty the physical object expresses and represents the immaterial. The material object, that which is distinctly perceived . . . is a symbol through which, or on which, appear the signs of spiritual law. . . . The twin, and in this case interchangeable, ideas of symbolization and expression grant Ruskin the means of reconciling material and immaterial, for they grant him a way of showing that the beautiful object is beautiful because it is spiritual."[22]

This reconciliation of the material with the spiritual requires faith. Ruskin's attention to physical detail would not be so intense if the passage to the spiritual were so easy. Even when making his strongest statements that this passage can be made, Ruskin presents it only as a possibility, an ideal conclusion to an arduous process only just begun. "The fact of our deriving constant pleasure from whatever is a type or semblance of divine attributes, and from nothing but that which is so . . . seems a promise of a communion ultimately deep, close, and conscious, with the Being whose darkened manifestations we here feebly and unthinkingly delight in" (4:144–45). *Modern Painters* strives to achieve this desired communion, and it is in the famous purple passages, with

---

22. *The Aesthetic and Critical Theories of John Ruskin,* p. 178.

their extended use of metaphor, that the writer assaults the boundaries between the sacred and the profane. An example from *Modern Painters I* shows the doubleness inherent in the assault, and highlights several of the problems I have been discussing. The description is of a Turner painting of Venice.[23]

> But let us take, with Turner, the last and greatest step of all. Thank heaven, we are in sunshine again,—and what sunshine! Not the lurid, gloomy, plague-like oppression of Canaletti, but white, flashing fulness of dazzling light, which the waves drink and the clouds breathe, bounding and burning in intensity of joy. That sky—it is a very visible infinity,—liquid, measureless, unfathomable, panting and melting through the chasms in the long fields of snow-white, flaked, slow-moving vapour, that guide the eye along their multitudinous waves down to the islanded rest of the Euganean hills. Do we dream, or does the white forked sail drift nearer, and nearer yet, diminishing the blue sea between us with the fulness of its wings? It pauses now; but the quivering of its bright reflection troubles the shadow of the sea, those azure, fathomless depths of crystal mystery, on which the swiftness of the poised gondola floats double, its black beak lifted like the crest of a dark ocean bird, its scarlet draperies flashed back from the kindling surface, and its bent oar breaking the radiant water into a dust of gold. Dreamlike and dim, but glorious, the unnumbered palaces lift their shafts out of the hollow sea,—pale ranks of motionless flame,—their mighty towers sent up to heaven like tongues of more eager fire,—their grey domes looming vast and dark, like eclipsed worlds,—their sculptured arabesques and purple marble fading farther and fainter, league beyond league, lost in the light of the distance. Detail after detail, thought beyond thought, you find and feel them through the radiant mystery, inexhaustible as indistinct, beautiful, but never all revealed; secret in fulness, confused in symmetry, as nature herself is to the bewildered and foiled glance, giving out of that indistinctness, and through that confusion, the perpetual newness of the infinite, and the beautiful. (3:257)

The passage begins with almost a direct vision of heaven, of pure, "dazzling," and "full" light, a light that sustains life. The "waves drink" the light and the "clouds breathe" it. That sunshine turns the world below to fire —the water and clouds are "burning"—in a suggestion of a medieval progression of elements by which earth and water, first changed to fire, will eventually merge with air. The clouds direct the light to the earth and water below, while

23. The passage quoted appeared in the first two editions of *Modern Painters I* (1843, 1844) and was deleted in the third edition (1846) and thereafter. In the preface to the third edition, Ruskin writes that he has cut out passages that "required modification or explanation" (3:53). Throughout his career, Ruskin habitually apologized for the extravagance of his prose effusions (after the fact), while defending the beliefs or opinions that prompted those effusions. The preface to the third edition of *Modern Painters I* contains one such apology: "If I were now to bestow on this feeble essay the careful revision which it much needs . . . it would not be to alter its tendencies, or modify its conclusions, but to prevent indignation from appearing virulence on the one side, and enthusiasm partizanship on the other" (3:53). My choice of this passage has been governed by the attempt to find as extreme an example of Ruskin's purple prose as possible.

also "guid[ing] the eye" of the human beholder. Ruskin interprets the scene as the world moving toward light, and his use of the "we" indicates that the observer is being drawn into the scene as well. The white sail of a boat "troubles the shadow of the sea"; the oar of a gondola transforms the water into a "dust of gold." Both the boat and the gondola are metaphorically described as birds, a fitting image since they bring the light of heaven to the water on which they are perched. (Birds traditionally suggest transcendence of the terrestrial.) Furthermore, the synecdoche by which the boat is only identified as "the white forked sail" makes the reference ambiguous, since the description also fits the light that is flowing toward the viewer through the clouds. Stressing motion, the passage has, thus far, decreased the distance between earth and sky, darkness and light, viewer and viewed, as light descends to permeate this world. Turner's art overcomes the dualism between earth and heaven by transfiguring this world in the revealing glow of the sun. Ruskin's prose achieves a similar transfiguration through the metaphors that emphasize how one thing can be described in terms more usually applied to quite a different thing. Metaphor emphasizes that the difference between things can be overcome.

But then Ruskin turns to the city, the palaces of Venice, and his description almost completely reverses itself. Although their towers seem to indicate a desire for heaven's light in their reaching to the sky "like tongues . . . of eager fire," the palaces' most striking feature is their resistance to the union between heaven and earth offered by light. Far from partaking of light's clarity, the palaces are "indistinct," "like eclipsed worlds," and "never all revealed." They resist incorporation into the realm of light or into the realm of language; they are impossible to portray or describe precisely. We learn only of their mysterious indistinctness, and the only metaphor used in describing them is that one image—"tongues of eager fire"—that works to include the towers in the communion with light.

The tenuous thread that holds together the two halves of this passage is mystery. The clear bright light is "dazzling," "measureless," "unfathomable," while the dark "grey domes" point to the "infinite" in their "perpetual newness" and by their very "confusion." The temptation is to accuse Ruskin himself of hopeless confusion, but the grounds for the muddle lie, as I have been trying to suggest, in the exigencies of symbolic language itself. The terrestial landscape takes on light so readily in the first half of the passage that it can only sustain its difference from the celestial by its resistance to light in the second half. (Certainly our reaction to many Turner paintings must be that light is threatening to swallow up the whole world.) Ruskin expresses this dual impulse to union and to differentiation both semantically and syntactically when he writes, "The more we know, and the more we feel, the more we separate; we separate to obtain a more perfect unity" (3:37). Ruskin's initial enthusiasm for union makes him stress the sharing in light of all things in this world, but his subsequent retreat serves as a reminder that he wants to preserve this world as well. His realism takes as its focus the individual thing in all its uniqueness and thus works against the dissolution of the symbol in favor of what it stands for. Ruskin, at least in his early writings, does not evidence Carlyle's apocalyptic bent. The act of union in the symbol is the means by which we learn the deeper significance of this world, but is not, and cannot be allowed to become, the world itself.

In practice, then, representation reveals a necessary, a desired, and yet a disturbing doubleness. (Carlyle has phrased that doubleness as a simultaneous "revelation and concealment.") There always remains the possibility that, using words or images as symbols, the artist is not moving toward God, but only deeper into debilitating obscurity. Ruskin's analysis of modern painting's "cloudiness" makes this ambiguity most obvious. Modern painting evidences "a general profanity of temper in regarding . . . nature; that is to say, a total absence of faith in the presence of any deity therein" (5:320). Obscurity and mystery might, very simply, signify total lack of insight, might only denote ignorance. "The profoundest reason of this darkness of heart is, I believe, our want of faith" (5:322). Realism, accurate portrayal of the natural thing, may be indicative of the utmost profanity. (Thus Rossetti's poetry appears "fleshly" when the passage from the material into the spiritual is not achieved, when the real thing's symbolic function is not readily apparent.) The artist displays all his ingenuity in the painted image, the poetic word, precisely because that image, that word, is all he has; the sign points to nothing beyond itself. The rest is darkness. And in the darkness of the modern period, the obscurity that afflicts all signs makes the religious sign indistinguishable from the faithless, unmeaning artifact.

Ruskin, to distinguish the "cloudy" Turner from the other modern painters who merely look like him, insists on a hierarchy of three possibilities: the "ignoble mystery" of ignorance, the clarity of "perfect intelligibleness," and the "noble mystery" of the "greatest men" who "must struggle through intelligibility to obscurity" (6:96). "Noble mystery differs from ignoble, in being a veil thrown between us and something definite, known and substantial; but the ignoble mystery is a veil cast before chaos, the studious concealment of Nothing" (6:94). This definition is meant, clearly, to apply to the physical landscape a painter portrays. Poor painters use obscurity to hide their ignorance, their failure to observe the landscape carefully and accurately. But if "noble mystery" only "veils . . . something known and substantial," then what is the need or source of its obscurity? Ruskin moves here from the physical to the spiritual without indicating the fact of or means for such a movement. On the material worldly plane, Turner's use of clouds is justified because this painter "knows thoroughly what the object is" (6:94) that hides behind the intervening mist. Bad painters use such mists to cover their ignorance of the hidden physical object. But on the spiritual plane—and surely Ruskin has

moved to this plane when he talks of a "cloudiness . . . *past* clearness" (6:96)
—"noble mystery" must reflect our innate inability to see anything clearly;
this veil is not justified because the artist knows the object behind it, but
because, as Ruskin has argued, men can never know that object, God.

In other words, Ruskin (very much like Browning) needs the image in
painting and in poetry both to function faithfully as a representative (the cloud
blocking the sun represents, by analogy, our limited understanding blocking
full perception of God) *and* to represent its own limits (the obscurity of the
cloud marks the obscurity of earthly representation itself). Language and art,
the word and the image, represent their own limits when they confess, by
obscurity (mystery), that the painted image or word is not the thing itself. The
artist who has "travelled past clearness" into "noble mystery" is the artist
whose signs proclaim their failure to represent clearly and adequately the truth
they nonetheless announce: the union of man and God. The "mystery" of the
image in art is not only its affording us passage into the realm of higher truths,
but also its inability to embody those truths. The word can represent those
truths, but only while reminding us that the representative is not the thing
itself; the representative can aid our comprehension and our perception of a
thing or a concept, saying that it is something *like* this, but the representative
cannot say that the thing or concept *is* this. Thus, representation maintains the
dualism characteristic of existence in this world, while also indicating the
distant prospect of the apocalyptic romantic marriage. Ruskin makes much less
radical claims than Coleridge or even Carlyle for what the word as a mediator
between and meeting place for the sacred and the profane can achieve. For
Ruskin, revelation of the spiritual is never as direct as Coleridge and Carlyle
at times make it out to be. Conversely, Ruskin is much more interested in and
reliant on direct perception of natural objects than either Coleridge or Carlyle.

The mystery of clouds, then, is the mystery of representation itself, the
process by which something different from the subject of discourse is the agent
of that subject's presentation. And the mystery of representation is absolute
when, as in Ruskin's case (and Browning's), the subject of discourse is defined
as incapable of being directly presented in language. This inability to represent
directly is positive insofar as it preserves the distinction between human and
divine, granting each its right to exist, while also establishing the possibility
—its limits and conditions—of communication between them. This inability
is negative insofar as the stated object of human desire is placed outside the
limits of human endeavor and language; men can only have worldly and
wordy representatives of the divine, never the divine itself.

The modern reader is likely to complain that he cannot accept as adequate
a theory of representation that rests its claim on the "mysterious" fact that
representation works, that we somehow manage to understand statements
about things we have never seen and experienced by way of signs that are not
those things. Yet, in spite of the recent emphasis on linguistic systems as

man-made, the actual origins of such systems have remained a mystery even in our enlightened century. The deconstructionists discuss how words shift or lose meaning within a given system, but refuse to handle the question of how a workable system was ever established.[24] Locke's insistence that we always keep words' meanings firmly in grasp, Coleridge's desire for a magical word that partakes in the reality it designates, and Ruskin's determined faith in a mystery whose secret eludes human comprehension are all responses to the perceived frailty of systems of signification. This mechanism we do not truly understand might break down at any time, so various programs are put forward to make the system more stable. The deconstructionists take their place within the same tradition, although they prefer to emphasize signification's frailty rather than to suggest ways to combat it. (Obviously, however, these writers have some stake in the system's continued ability to function.) I have stressed, thus far, Ruskin's faith in representation and his finding a positive purpose even in that difference between representative and represented which seems to pose the greatest threat to successful representation. But Ruskin's faith is hardly constant and, as he himself was the first to proclaim, deserts him altogether at stages of his later career. Ruskin's fight with madness and his final descent into complete silence draw the interest of modern readers in a way the moral pieties of his early work often do not, but the fact remains that much of the later work is unreadable. Ruskin's madness, like Rossetti's despair, can be taken as an emblem of the Victorians' anguished efforts to reach a reality beyond self that can never quite be grasped. Able to recognize difference and distance from the divine as a "happy Fall" in his early writings, Ruskin begins to battle indirection frantically once he loses the ability to anchor the sign to the unseen truth it signifies. The material forms the world presents to him seem ever more bizarre and grotesque, ever further from the God of light he seeks.

A discussion of Ruskin's later career should begin by noting that his loss of faith can be overestimated. Throughout the last thirty years of his working life (1860–1890), Ruskin periodically offers statements of faith and makes typological interpretations that resemble those found in *Modern Painters, The Stones of Venice,* and other early works.

Ruskin's loss of faith manifests itself in two ways that, at first glance, seem absolutely contradictory. His repudiation of indirection leads him, at times, to celebrate the virtues of a plain style in which the difference between words and their meanings is kept to a minimum. But his later works more

---

24. For a description of the way words lose or change their meaning within an established linguistic system, see Jacques Derrida, "White Mythology: Metaphor in the Text of Philosophy," *New Library History* 6 (1974): 5–74. But Derrida is adamantly unwilling to explain how the "differences" between signs guarantee their ability to signify even though they are unstable, or to account for the establishment of differences. He falls back on what seems an almost mystical insistence that differences are always "already there." For the fullest discussion of this recurrent position in Derrida, see the essay "Differance," *Speech and Phenomena* (Evanston: Northwestern University Press, 1973), pp. 129–60.

often puzzle readers because things and words carry so many meanings. Natural things do not lose their meaning for Ruskin as much as he loses his confidence that he possesses the correct method for discerning that meaning. Where once things pointed fairly clearly to God's hand in nature, now a thing's meanings are various and multiple. When in reasonably firm command of these multiple meanings (*The Queen of the Air* is the prime example), Ruskin can be a charming and enlightening explicator of texts, but in *Fors Clavigera* we often witness his inability to sort out the crucial from the trivial or the plausible from the implausible when presenting the paths his thoughts take when confronted with this object or that name. If a naturalistic realism makes the object in nature mean too little for Ruskin's taste, the hazard of things meaning too much threatens him at the other end of the scale. Ruskin's own comments on this loss of control—and the resultant failure to make contact with his audience—are often quite moving, and should be a reliable antidote to any attempt to celebrate his madness as true insight instead of unbearable pain. "Now, it is true, that my writing may be obscure, or seem only half in earnest. But it is the best I can do; it expresses the thoughts that come to me as they come; and I have no time just now to put them into more intelligible words. . . . And, literally, no one answers. Nay, even those who read, read so carelessly that they don't notice whether the book is to go on or not" (27:293). Overdetermination is not the same thing as indeterminancy; a thing's or word's ability to signify, even to signify a variety of meanings, still depends on its carrying a fairly small number of significances. The later Ruskin sometimes loses entirely the ability to make a thing meaningful to his audience. But it seems to me that his labored pursuit of a thing's or word's significance is always in the name of discovering its "true" meaning. His endless etymological ponderings present his hope that origins might be the clue to determinate meanings in a world that has become frighteningly indeterminate.[25] Whether pursuing the many meanings a thing (or word) has acquired or making the Lockean plea that we use signifiers carefully, Ruskin's goal remains the delineation of a fixed range of reference that will guarantee the word's ability to make sense.

As might be expected, recent criticism has been full of praise for the Ruskin who presents multiple meanings.[26] In *The Queen of the Air* Ruskin develops a notion of myth that comes close to modern understandings of the

25. For a more favorable assessment of Ruskin's etymological investigations, see Northrop Frye, *Anatomy of Criticism* (Princeton: Princeton University Press, 1957), pp. 9–10.

26. For example, see Harold Bloom's introduction to *The Literary Criticism of John Ruskin* (New York: W. W. Norton, 1965). Bloom finds *The Queen of the Air*, with its pursuit of multiple meanings, the most significant of Ruskin's works for modern critics (xxiv). Guy Davenport, "The House That Jack Built," *Salmagundi*, no. 43 (1979), 140–55, finds in *Fors Clavigera* features—such as serial structure, the interweaving of public and private symbols, and the continual reopening of discussions seemingly closed in earlier installments—that resurface in many modern works, particularly Pound's *Cantos*.

term and reveals a sensitivity to what Freud calls the "antithetical sense of primary words." Reasonably in control of his multiple meanings here, Ruskin can identify Hermes, the god of clouds, as both a deceiver and a guide, without feeling a need to assert one function over the other and without offering so many meanings (as in the discussions of Ursula in *Fors Clavigera*) that the figure is rendered totally obscure. The doubleness of clouds holds. "The snatching away by the clouds is connected with the thought of hiding, and of making things seem to be what they are not; so that Hermes is the god of lying, as he is of mist; and yet, with this ignoble function of making things vanish and disappear, is connected the . . . authority of leading souls in the cloud of death" (19:320). In this case, Ruskin is able to find "the gentle and serviceable Hermes" even among legends that reveal him as "deceitful" (19:322), but such is not always possible. The "lying" nature of clouds, their "making things seem to be what they are not," troubles the later Ruskin in various ways and with various results to which I will now turn. "The Mystery of Life and its Arts" (1868) offers a convenient place to begin. The lecture presents the by-now-familiar equation of clouds with mystery, but extends the scope of the association by claiming "human life" is a mystery as well.

> But it is not always that . . . we can enter into any true perception that this human life shares in the nature of it, not only the evanescence, but the mystery of the cloud; that its avenues are wreathed in darkness, and its forms and causes no less fantastic, than spectral and obscure; so that not only in the vanity which we cannot grasp, but in the shadow which we cannot pierce, it is true of this cloudy life of ours, that "man walketh in a vain shadow, and disquieteth himself in vain." (18:146–47)

Ruskin no longer finds any comfort in this obscurity. He has become convinced that Victorian society willfully creates this distance between itself and God. We, he tells his audience, "have walked after the imagination of our evil hearts, instead of after the counsels of Eternity, until our lives—not in the likeness of the cloud of heaven, but of the smoke of hell—have become 'as a vapour, that appeareth for a little time, and then vanisheth away' " (18:179). Viewing contemporary society, Ruskin only finds "ignoble mystery"; all human talk and action has worked to obscure perception of the divine. Imagination has been leading men astray. The cloud is not pierced because no one wants to pierce it. Those mysteries that the Ruskin of *Modern Painters* identified as the nature of human existence are now understood as social creations, hardly inevitable. Men have used the excuse of ignorance and obscurity to justify acting in their own interests rather than "after the counsels of Eternity."

Within a culture that fosters mystery for its own selfish ends, words become particularly dangerous. Given the slightest pretext, the audience will focus attention on words rather than on what they denote. Ruskin decides, rather bitterly, that he found favor with Victorian readers only because they could enjoy the felicities of his style while ignoring what he had to say. "People thought of the words only, and cared nothing for their meaning" (18:146). His readers have loved him for all the wrong reasons, for his ability "to set his words sometimes prettily together" (18:196). The ineffectiveness of words, their deflection of energy away from their meaning to themselves, is underlined by Ruskin's informing his audience that all his "pretty" words about Turner and about architecture have brought no positive results. Turner —who, Ruskin says, "discouraged me scornfully"—was right when he proclaimed "the uselessness of talking about what people could not see for themselves" (18:148). This attack on words with its final retreat to what can be plainly *seen* is recognizably in the Lockean tradition.

The question of how, when, and why Ruskin shifted his attention from aesthetic to social issues is a vexed one that need not detain us here. What is important to recognize is that for Ruskin as social critic the failure to apprehend the truth is a social choice, not evidence of an inevitable epistemological difficulty. His historical studies seem to have led Ruskin to the conclusion that not only do different eras know different things and have different blind spots, but also that what they know or do not know reveals basic desires. As a writer he is determined to fight such willful obscurity, and that fight involves his speaking his piece plainly. "Happily, therefore, the power of using such pleasant language—if indeed it ever were mine—is passing away from me; and whatever I am now able to say at all, I find myself forced to say with great plainness" (18:146). Chances are that his message will be ignored because unpleasant, but the ability to focus delight on his style will no longer facilitate his readers' evasion of his meaning. "I could be of great use to you—infinite use—with brief saying, if you would believe it; but you would not, just because the thing that would be of real use would displease you" (18:168).

Ruskin recognizes that social mysteries, polite or otherwise, serve to keep the middle class from ever seeing the suffering its way of life has inflicted on English workers. "Whenever in any religious faith, dark or bright, we allow our minds to dwell upon the points in which we differ from other people, we are wrong, and in the devil's power" (18:185). The violence implicit in this attack on differences is more explicit in the last passage of *Unto This Last*. Veils must be torn away so that the plight of the workers, our fellow men, can be fully seen. "Raise the veil boldly; face the light; and if, as yet, the light of the eye can only be through tears, and the light of the body through sackcloth, go thou forth weeping, bearing precious seed, until the time come . . . when, for earth's severed multitudes of the wicked and the weary, there shall be holier reconciliation than that of the narrow home, and calm economy" (17:114). All that stands between the British public and the truth must be swept away. Many of the later works reveal a similar impatience with intermediaries, with veils, as the truth behind appearances recedes from Ruskin's grasp, or, when he believes he sees it clearly, his audience persists in willfully ignoring it. Apocalyptic desires, with their accompanying violent imagery, usually indicate that more peaceful means of making the truth appear have proved insufficient.

Often unable to pierce the cloud himself, and convinced that his society does not even desire to pierce it, Ruskin considers the possibility "that the cloud . . . has no strength nor fire within; but is a painted cloud only, to be delighted in, yet despised" (18:151). But this possibility is too terrible for him. Appearances must be tied to some meaning behind them. (As an aside, we might note that Ruskin's economics work on the same basis. He wants to deny relative values established by a market of exchanges in favor of an absolute and stable standard of "use.") The "painted" varieties of clouds, the infinite forms of nature that have so delighted him, can only be legitimate sources of pleasure when anchored to transcendent meanings. The play of free-floating forms holds no appeal for Ruskin; the clouds are significant because they are firmly placed between heaven and earth even as they drift across the sky.[27] When the meanings behind appearances become hard to find, Ruskin is more likely to blame the observer (either his guilty self or his guilty contemporaries) than to conclude those meanings do not exist. (Once again, we see here the similarity between the later Ruskin and Rossetti.)

> It became to me not a painted cloud, but a terrible and impenetrable one: not a mirage, which vanished as I drew near, but a pillar of darkness, to which I was forbidden to draw near. For I saw that both my own failure, and such success in petty things as in its poor triumph seemed to me worse than failure, came from the want of sufficiently earnest effort to understand the whole law and meaning of existence. (18:151–52)

By 1884, the "pillar of darkness" has become the "storm-cloud," and the guilt of failing to see through the clouds has been extended from Ruskin himself to the whole nineteenth century. The plainest style possible is necessitated by the growing inability to understand the figural significance of things or poetic language. Ruskin begins the famous (or infamous) lecture on the storm-cloud by insisting that his title is no metaphor. "I might, indeed, have meant, and it would have been only too like me to mean, any number of things by such a title;—but tonight, I mean simply what I have said, and propose to bring to your notice a series of cloud phenomena, which, so far as I can weigh existing evidence, are peculiar to our own times" (34:9). Here Ruskin takes an almost purely Lockean position. His lecture, and the existence of the

27. Ruskin's resistance to the notion that clouds cannot be fixed, but are always moving, is indicated by his chastising, in the lecture on the storm cloud (34:11–12), the "blockhead" who had denied that clouds can be "stationary."

storm cloud, demonstrate how men can no longer handle the doubleness of natural signs. The figure in the metaphor, the appearance of the cloud, no longer successfully represents. Men are no longer capable of perceiving what lies beyond appearance.

Yet, of course, Ruskin's whole demonstration of this breakdown of representation is conducted in a figural discourse that requires our recognition that the storm-cloud points to a truth beyond itself. Ruskin's editors back up his claim that the physical facts justify his lecture, but such loyalty (even if true to the facts) is beside the point. A physical reality or not, the storm cloud quickly becomes metaphorical for Ruskin—in spite of his opening disclaimer. "Far and away more important to you than all the physical laws" of perception, there is "a *moral* Science of Light" (34:27), and the physical darkness of the storm cloud can only be correctly interpreted in relation to this moral science.

> Blanched Sun,—blighted grass,—blinded man.—If in conclusion, you ask me for any conceivable cause or meaning of these things—I can tell you none, according to your modern beliefs; but I can tell you what meaning it would have borne to men of old time. Remember, for the last twenty years, England, and all foreign nations, either tempting her or following her, have blasphemed the name of God deliberately and openly; and have done iniquity by proclamation, every man doing as much injustice to his brother as it is in his power to do. Of states in such moral gloom every seer of old predicted the physical gloom. (34:40)

Seers of old, versed in the correct understanding of the moral significance of natural facts, could have read the meaning the moderns fail to perceive.

Ruskin links modern evil with the misuse of language: "blasphemy" and "iniquitous proclamation." The evil of the storm cloud is the evil of language that no longer contains truth the way the clouds of old contained light, a language that cannot refer to a truth beyond itself. Words have become completely earthly and profane, no longer opening out toward the eternal. "In plague-wind, the sun is choked out of the whole heaven, all day long, by a cloud" (34:39). In earlier lectures Ruskin derided the social mystery of false distinctions, but here he confronts a language that makes no distinctions at all. Conveying no light, the language of the storm cloud fosters a chaos of nondifferentiation, a world with no moral hierarchy, only the virtual civil war of a society that pits each man, indiscriminately, against his neighbor. The cloud of light maintains the distinction between man and God, but the storm cloud leaves man divorced from the divine in a world of no distinctions.

In the face of such chaos, the writer's task is to speak plainly in order to restore a language that can make basic, necessary distinctions. In *Fiction, Fair and Foul* (1880), another text in which Ruskin discusses the total collapse of language (here in relation to contemporary fiction), the following (Lockean) prescription on style is offered: "Choice of the fewest and simplest words that can be found in the compass of the language, to express the thing meant: these few words being also arranged in the most straight-forward and intelligible way" (34:335). The call for plain speech in the later Ruskin involves a disparagement of his own earlier excesses. The footnotes Ruskin added to *Modern Painters II* in 1883 often make fun of his youthful pleasure in figural language. But there is also a sense in which those footnotes reflect the older writer's loss of faith in his audience's ability to handle metaphor, to read intelligently and sensitively. For example, one note reads: "Some sense in this bit at last! The six pages of metaphor we have just gone through mean, in all, little more than that the best authors express the mind, more than the person or manners, of men or heroes" (4:253n). At a time when Ruskin was struggling with madness, was fighting to retain some control over the significance of words and images, it is hardly surprising that he would praise a lucid style, or that, in *Praeterita,* he decides finally not to include that confession of a love of clouds and other inessential decorations.

Yet, even at the end, Ruskin had not lost all sight of the greater, transcendent possibilities afforded by language to those who possess faith in the sign's ability to reveal something beyond itself. In *Fiction, Fair and Foul,* he follows the recommendation of a spare style with a statement about the kind of language open to the greatest writers (even while lamenting that none such now exist): "Utmost spiritual contents in words; so that each carries not only its instant meaning, but a cloudy companionship of higher and darker meaning according to the passion—nearly always indicated by metaphor" (34:336). And in the lecture on the storm cloud, although unable to state the dream right now, Ruskin can quote from an earlier work (an Oxford lecture of 1872) to place before his audience that ideal toward which all perception of things in this world and all use of language should be aimed.

> The "Fiat Lux" of creation is therefore, in the deep sense, "fiat anima," and is as much, when you understand it, the ordering of Intelligence as the ordering of Vision. It is the appointment of change of what else had been only a mechanical effluence from things unseen to things unseeing,—from Stars, that did not shine, to Earth, that did not perceive,—the change, I say, of that blind vibration into the glory of the Sun and Moon for human eyes: *so making possible the communication* out of the unfathomable truth of that portion of truth which is good for us, and animating to us, and is set to rule over the day and over the night of our joy and our sorrow. (34:27, my emphasis)

5

Dickens: Fancy and the Real

To turn from Carlyle and Ruskin to Dickens, George Eliot, and Browning is to move from writers who explicitly discuss theoretical issues surrounding representation to writers who develop strategies of representation in works in which representation is not a specific topic of discourse. The distinction is hardly absolute, since, as I have tried to show, Carlyle's and Ruskin's rhetorical practice reveals much about their attitudes toward and beliefs about representation. Conversely, Dickens's, Eliot's, and Browning's discussions of their artistic practice provide crucial information about what they hoped to achieve and the methods they thought most likely to bring success. Nevertheless, my focus in the next three chapters will be on modes of representation developed in the process of writing novels and poems. Dickens, George Eliot, and Browning necessarily encountered some of the problems and contradictions discussed in the previous three chapters (as well as in the Introduction), but they developed certain working strategies that allowed them to continue shaping coherent works of art in the face of those problems.

The emphasis here is pragmatic. To a greater degree than Rossetti, Carlyle, or Ruskin, these three writers found representational practices that *worked*. To a certain extent, their success is based on their ability to derive some benefit from the difference between word and world, to adopt a romantic (accepting) attitude toward the independent energies of the word. But all three remain Victorian in their continued allegiance to the empiricist insistence on the word's subordination to a greater reality; the constructions of mind remain answerable to something beyond it.

Dickens made one of his few public pronouncements about the goals of his writing in "A Preliminary Word" to *Household Words*. He pledges to his readers that his new magazine will "tenderly cherish the light of Fancy which is inherent in the human breast" and will "show to all, that in all familiar things, even in those repellant on the surface, there is Romance enough, if we find it out." In the preface to *Bleak House*, the first novel he published after beginning *Household Words*, Dickens reiterates his position: "I have purposely dwelt upon the romantic side of familiar things" (xiv).[1] The championship of

---

1. The passage from *Household Words* is quoted from *Charles Dickens*, ed. Stephen Wall (Baltimore: Penguin Books, 1970), p. 90. Passages from the novels are from the *New Oxford Illustrated Dickens*, 21 vols. (London: Oxford University Press, 1947–1958), and are cited parenthetically in the text, with book, chapter, and page numbers given for passages from *Hard*

fancy becomes a central tenet of Dickens's artistic program, most notably in *Hard Times,* a novel devoted to proving the necessity of fancy in a world "chained . . . to material realities, and inspired . . . with no faith in anything else" (2:7, 127). In accord with the prescriptions of Carlyle and the goals of the romantics, Dickens understands art's task as the revelation of truths apart from "material realities." In a letter to John Forster, Dickens distinguishes his own practice from a "realism" that devotes itself to reproducing the observable features of daily life.

> It does not seem to me to be enough to say of any description that it is the exact truth. The exact truth must be there; but the merit or art in the narrator, is the manner of stating the truth. As to which thing in literature, it always seems to me that there is a world to be done. And in these times, when the tendency is to be frightfully literal and catalogue-like—to make the thing, in short, a sort of sum in reduction that any miserable creature can do in that way—I have an idea (really founded on the love of what I profess), that the very holding of popular literature through a kind of popular dark age, may depend on such fanciful treatment.[2]

Dickens's persistent championing of fancy has led critics to categorize his work apart from the tradition of nineteenth-century realism.[3] But the question of Dickens's relation to realism has not been settled to everyone's satisfaction. Recent reassessments range from identifying Dickens as a primary example of the realistic tradition to denying that his work has any realistic elements.[4] The letter to Forster does, after all, recognize the need for "exact truth," while the author of *Bleak House* uses the preface to continue his public debate with George Lewes about the possibility of spontaneous combustion, assuring the reader that he "took pains to investigate the subject and found fully docu-

---

Times, Little Dorrit, A Tale of Two Cities, and *Our Mutual Friend,* while chapter and page numbers are given for passages from *David Copperfield, Bleak House,* and *Great Expectations.*

2. John Forster, *The Life of Charles Dickens* (London: J. M. Dent & Sons, 1966), 2:279.

3. For a Victorian attempt to differentiate Dickens's work from that of more "realistic" writers, see G. H. Lewes's famous assessment of Dickens's career, reprinted in *The Dickens Critics,* ed. George H. Ford and Lauriat Lane, Jr. (Ithaca: Cornell University Press, 1961), pp. 55–74. See Richard Stang, *The Theory of the Novel in England, 1850–1870* (New York: Columbia University Press, 1959), pp. 153–59, for a short summary of the ways Dickens appears different from his contemporaries who espoused "realism."

4. John Romano, *Dickens and Reality* (New York: Columbia University Press, 1978), presents the case for considering Dickens a mainstream realist, while J. Hillis Miller, "The Fiction of Realism: *Sketches by Boz, Oliver Twist* and Cruikshank's Illustrations," in *Dickens Centennial Essays,* ed. Ada Nisbet and Blake Nevius (Berkeley: University of California Press, 1971), pp. 85–154, argues that Dickens's work cannot be said to rely on any prior reality. Between these two comes Robert Newsom, *Dickens on the Romantic Side of Familiar Things: "Bleak House" and the Novel Tradition* (New York: Columbia University Press, 1977). Newsom discusses the interplay "between the empirical and the fictional" (150) in *Bleak House.*

mented cases of the phenomenon" (xiv).[5] Moreover, just at that point in his career when Dickens begins to champion fancy, he begins to write those novels —*Bleak House, Little Dorrit,* and *Our Mutual Friend*—that struck his contemporaries and strike modern readers as a turning away from the careless comedies of his youth.

The benevolent grandfather figures of the early novels (Brownlow, old Martin Chuzzlewit, the Cheerybles) made certain that all ended well, but the later novels examine more fully the cruel effects of Victorian commercial society on its members and find escape from that society into a comic refuge less easy to achieve. *Dombey and Son,* in which the father figure does not protect the younger characters but must be saved himself, is usually seen as the point of transition from the "early" to the "late" Dickens. While the differences between "early" and "late" can be exaggerated, I do think there are some significant structural elements that recur in the novels written after *Dombey and Son,* elements that do not appear in the earlier novels. Without pressing too hard for a connection that cannot be proved, I would like to suggest that the timing of "A Preliminary Word"—published when *David Copperfield* was eight installments from completion—is significant. In his autobiographical novel, I will argue, Dickens develops a new strategy of representation, one almost forced upon him by the difficulties involved in trying to be "true" to his past while also engaged in writing a work of fiction. An examination of *David Copperfield* reveals the very process by which the new representational strategy came into being. After a close look at *Copperfield,* I will briefly indicate how its essential features resurface in the later novels.

David Copperfield distinguishes reality from fancy along fairly predictable lines. Reality designates the world of perceivable fact, whereas fancy refers to what the imagination adds to the facts offered to it by the senses. Applied to the use of language, this distinction links reality with a style that works to assure language's ability to repeat or represent accurately in words the world of things, while fancy leads to an extravagant style that highlights the difference between the world of objects and the linguistic world. Reality is empirical, while fancy designates the nonmaterial mental processes associated with the romantic praise of the imagination. The novel presents the distinction between realism and fancy as follows:

5. Dickens and George Henry Lewes exchanged a series of letters on the factual basis of spontaneous combustion. The interesting thing about the controversy is how seriously Dickens took it; he felt it was his responsibility to his readers to present only incidents that might actually occur. Dickens had no interest in presenting the more obvious defense that the incident fits his needs in a work of fiction. For a full account of the controversy, with a reprinting of the letters exchanged, see Gordon S. Haight, "Dickens and Lewes on Spontaneous Combustion," *Nineteenth-Century Fiction* 10 (1955): 50–61. (*Nineteenth-Century Fiction* will be abbreviated *NCF* in subsequent notes.)

When my thoughts go back now, to that slow agony of my youth, I wonder how much of the histories I invented for such people hangs like a mist of fancy over well-remembered facts! When I tread the old ground, I do not wonder that I seem to see and pity, going on before me, an innocent romantic boy, making his imaginative world out of such strange experiences and sordid things. (11, 169)

"Fancy" is contrasted to "fact" here, just as it will be in *Hard Times,* but in this case the narrator's sympathy is with fact. Fancy is understandable in the "romantic, innocent" child, especially since he needs to retreat from a world of "sordid things" that he cannot hope to change. But for an adult, for a narrator who wishes to present the facts about his life clearly and accurately, fancy only threatens the integrity of his narrative. David must sift through his memories, separating fact from fancy. The only crime to which David ever admits is that he was "romantic." At the end of his narrative, he will attribute the troubles of his adult life to following the dictates of a childish, "heedless fancy" (62, 862). David's progress leads him from a childhood "romanticism" toward a staunch reliance on and, at times, stoical acceptance of "the reality principle," a movement rendered thematically as the maturation of an "undisciplined heart."[6] Or, at least, that is the way David likes to represent his progress. As we shall see, fancy has more to do with David's story than he, as a realistic narrator, is prepared to admit.

A realistic narrative must establish what is indisputably "real." In both Dickens and George Eliot, the original premise is that reality is what is immediately available to the senses rather than some invisible spiritual truth. The novelists, unlike the poets or Carlyle and Ruskin, only develop their allegiance to spiritual truths after discovering some deficiency in the material realm they originally accept as sufficient for their needs. The second chapter of *David Copperfield,* entitled "I Observe," establishes the primacy of the visual. The chapter begins: "The first objects that assume a distinct presence before me, as I look far back, into the blank of my infancy, are my mother . . . and Peggotty" (2, 13). Seeing things is the way they are established as "objects," separate from the perceiving self, yet present to that self, and as immediately real as it is.

Memory is another kind of seeing, as the phrase about looking back in the passage just quoted indicates. If memory's "seeing" is not merely metaphorical, but as accurate and dependable as the original seeing, then the narrative

6. The classic statement of the theme of the "undisciplined heart" is Gwendolyn Needham's "The Undisciplined Heart of David Copperfield," *NCF* 9 (1954): 81–107. James Kincaid's reading of the novel in chap. 7 of *Dickens and the Rhetoric of Laughter* (Oxford: Clarendon Press, 1971) offers an important qualification to Needham's essay. Kincaid argues, and my discussion follows his on this point, that David's movement to discipline is, at the very least, an ambiguous one, if not completely lamentable. The realistic narrator is priggish in his suspicion of fancy, as evidenced by his uneasiness with Micawber.

as a "written memory" (58, 817) will simply record the discoveries of that looking back. David takes pains to characterize himself as an exceptionally observant person. "I looked at nothing, that I know of, but I saw everything, even to the prospect of a church upon his china inkstand, as I sat down—and this, too, was a faculty confirmed in me in the old Micawber times" (27, 402).

The primary reality of the visual is asserted by contrasting it to the fanciful in a passage that introduces several of the novel's most central concerns.

> One Sunday night my mother reads to Peggotty and me in there [the room in which the father's funeral was held], how Lazarus was raised up from the dead. And I am so frightened that they are afterwards obliged to take me out of bed, and show me the quiet churchyard out of the bedroom window, with the dead all lying in their graves at rest, below the solemn moon.
>
> There is nothing half so green that I know anywhere, as the green of that churchyard; nothing half so shady as its trees; nothing half so quiet as its tombstones. The sheep are feeding there, when I kneel up, early in the morning, in my little bed in a closet within my mother's room, to look out at it; and I see the red light shining on the sun-dial, and think within myself, "Is the sun-dial glad, I wonder, that it can tell time again?" (2, 14)

The visual fact of the quiet churchyard is presented to the child to quell the fanciful fears awakened by the story. The clarity of daytime vision is contrasted to the fancies of nighttime, romantic visions developed in the dark when nothing real can be seen. The return of the sun at dawn means the return of the outside world to the child—and this daytime world of consciousness and visual perception is the world of time. Only with the sunrise does time begin, as the question to the sundial indicates. David associates consciousness with the ability to see things. "I felt so sleepy, that I knew if I lost sight of anything, for a moment, I was gone" (2, 16). Consciousness is that condition in which we remain aware of the outer world, and the most important awareness is visual.

Yet, interestingly enough, the reality that so completely dominates David's childhood vision, the landscape that seems more green, more shady, more quiet that anything else, is the churchyard, with its reminders of death, particularly the gravestone that marks his father's resting place. David is quieted by being assured that the dead remain dead, that the story of Lazarus is not real.[7] In a world of objects present to his sight, the child is fascinated

7. Mark Spilka, "*David Copperfield* as Psychological Fiction," *Critical Quarterly* 1 (1959): 295, reads David's reaction to the Lazarus story as a fear of the father's return, a fear about to be realized in Murdstone's appearance, which destroys the close union David enjoys with his mother. Jack Lindsay, in his excellent *Charles Dickens: A Biographical and Critical Study* (London: Andrew Dakars, 1950), sees the churchyard (a prominent image in Dickens's, as in David's and Pip's, early memories) as "both the lost Eden and the dark spot of the death wish" (34). What requires explanation is the child's fascination with the dead father, along with his strong wish that the father remain dead.

by the object—a tombstone—that is a memorial to an absent object. This passage already suggests the limits of a reliance on a purely visual apprehension of reality. An historical world has a depth that cannot be comprehended by the purely visual; things that are absent, which cannot be seen now, bear on the significance of that which is seen in the present moment. But, at this early stage in the narrative, explicit awareness of this complication is avoided, while David celebrates, as Wordsworth was wont to do, the immediate union of the child with his surroundings. He avoids confronting the dualism that follows from recognizing that mind, with its imaginings and memories, is an alien in a world of static, present objects.

Aural perceptions do not receive as much attention as visual ones, but they are also classed among immediate perceptions of the real in the novel. Hearing is most important when sight is deprived; in normal cases, hearing is simply linked with seeing, since we hear as well as see the person speaking in front of us. However, when locked into his room after biting Murdstone, David has to rely entirely on hearing to gain information of the outside world. "I listened to all the incidents of the house that made themselves audible to me; the ringing of bells, the opening and shutting of doors, the murmuring of voices, the footsteps on the stairs; to any laughing, whistling, or singing, outside, which seemed more dismal than anything else to me in my solitude and disgrace" (4, 59). Hearing, like seeing, involves a perception of the present moment; the sound is heard in the moment in which it is produced. But since seeing is primary, when we cannot see what is making a sound we must interpret the noise in order to understand who or what caused it. Thus aural perception, when unaccompanied by the presence of the causal agent to sight, already involves a distance from the external world, albeit a spatial not a temporal distance. The primacy of sight rests on its exclusion of all such distance, its immediate union of self and world.

The clarity of daytime vision is often contrasted to the confusion of dreams, but such is not the case in David's narrative. Several chapters (including 6, 7, 8, 14, 24, and 26) in the first half of the novel end with David's falling asleep, and with a short account of his dreams. The last paragraph of chapter 7 is fairly typical: "I had many a broken sleep inside the Yarmouth mail, and many an incoherent dream of all these things. But when I awoke at intervals, the ground outside the window was not the playground of Salem House, and the sound in my ears was not the sound of Mr. Creakle giving it to Traddles, but was the sound of the coachman touching up the horses" (7, 106). The dreams in the novel break down into isolated perceptions, in this case both visual and aural, that have no plot, and are usually simple repetitions of the images of the day just past. Focusing on the imagistic content of dreams assures their "incoherence" in terms of narrative structure, which places dreams in an odd position, epistemologically, in the novel. Dreams are "realistic" insofar as they present aural and visual images; as such, the dreams in the narrative are usually easily recognizable as representations of David's experiences. However, dreams are nonrealistic, "fanciful," insofar as these images float free of context, notably narrative context.

This odd position of dreams is tied to the commitment of David's narrative to the factual as opposed to the fanciful quality of memory; it is important to David as narrator that the memories presented in the narrative be established as accurate. The images of memory are, in several ways, clearly akin to those of dreams, so the narrative takes pains to establish the perceptual accuracy of both. The difference between memory and dream is that memory can construct a coherent narrative account by which its images are organized temporally.

Dream images and memory are most obviously akin in being less imme-diate than the images of sense perception. Hume has offered the traditional distinction between the two types of images by calling those of dream and memory "ideas" and those of sense perception "impressions." Hume's insistence that impressions are always more "lively" than ideas is questionable, since a vivid dream or memory is often more pronounced than a weak sensory perception.[8] David offers his own counterexample to Hume when he writes of Traddles: "His honest face . . . impresses me more in the remembrance than it did in the reality" (41, 593). This ability of memory to see details clearly, perhaps even more clearly than seen at the moment of original perception, is crucial to the narrative's insistence on its accuracy.

"Ideas" (in Hume's sense) are suspect because they do not rely on the object's presence, whereas an "impression" is generated by an object present to the perceiver. The problem with second-order images, those "ideas" formed in the object's absence, is that their faithfulness to the thing represented is not immediately verifiable; these ideas might be fanciful. (Language, in almost every instance of its use, presents the same problem as second-order images since words usually refer to some thing or some concept not present to the speaker or his audience.) In *David Copperfield,* that fancy alters or remakes the world of fact is assumed, but the narrative tries to keep memory, and even dream images, out of fancy's camp. Of course, some dream distor-tion is admitted, but since dream images are similar to those of memory, the clarity of dreams is stressed in order to help establish the reliability of memory.

Thus, when David comes to narrate an "event [the storm that kills Ham and Steerforth] in my life, so indelible, so awful" (55, 784) that his whole

8. See David Hume, *An Inquiry Concerning Human Understanding* (New York: Bobbs-Merrill, 1955), pp. 26–27.

narrative has been directed toward it, he combines dream and memory to assert the faithfulness of his narration to the original:

> For years after it occured, I dreamed of it often. I have started up so vividly impressed by it, that its fury has yet seemed raging in my quiet room, in the still night. I dream of it sometimes, though at lengthened and uncertain intervals, to this hour. I have an association between it and a stormy wind, or the lightest mention of a sea-shore, as strong as any of which my mind is conscious. As plainly as I behold what happened, I will try to write it down. I do not recall it, but see it done; for it happens again before me. (55, 784)

Determined to validate the accuracy of his narrative, David appeals to the perceptual situation in which the object is present to the viewer. Memory can "see" so clearly that David can insist that the original event is not temporally distance, not permanently lost in the past, but exists in the present, and because present, is seen. "I do not recall it, but see it done; for it happens again before me." In this instance, there is no temporal absence; the event has been present in dream and memory to David throughout the years since it took place.

This is the "realism" for which David's narrative strives: a point where the images of memory are overwhelmed by the lost object's return to presence, to immediate perception. The relation of this "realism" to empiricist epistemo-logical schemas is obvious, but we should also note the nostalgia inherent in this attempt to recover fully a distant past. The nostalgic desire for a lost past, and for a lost ability to exist immediately in the world, surfaces in many romantic autobiographies, including *The Prelude* and *The Mill on the Floss*. Both empiricism and romanticism resist, at times, the mediation of an image —be it linguistic, oneiric, or of memory—between the self and experience. By locating the real in immediate sensory perception, David can only assert the reality of his memory when it yields to such immediacy. Ideally, the images of memory, and the words David uses to convey those images, are transparent, opening toward an apprehension of the event that was their genesis—an apprehension that is the same as having actually witnessed the event. David's narrative, then, reveals a desire for a "naive realism" in which all mediation (with its unwelcome reminder of the separation of mind from world) is rendered unnecessary. The most simplistic realism would attempt to guarantee that all representations are exact copies of the original and that words, specifi-cally, serve as transparent denominations of things. Realism of this type is essentially hostile to time (hence its link with nostalgia); its most fundamental desire is to regain the past, denying that anything is lost irrevocably. This demand for the lost object's return to presence means the repudiation of all representation, all substitutes, in favor of the thing itself. By making the word or the image (of memory or dream) perfectly equivalent to the thing, one would overcome the loss of the original object; it would always be available through the easily accessible word or image.[9] It is the impossibility of this demand that the representative be identical with the represented, an impossibility recognized dimly in David's narrative even while he strives to achieve the impossible, that leads to Dickens's acceptance of representation, with its built-in difference between sign and signified. And in discovering a use for that difference, Dickens is able to convert the fall into mediation into a "happy fall," is able to discover the advantages of "fancy." The necessity of approaching the past through the indirection of representative images and words will confer some benefits as well as pain.

Naive realism's hostility to time, its attempt to deny loss and death, is one reason Dickens eventually abandons it; another reason is its hostility to words. The realist appeals to silence, the mute apprehension of actual things. David evidences some of the realist mistrust of words, of their tendency to get between the perceiver and that which is to be perceived. In search of a transparent style, David often expresses his belief that metaphorical and rhetorical flourishes crowd out the real. A simple instance occurs in one of his attempts to be "serious" with Dora. He tells her, "We infect everyone about us," and then comments on this way of stating his "meaning": "I might have gone on in this figurative manner, if Dora's face had not admonished me that she was wondering with all her might whether I was going to propose any new kind of vaccination, or other medical remedy, for this unwholesome state of ours. Therefore I checked myself, and made my meaning plainer" (48, 693). Figurative language is directly contrasted with making one's meaning "plain," and David, as usual when he is explicit about the type of language he prefers, chooses the latter. (Of course, his narrative as a whole is full of metaphors, just as it has a "style," but they are never explicitly acknowledged.)

David's "transparent style" is implicitly contrasted with Micawber's use of language throughout the novel. Style as tyranny, as the imposition of one's particular point of view on another, is represented by Micawber, which is why this comic figure is almost as threatening a father figure as Murdstone. Micawber's extravagance, both financial and linguistic, is dangerous in its subjection of other people. Traddles "loans his name" (28, 423) to Micawber; this ominous phrase combines the linguistic and financial, placing Traddles within the world Micawber has constituted to serve his own purposes. David must avoid Traddles's mistake, must hold on to his own name, and forge a style of his own. The Micawbers belong to the warehouse world, a world to which David is introduced by Murdstone, and from which he must escape.

Both Murdstone and Micawber try to impose a certain world upon the

9. Jacques Derrida has persistently called attention to the recurrent desire in Western writing to avoid the difference between word and referent in order to avoid the displacement of the thing by the word that comes to stand for it. My reading of *David Copperfield* is particularly influenced by Derrida's *Of Grammatology*.

child, a world most easily identified by its language. Murdstone's puritanical vocabulary is as distinctive as Micawber's florid style. David must reject both as inadequate; the process of maturation is, in part, the process of developing his own style. However, that style is never recognized as one. Rather, the narrative acts as if its own style were transparent, had no tinge of self. Like Ruskin in "The Mystery of Life and its Arts," David counters the discovery that some people use language to order the world according to their desires with an insistence that he speaks the truth plainly. The Murdstone and Micawber languages are idiosyncratic and, hence, objectionable. Their styles are personal, imply a refusal to participate in the human community, and are unaccountable to a reality independent of self. David, using ordinary language, establishes a pure communication with others, a style that simply states what has happened.

The most complete denunciation of words, and of their being used to obscure meaning and to prevent a clear apprehension of the real, comes in a description of Micawber. This passage is worthy of the third book of Locke's *Essay Concerning Human Understanding* in its plea for a plain style in which words are fitted to things.

> Mr. Micawber had a relish in this formal piling up of words, which, however ludicrously displayed in his case, was, I must say, not at all peculiar to him. I have observed it, in the course of my life, in numbers of men. It seems to me to be a general rule. . . . We talk about the tyranny of words, but we like to tyrannise over them, too; we are fond of having a large superfluous establishment of words to wait upon us on great occasions; we think it looks important, and sounds well. As we are not particular about the meaning of our liveries on state occasions, if they be but fine and numerous enough, so the meaning or necessity of our words is a secondary consideration, if there be but a great parade of them. And as individuals get into trouble by making too great a show of liveries, or as slaves when they are too numerous rise against their masters, so I think I could mention a nation that has got into many great difficulties, and will get into many greater, from maintaining too large a retinue of words. (52, 754)

A remarkable passage, in which we find a writer complaining that we have "too large a retinue of words," many of which are superfluous. Our extravagance with words (delineated by the use of an elaborate analogy between liveries and words) is declared "a general rule," but David's critique makes it clear he feels he avoids the worst abuses. Micawber's use of language, marvelous though it is, is finally seen as abusive, and in keeping with his ambiguous status as neither hero nor villain he is packed off to Australia at the end of the novel.

Yet this hostility to words is not consistently maintained throughout the narrative, and in considering David's attitudes toward language we will discover the implicit critique of naive realism found in this novel that struggles to be realistic. Even Micawber will be found to have a legitimate role in those instances when the novel relies on, rather than bemoans, the difference between words and things.

The first indication of this difference is the child's fascination with the physical properties of words. David's reliance on sensory perception insures that words, as peculiar sensory experiences, will interest him. Spoken words can be heard, but not seen; written words can be seen, but not heard. David experiences the material existence of the spoken word when trying to communicate with Peggotty through the keyhole after he has been locked in his room for biting Murdstone. "I was obliged to get her to repeat it, for she spoke it the first time quite down my throat, in consequence of my having forgotten to take my mouth away from the keyhole and put my ear there; and though her words tickled me a great deal, I didn't hear them" (4, 60). This experience suggests that when the material qualities of words attract our attention, we begin to lose our sense of what the words mean. The word's existence in itself as a material thing conflicts with its function as a sign of something else.[10]

David is also fascinated by the appearance of the written word. "To this day, when I look upon the fat black letters in the primer, the puzzling novelty of their shapes, and the easy good-nature of O and Q and S, seem to present themselves again before me as they used to do" (4, 53). Written letters "present themselves" to the viewer as objects in their own right, as physical things having form, color, and so on. The struggles to learn shorthand repeat this preoccupation with the physical shapes of signs, as well as suggesting that when the signs' novelty wears off, we become less aware of their physical appearance and more willing to see them only in terms of what they serve to represent: "The most despotic characters I have ever known; who insisted, for instance, that a thing like the beginning of a cobweb, meant expectation, and that a pen-and-ink sky-rocket stood for disadvantageous" (38, 545). Of course, if the fact that the sign looks like a skyrocket is emphasized, its standing for disadvantageous will seem absurd. These "arbitrary characters" (38, 545) become "despotic" the moment David looks at them as if they were not arbitrary, as if their physical appearance were a clue to their meaning.

David's naive perceptual experience of letters and words as physical objects, while conforming to his tendency to privilege sensory perception, involves the recognition of the word's essential difference from its referent.

10. Sigurd Burckhardt, *Shakespearean Meanings* (Princeton: Princeton University Press, 1968), chap. 2, offers a clear account of how words' material existence is stressed in poetry. Rhymes "call attention to the purely sonant nature of words. They aid the poet in weighting the balance on the side of sound and thus giving words body, which simply as signs they lack" (27). For Burckhart, poetic language always works to call into question the normal acceptance of the "transparency" of language. Poetic language opens up a disturbing distance that reminds us that word and thing are not one and the same. My argument is that certain elements of *David Copperfield* focus the reader's awareness on that distance.

And this essential difference must undermine a simple realism. There can be no exact repetition; a repetition in words or in memory is a repetition by representative, a repetition with a difference. David's narrative hedges on this point: it both accepts and denies that repetition always carries a difference with it. David, as we have seen, insists that an exact repetition is possible when he narrates the events surrounding Ham and Steerforth's deaths. But other experiences, in particular the failure of his first marriage, will lead David to question the possibility and even the desirability of exact repetition.

The hostility toward a differential view of language is, as I suggested above, a hostility to time. Where there is a difference between the word and the thing, the word marks the place of the thing's absence. Where the word is, the thing once was. The word re-presents the thing in the present, but the thing itself is lost. The fall into language, into mediation, is the fall into history, where man—in the theological vision of Carlyle, Ruskin, Rossetti, and Browning—is separated from the eternal; in the more secular visions of Dickens and George Eliot, existence in history marks the separation of man from the happy past of childhood and the envisioned future of a more suitable social order. The historical nature of experience forces on Dickens the need to represent absent entities, just as the invisibility of God necessitates Carlyle's and Ruskin's similar reliance on representation. Within time, difference marks loss; if only the word, and not the thing, can be called to presence, then difference marks death. What cannot be repeated is dead.

David Copperfield is obsessed with the fleeting nature of all experience, especially moments of happiness. One of the novel's most perfect moments is the happy scene following Emily's acceptance of Ham, a scene interrupted by the entrance of David and Steerforth into Mr. Peggotty's boat. As David finishes describing the scene, he adds: "The little picture was so instantaneously dissolved by our going in, that one might have doubted whether it had ever been" (21, 311–12). The brute facts of time and change, carrying the message of death (whose symbol is the sea), seem to overwhelm all human constructions. Peggotty's boat is a refuge from the sea, but it is destroyed in the storm that kills Ham and Steerforth. The dissolution of that happy scene points toward the larger dissolutions in the novel; the narrative can only reconstitute the scene in words. Words do not die, they can be said again, but things and situations do not enjoy the same immunity to time. The child, in a world of immediate perception, also lives in a world of an eternal present. "As to any sense of inequality, or youthfulness, or other difficulty in our way, little Em'ly and I had no such trouble, because we had no future. We made no more provision for growing older, than we did for growing younger" (3, 37). An exact repetition, if possible, would restore the child's world. Language is resented for its marking the loss of a world in which the whole is completely present. Language introduces a world in which reality is dispersed over time and space, with only a small fragment of the totality present in any particular moment. Most of reality is only present to us in the words that represent absent things. The eternal and full present of the child is lost, and mourned.

Both the psychologist and the theologian will recognize the narrative's presentation of that loss. The child loses his mother and is expelled from a garden "where the fruit clusters on the trees, riper and richer than fruit has ever been since, in any other garden" (2, 15). David's first marriage must be seen as an attempt to regain this lost paradise,[11] with Dora slated to play the role of the lost mother. But a repetition of that earlier happiness is impossible, and David comes to admit, uneasily to be sure, that loss is inevitable. "What I missed, I still regarded —I always regarded—as something that had been a dream of my youthful fancy; that was incapable of realisation; that I was now discovering to be so, with some natural pain, as all men did" (48, 697). The "disciplined" David gives up the dream that time and death can be overcome, accepting Agnes, the bride whose habitual gesture of "pointing upward" (44, 877) links her with a peaceful acceptance of death.[12] But the dream of a perfect and eternal present is not renounced without suggesting that life is a prison. Describing the death of his and Dora's child, David writes: "The spirit fluttered for a moment on the threshold of its little prison and, unconscious of captivity, took wing" (48, 698). Imprisoned in time, men are barred from eternal union with the dearest objects of perception.

Once the historical nature of experience is accepted, language is not only necessary, but can be recognized as the source of many benefits. Even if words do, at times, confuse rather than clarify, they alone make meaning possible. The child David sees Murdstone's visits to his mother, but remains completely innocent of their significance. "No such thing came into my mind or near it. I could observe, in little pieces, as it were; but as to making a net of a number of pieces, and catching anybody in it, that was, as yet, beyond me" (2, 21). Immediate perception is always of "little pieces" because it only registers what is present. Meaning can only be grasped when the connections between disparate events are explored; most of these events are, necessarily, no longer perceptually available. Language provides the "net" in which the various pieces supplied by perception can be caught and put together.

The limits of sight, which is the child's only reliance, are suggested by David's inability to see anything through the telescope (2, 23). Living in the present, the child is unable to use his past to discover patterns that would allow him to understand what is about to happen. His exile in the present means that

11. In Hablot K. Browne's illustration of David's meeting with Dora at her aunt's house, a copy of *Paradise Regained* is prominently displayed on the bookshelf.

12. Agnes "points upward" both when Dora dies and when David anticipates his own death in the novel's final sentence. Alexander Welsh, *The City of Dickens* (Oxford: Clarendon Press, 1971), chap. 13, discusses in detail Agnes's connection with death.

his perception of objects is especially intense and particularly innocent, but his understanding of the present's relation to a whole sequence of events, by which its meaning is constituted, is limited.

Language also grants the ability to share these grasped meanings with others. The whole subplot of the Strongs' marriage makes this point: open statements of one's feelings form the basis of love and community. David learns the same lesson in his courtship and marriage of Dora. His secret engagement only leads to trouble, while his openness with Dora's aunts makes the marriage possible. Once married, he is oppressed by all the things he cannot talk about with his wife. "It would have been better for me if my wife could have helped me more, and shared the many thoughts in which I had no partner; and that this might have been; I knew" (48, 697). The community established by language is an important consolation for what has been lost in entering the realms of language and history. David's narrative tries to create with the reader that ideal openness of expression that he also achieves in his second marriage. Since the experiences of individuals vary, only language can establish a community in which one can share what has been present to him by representing it in words to another.

We find here another reason for David to disparage Micawberlike language. Words must transcend self in order to form the basis of the social world. Reality (or "fact" as Carlyle and Dickens so often call it) functions as a crucial corrective to the illusions of self-interested vision for almost every writer in the Victorian period. For the ethical (often biblical) truths on which Carlyle and Ruskin rely, Dickens and George Eliot usually substitute a more secular, social morality. And their usual justification for their moral prescriptions is that adherence to these principles would allow the formation of a more perfect human community. They use the needs of that community to deny the extravagance of individual desires, as well as to explain the relation of their fictions to actual conditions in contemporary Victorian society. This rather different basis for their "realism" distances Dickens and George Eliot somewhat from the more mystical (even where not traditionally religious) concerns of Carlyle, Ruskin, and the poets. But for all these writers the most significant reality to which the individual must pay heed is nonmaterial, not immediately perceivable, and must be represented through the use of intermediate symbols.

Finally, language affords David the ability to discover the significance of his own life through its repetition in the autobiographical narrative he offers to his readers.[13] When the past is relived and memory used to recognize the present's novelty (its difference), the "mistaken impulses" of the past can be

13. The analogy between this process of narrative repetition and the dynamics of the Freudian "talking cure" are striking, a point that suggests how strongly Freud's methods partake of a nineteenth-century understanding of temporality. Freud, of course, is much more willing to accept the word's magical powers than Dickens is.

overcome. Aunt Betsey sums up the novel's whole message concerning repetition and memory when she states: "It's in vain, Trot, to recall the past, unless it works some influence upon the present" (23, 347). The difference between the original and its repetition can be a saving difference, not one that must be lamented. Exact repetition is obsessional, leaving no room for growth or progress; repetition with a difference is liberating. David's fear of exact repetition is apparent in his reaction to the story of Lazarus; he does not want the resurrection of the dead, but only the memory of the dead. His father's tombstone is a comforting and significant monument in the child's world, but a returned father is a terrifying thought. In more obvious cases David does not as readily admit his desire that the dead remain dead. (As I have noted, at times he explicitly desires the opposite.) But even when regretting his mother's fate, David's narrative shows his becoming reconciled to the fact of loss, learning to accept the substitutes time offers him. David writes: "How blest I was in having such a friend as Steerforth, such a friend as Peggotty, and such a substitute for what I had lost as my excellent and generous aunt" (22, 321).

David must accept the fact of loss and the substitutes time offers him. From a Freudian perspective, we might say that all later love objects are representations of the original love object, the mother. But comedy is only possible if David accepts the difference from the original object of these later representations. Tragedy results when the self refuses to be reconciled with the substitutes time offers; tragedy posits an irreconcilable contradiction between what men want and what they can have. The comic marriage (so prevalent in romantic literature) offers a vision of possible reconciliation. Marriage in *David Copperfield* overcomes the distance between the self and the lost object it desires by offering a new object. This new object functions like a word, since it is not just itself, but also a sign of the original object. The new object carries the mark of difference, of death, since it reminds David of the loss of the original object even while consoling him for that loss. To accept the new object requires the renunciation of a naive realism (the insistence that the representative *be* the thing) and implies the acceptance of death.[14] Time offers new possibilities to the novel's hero, but these can be seized only if he is reconciled to living in situations that are not the same as those of his past. David's first

14. My discussion of David's relation to loss and death should be placed alongside Robert E. Lougy's excellent essay "Remembrances of Death Past and Future: A Reading of *David Copperfield*," *Dickens Studies Annual* 6 (1977): 72–101. (*Dickens Studies Annual* will be abbreviated *DSA* in subsequent notes.) Lougy discusses several scenes on which I also touch: in particular, the child's fear of the father's return and David's narration of Ham and Steerforth's deaths. Lougy, however, is more interested in how the deaths of others serve to illustrate to David his own mortality, and he portrays David as attempting to avoid this lesson. Lougy also sees the novel's ending as a retreat from the more honest confrontations with death contained in earlier episodes. My differences from Lougy are, I trust, clear. I wish to emphasize how David experiences language as carrying death within itself, and how he finds that language offers certain compensations for the consciousness of loss and death that it imposes.

marriage serves to make clear that an exact repetition is neither possible nor desirable, thus preparing him for his second, more successful, marriage.

Representation becomes the very source of the future. The representative's difference is what pulls David from the past into a new life. Words, in their difference from things, necessarily change the world in the act of representing it. It is not surprising that Dickens should learn this lesson in writing an autobiographical novel; I will argue in the next chapter that George Eliot makes a similar discovery in writing *The Mill on the Floss*. The autobiographer, whether writing a straight autobiography or a fictional one, must inevitably recognize the difference between his life and the shape that life assumes once narrated. And more often than not that difference will be experienced as liberating, as enabling a vision of one's past more satisfying than a collection of random memories. In any case, I think that Dickens's experience in writing *David Copperfield* led him to a new awareness of the word's own energies. The word's difference (which might be called its own inherent content) makes a difference, causes things to happen. In accepting that difference and even relying on it, Dickens adopts the romantic veneration of the word's ability to organize and direct thought. The gap between mind and world can be made fruitful if mind's separate energies are brought to bear on the real, altering its shape in constructive ways. The Strongs' marriage offers a minor instance of the way the reinterpretation involved in representing the past to oneself works. When Dr. Strong says, "Much that I have seen, but not noted, has come back upon me with new meaning" (42, 618–19), he echoes a very similar statement made earlier by David: "And now, I must confess, the recollection of what I had seen on that night when Mr. Maldon went away, first began to return upon me with a meaning it had never had, and to trouble me" (19, 281). The Strongs' difficulties suggest the danger of misinterpretation, but also indicate that the significance of the past can be altered by the understanding of it developed in the present.

David's narrative recognizes the special role stories, and art, play in granting this ability to change our understanding of the past. After the first time he ever goes to the theater, David is "filled with the play, and with the past—for it was, in a manner, like a shining transparency, through which I saw my earlier life moving along" (19, 286). The play's ability to recall the past is in no way linked to any resemblance between it (he has seen *Julius Caesar*) and that past, but, it would seem, results from the play's existence in a realm a step removed from reality. Representation takes place in time, but it is also a way of stepping back from complete immersion in the present. The play invites David to run his eye over the whole of his experience. And the state of mind produced by the play gives David the "confidence" that "at another time [he] might have wanted" (19, 287) to speak to Steerforth when he sees him that night at the hotel. Stories not only evoke the past, but point toward the future as well. From his childhood readings, David derives "visions" of other times and places that appear "as if they were faintly painted or written on the wall" of his room (10, 135). In the retreat from time (even while it is within time) that is the space of art, the future, as well as the past, can be written. And it is this writing that David's narrative of his "personal history" undertakes.

A more direct liberation into the future by way of story is David's repetition, while working at the warehouse, "again and again, and a hundred times again . . . of that old story" of his birth and Aunt Betsey's part in it (12, 176). He focuses on his mother's belief that his aunt had touched her hair "with no ungentle hand," a belief that "might have been altogether my mother's fancy and might have had no foundation whatever in fact" (12, 176). However, as Dickens will insist throughout the 1850s, this element of fancy is precisely what makes stories liberating. Whether this part of the story is true or not, the reader never discovers; it is enough to know that David acts upon this interpretation, running away to Dover—and that the "fancy" is repeated after his arrival. "It might have been a dream, originating in the fancy which had occupied my mind so long, but I awoke with the impression that my aunt had come and bent over me, and had put my hair away from my face, and laid my head more comfortably, and had then stood looking at me. The words, 'Pretty fellow' or 'Poor fellow,' seemed to be in my ears, too; but certainly there was nothing else, when I awoke, to lead me to believe that they had been uttered by my aunt, who sat in the bow-window gazing out to sea" (13, 196). Whether the incident is fact or fancy is irrelevant to its allowing another interpretation of Aunt Betsey's character, one that gives David hope, and which furnishes support for his new beginning. Fancy designates those energies of mind that confront the "facts" and refuse to accept them as unalterable. David endorses the fancy that propels him to run away from the warehouse; he is less sympathetic (although not completely hostile) to the fancies that govern his love for Dora, the child-wife who seems his mother come to life again.

Aunt Betsey insists that the past must be recalled to influence the present when relating her own "past history" (23, 347), finding in her neglect of David's parents a reason to aid him. Part of David's recovery after Dora's death is attributed to his writing a semi-autobiographical novel (58, 816). When reinterpretation and the acceptance of substitutes for desired objects of the past are affirmed, writing and its ability to represent, even with a difference, are affirmed. David fluctuates between accepting the difference inherent in writing and struggling to overcome that difference to "see" his past as if it were present. This fluctuation leads to David's appreciation of fancy in some contexts and his characterization of it as childish in others. Fancy is aligned with difference, with what imagination adds to the materials given it by perception, and the narrative cannot lose its suspicion that representations are, in some way, unreal; they are just words and as such are not a very good consolation for the lost object. David manifests, at times, the same frustration with having only representatives and not the thing itself that we find in the work of Rossetti, Carlyle, and Ruskin.

David Copperfield also evidences the recurring Victorian suspicion that fancy is self-indulgent; when the mind represents the world to itself, it will represent it according to the self's desires and not in accordance with the way things really are. I suspect that Dickens would have been particularly uneasy on this score in writing a novel in which the events of his life are altered so as to make his history much more pleasant. David effects a heroic escape from the blacking warehouse, while Dora's father, and later Dora herself, die at convenient moments. The narrative's attempt to present itself as a reporting of the facts, as distinct from the fanciful utterances of Micawber, keeps David from celebrating fancy as unabashedly as Dickens will do in later novels. David's narrative is sensitive to the fact that talking about oneself can be a way of imposing one's own view of self on the listener and an attempt to shape the world to one's own ends. The novel begins with a coy disclaimer that the narrator is setting himself up as a hero; the reader will decide whether David is the hero of his own book.

David's continued uneasiness with the place of fancy leaves the most complete demonstration of the word's power to Mr. Micawber. In his denunciation of Uriah Heep, Micawber characteristically depends on language to provide him with the energy necessary to carry out his arduous task. The name *Heep,* repeated time and again, carries within it all the reasons for Micawber's activities, and is called upon whenever he requires fresh inspiration. David describes Micawber's reliance on the word: "With this last repetition of the magic word that had kept him going at all, and in which he surpassed all his previous efforts, Mr. Micawber rushed out of the house" (49, 712). By a significant displacement, Micawber is able to practice the repetition about which David himself is uneasy, and by means of that repetition Micawber causes Heep's downfall and the Wickfields' liberation, a feat the novel's hero has been unable to effect. In Micawber the narrative recognizes the necessity of repetition, even while remaining unable to endorse it unconditionally, or to recognize explicitly its own act of repetition in repeating the narrator's past in the words of its tale.

In union with an audience who will endorse his transforming words— the readers to whom David appeals in his opening sentence—the writer can change the world. In *David Copperfield,* Dickens is still shy of this power, afraid that the writer's changes are "fanciful." In subsequent years, as his disillusionment with contemporary England grows, Dickens will turn to "fancy" more readily as an escape from that "real" England, and as a possible means of transforming it. But, with the possible exception of *Hard Times,* Dickens always remains wary of the power of the imagination; the use of that power must be carefully circumscribed within a communal situation that transcends the self and its desires. For Esther Summerson, Arthur Clennam, Charles Darnay, and John Harmon the past is not a lost paradise they wish to regain, but an imprisoning determinism from which they are trying to escape. These characters experience little of the nostalgia found in David's "Retrospective" chapters. For them, the ability to transform the past must be seen as completely positive. But the willfulness and aggression involved in the obliteration of the past disturbs Dickens; much of that aggression is displaced onto minor characters, but the later heroes and heroines must earn their liberation through an encounter with death. And in *Great Expectations* the hero is not purged of his aggressive attempt to shape life to his own desires and is left a prisoner in the real world his narrative has revealed to him and his audience.

With the exception of *Hard Times,* the novels that follow *David Copperfield* use repetition as the basic structuring principle of the plot. Repetition with a difference opens the way for a possible future, for the establishment of a new reality, a new (comic) society. These later novels seem so realistic in part because they present in such detail the case against the society characters face at the beginning of the novel. "Fancy," which makes the saving repetition possible, is required to transform the grim reality of contemporary English society. The saving repetition is always in some way a re-presentation. The hero's or heroine's relation to the past must be represented by a reenactment that finally breaks the past's hold over him or her. Seeing the past in a new way, representing it with a changed emphasis, effects this transformation.

I want to begin with the exception—*Hard Times*—before discussing in some detail how the pattern of repetition works itself out in the later novels. That the novel most explicitly committed to championing fancy does not follow the pattern of the other works is surely significant. All the other novels, as I will suggest, demonstrate an uneasiness with fancy's power similar to the uneasiness found in *David Copperfield. Hard Times* avoids that uneasiness by forgoing the most potent use of fancy: repetition. Instead, Dickens returns to the basic transformational device of his earlier plots (used, for example, in *Martin Chuzzlewit* and *Dombey and Son):* conversion.

Both the rhetorical style and the basic argument of *Hard Times* link it to a realism that Carlyle and Ruskin would have found familiar. (The novel was, of course, dedicated to Carlyle, while Ruskin, in a famous note to *Unto This Last,* expressed his approval of it.) The "return of the repressed" describes the plot of *Hard Times;* repressed fancy will return inevitably, the novelist argues, because "fancy" perceives a reality greater than the "facts" that Gradgrind espouses. The paradox here is familiar—and straight from Carlyle. What men deem most real is actually less real than those spiritual qualities they are likely to scorn as "imaginary." Dickens takes up arms in the battle over the right to use the word *reality,* so that when *fancy* and *fact* are contrasted in *Hard Times* the meanings assigned to each term are drastically different than the meanings assigned to them in *David Copperfield.*

> Cultivate in them, while there is yet time, the utmost graces of the fancies and affections, to adorn their lives so much in need of ornament; or, in the day of your triumph, when romance is utterly driven out of their souls, and they and a bare existence stand face to face, Reality will take a wolfish turn, and make an end of you. (2:6, 162–63)

The novel simply illustrates this warning. "Reality" will not allow the continued suppression of such a vital element within it. The "natural prompting" of the "heart" (2:12, 216) must be served. Once Dickens aligns *fancy* with *nature,* he is able to insist on the *realism* of his undertaking even when he is being most imaginative. Given this twisting of terms, he can compare *nature* favorably with *art* and see his own novel as squarely on the side of nature without feeling he has contradicted his celebration of fancy. The artificial world is the one built by the champions of *fact;* the examples Dickens offers of *art* are the machines and factories of Coketown. "Never fear, good people of an anxious turn of mind, that Art will consign Nature to oblivion. Set anywhere, side by side, the work of God and the work of man; and the former, even though it be a troop of Hands of very small account, will gain in dignity from the comparison" (1:11, 69). The nature created by God, including fancy and affection, will eventually triumph over the deformities of the man-made. *Hard Times* adopts the apocalyptic rhetoric found in Carlyle, a rhetoric also found, to some extent, in the other "late" novels, when the narrator fulminates against such purveyors of false values as the dandies of Chesney Wold, the Barnacles, the aristocrats of the ancien régime, and the Veneerings. But *Hard Times* also reveals Dickens's deep-rooted fear of apocalyptic violence, most notably in his hostility toward any potential action by the victimized workers. The ineffectual and pacific Stephen Blackpool represents Dickens's best vision of a working man.

The other late novels often involve a return of a repressed reality, although that reality is defined rather differently than in *Hard Times.* That the imagination has the power to alter the world makes comedy possible, but the possible misuse of such power by an individual acting only to serve his or her selfish needs troubles Dickens. Like all the Victorians, Dickens must identify and make apparent a reality that transcends the self. In *David Copperfield* he had lost the ability to identify reality with the objects revealed by perception since perceptual reality is capable of alteration by the mind of the perceiver. *Hard Times* sidesteps the issue of the mind's role in the creation of reality by appealing to spiritual and sentimental values that are real for all men in all times. But the other late novels address, albeit indirectly, the problem of the reality of a world made by man. Dickens, like George Eliot after him, will protect against the abuses of the selfish imagination by insisting that reality is a social product that is greater than any individual's conception of it. More than Eliot, Dickens is troubled by the aggression involved in man's alteration of the world he finds in perception, and the late novels must all find a way to justify the changes in the world that act to benefit the hero or heroine.

Bleak House provides an extended demonstration of the possible advantages and dangers of repetition. The third person narrator in the novel is trapped in the present tense. He gathers all the evidence needed to condemn contemporary society, confronting the "deadened world[s]" (2, 8) of Chancery and Chesney Wold. Apocalyptic in tone throughout, the third person narration looks forward to a future in which Chancery and Chesney Wold will no longer exist.[15] "If all the injustice it has committed, and all the misery it has caused, could only be locked up with it, and the whole burnt away in a great funeral pyre,—why so much the better for other parties than the parties in Jarndyce and Jarndyce!" (1, 7). The narrator's gathering of evidence and his hopes for an ending that never arrives link him to the suitors. "There is no now for us suitors," Richard Carstone tells Esther Summerson (37, 524); the calamity of Chancery suits is that they indefinitely prolong the present, the "now," even while radically devaluing it in relation to "vague things to come" (17, 233). The narrator also remains totally trapped in a present that never leads to that hoped-for future. His impassioned rhetoric matches Gridley's rage and Miss Flite's mad expectations—and is just as effective. Chancery does not collapse, even if the case does end; Chesney Wold is destroyed, but its end brings only an end of life that offers no joy for anyone. The third person narration ends with a vision of "dull repose," of a world "abandoned to darkness" (66, 875–76), and can offer no alternative landscape.

It remains for Esther's narrative to demonstrate how the death of the past can lead to a better future. From the outset, we learn that Esther's perceptions are influenced by her affections. "I had always rather a noticing way—not a quick way, O no!—a silent way of noticing what passed before me, and thinking I should like to understand it better. I have not by any means a quick understanding. When I love a person very tenderly indeed, it seems to brighten. But even that may be my vanity" (3, 15). The reality Esther presents will be influenced by her emotions—perhaps even by mistaken self-regard. Esther's "coyness," which has bothered so many modern readers of the novel,[16]

15. For discussions of the apocalyptic imagery in *Bleak House,* see Ann Y. Wilkinson, "*Bleak House:* From Faraday to Judgment Day," *ELH* 34 (1967): 225–47, and William F. Axton, "Religious and Scientific Imagery in *Bleak House,*" *NCF* 22 (1968): 349–61.
16. For various interpretations of Esther's "progress" see William F. Axton, "The Trouble

serves, in part, to assure the reader that her narration is not a mere willful imposition of self on the world. As we shall see, *Bleak House* shows much more awareness than *David Copperfield* that the social world consists of various selves who try to shape reality to their own wishes, and thus it becomes important to gain the reader's acquiescence with Esther's viewpoint.

Even though led by her affections, Esther does not reveal David's nostalgic attachment to her past. Esther's story begins when she buries her doll, to which she has confided her complaints about her life with Mrs. Rachael, and takes up her new life as Jarndyce's ward. Her ability to gain a future is dependent on this ability to bury, to accept the death of, the past. Her narrative is written in the past tense (unlike the third person narrative), seven years after the events it relates. And her repetition of the past in her narration is only very slightly tinged by the nostalgia found in David's "retrospective" chapters. Although Esther sheds tears over the buried doll, she is clearly happier with the new life she is given. Her narrative reveals, of course, that freeing oneself from the past is not as easy as throwing away childhood toys; Esther must eventually confront the facts of her past even though, at first, she would rather not know them. In the chapter entitled "Covering a Multitude of Sins," Esther turns down the chance to ask Jarndyce about her past, claiming that she is "quite content to know no more" (8, 99). But her "progress" (chapter 3) requires that she eventually learn the full truth about herself and her past. Her acceptance of that past allows her to become fully adult, fully herself, allows her to recognize that she loves Woodcourt, not Jarndyce.

Esther's movement to acceptance of her past is her movement from believing she were "better not born" to an ability to affirm her identity. "I knew I was as innocent of my birth as a queen of hers" (36, 516). This progress does not come without a price. Esther's new life, her freedom from the guilt imposed upon her by her illegitimacy, is only won through the death of Lady Dedlock, her mother.[17] The reinterpretation of the past is destructive in its changing the way the world is organized. Lady Dedlock has been protected by the world's ignorance of her sin. For years she had successfully governed the world's vision of her, but now the fact of her being Esther's mother is about to become public. The return of the repressed truth will overwhelm the limited, self-serving truth Lady Dedlock had imposed on the world. Esther,

---

with Esther," *Modern Language Quarterly* 26 (1965): 544–57; Alex Zwerdling, "Esther Summerson Rehabilitated," *PMLA* 88 (1973): 429–39; Judith Wilt, "Confusion and Consciousness in Dickens's Esther," *NCF* 32 (1977): 285–309; John Kucich, "Action in the Dickens Ending: *Bleak House* and *Great Expectations*," *NCF* 33 (1978): 88–109; and Michael Ragussis, "The Ghostly Signs of *Bleak House*," *NCF* 34 (1979): 253–80.

17. Lawrence Frank's excellent article "Through a Glass Darkly: Esther Summerson and *Bleak House*," *DSA* 4 (1974): 91–112, discusses Esther's recognition of her similarity to and difference from Lady Dedlock, thus suggesting the intimate connection between the fate of the two women in the novel.

of course, is distanced from actual participation in the exposure of her mother's secret, and in the death that results from that exposure. Tulkinghorn, Guppy, and Bucket perform the dirty work that is necessary to Esther's full happiness; Esther is right to claim that a "conspiracy" exists to make her happy (23, 351). But her illness, with its changing of her features, submits Esther herself to the law of death, to the necessary pain and renunciation that accompanies the surrender of the past in a new understanding of it. The favored Esther cannot benefit from a remaking of the past without paying some price.

Even while, on the whole, the novel endorses Esther's reshaping of her past, there remains some uneasiness that this tampering with the real is an aggressive act of self. The novel goes to great lengths to demonstrate Esther's passivity, less, I think, from Dickens's reliance on traditional notions about women than from an attempt to clear Esther of any suspicion of having manipulated or misused others in her remaking reality to better suit her needs. Heroes like Arthur Clennam and Charles Darnay are almost as passive as Esther, for essentially similar reasons, while the aggression that characterizes Dickens's next first-person narrator, Pip, makes *Great Expectations* quite different from any other Dickens novel.

Bleak House is not completely free from hints of the aggression more openly found in *Great Expectations*. All the later novels, in various ways, "displace" the aggression linked to altering the world as found. That Esther's life is dependent on Lady Dedlock's death is suggested by the novel even while Esther is carefully distanced from any guilt in causing her mother's death. Esther herself is the buried child of the novel, "bred . . . in secrecy from her birth" with "all traces of her existence" blotted out (17, 237). She is the reality Lady Dedlock has repressed, and, as a buried child, Esther is associated with the brickmaker's baby who dies in Ada's arms. The handkerchief that "covers" this dead child (in the chapter entitled "Covering a Multitude of Sins") later covers Lady Dedlock. The uncovering of Esther causes Lady Dedlock's death; Esther's knowledge of her innocence, of her right to live, can only be ratified if the guilt of Lady Dedlock's death is located elsewhere.

That elsewhere is Lady Dedlock. Running to her mother at the moment of her death, Esther misidentifies her as "Jenny, the mother of the dead child" (59, 811). The mistake reflects Esther's dim awareness that if she herself had died, her mother would have lived; Esther wants Jenny to have died in her mother's place, although it is the parent of the dead child who will live. Esther recognizes, to some extent, her role. "My echoing footsteps brought it suddenly into my mind that there was a dreadful truth in the legend of the Ghost's Walk; that it was I, who was to bring calamity upon the stately house." But she immediately repudiates this knowledge in the next paragraph. "Not before I was alone in my room for the night . . . did I begin to know how wrong and thankless this state [of thinking herself guilty] was" (36, 515). The novel endorses Esther's interpretation of the past as opposed to Lady Dedlock's, an endorsement based, in part, on Esther's innocence being truer to the "facts," while Lady Dedlock's reputation has been based on a lie. But the novel, by giving us two narratives, has also demonstrated that an active shaping of the world presented to the self must be undertaken in order to overcome the dead world of stagnant fact. Where any one reinterpretation is called for, there are bound to be many, and the clash among competing interpretations suggests a new source of social conflict.[18]

Individual interpretations become real when endorsed by the surrounding individuals who comprise society. The conflict between competing visions is settled by social endorsement. The reality that transcends the self in Dickens's later novels is a social reality; in order to complete his or her reinterpretation of the reigning social order the individual must find a community that enacts the new vision. Lady Dedlock's life collapses when the world no longer accepts the vision of her that she has offered. Even if unable to present contemporary England as converted to the new vision offered in his novels, Dickens does end them by presenting a small comic community that adopts the alternative vision embodied in the hero or heroine. To see society as constituted by the way a community envisions itself is to become more attentive to the rhetorical strategies by which to win others to one's own vision and to become more wary of the self-serving features of others' rhetoric. The plots of *Little Dorrit, A Tale of Two Cities,* and *Our Mutual Friend* also center around a significant act of repetition that allows for the creation of a new reality for the "saved" comic characters. The heroes of these three novels—Arthur Clennam, Charles Darnay, and John Harmon—all confront a "deadened" social world that seems likely to sustain itself unchanged forever. Mrs. Clennam remains the same throughout the long years Arthur has been in the East, while Mr. Dorrit has been in the Marshalsea for as long as anyone can remember; the ancien régime continues in the belief "that a system rooted in a frizzled hangman, powdered, gold-laced, pumped, and white-silk stockinged, would see the very stars out" (2:7, 102); old Mr. Harmon seeks to perpetuate his world even beyond his death by dictating in his will the conditions of his son's life. To overcome the burden of the past, each of the heroes must perform a significant repetition in which a saving difference allows a new future to be born. J. Hillis Miller has discussed at length how John Harmon manages to fulfill the conditions of his father's will even while changing its spirit so radically that he succeeds in forging his own life.[19] In *Little Dorrit* and *A Tale of Two Cities* the heroes

18. J. Hillis Miller's discussion of *Bleak House* in chap. 6 of *Charles Dickens: The World of His Novels* (Cambridge: Harvard University Press, 1958) centers on a consideration of the role played by repetition in the novel's structure. More recently, Miller has emphasized the "conflict of interpretations" in the novel. See his introduction to the Penguin edition of *Bleak House* (New York: Penguin Books, 1971).

19. See J. Hillis Miller, *Charles Dickens,* chap. 9.

reenact their parents' crimes, but place themselves in the role of the original victim. (Harmon's case in *Our Mutual Friend* is not so dramatic, but he, too, has distanced himself from his father's business by leaving his native land, and he must transform his father's intentions for him before he can safely inherit the family money.) Thus, Clennam goes to the Marshalsea for debt just as his family had placed the Dorrits there, while Darnay is locked away by the French revolutionaries as just payment for his family's imprisonment of Dr. Manette. Both heroes accept the burden of guilt they have inherited. At the beginning of *Little Dorrit,* Arthur begs his mother to "examine sacredly whether there is any wrong entrusted to us to set right" (1:5, 48), and he accepts his eventual imprisonment as punishment for having "slighted the whisper in my heart, that if my father had erred, it was my first duty to conceal the fault and to repair it" (2:27, 721). Similarly, Darnay confronts his uncle, renounces his inheritance just as Clennam quits the family business, and argues that the "world of wrong" (2:9, 117) done by the Darnay family must be redressed. Darnay declares himself "bound to a system that is frightful to me, responsible for it, but powerless in it; seeking to execute the last request of my dear mother's lips . . . to have mercy and to redress" (2:9, 117). In prison, Darnay accepts the logic that has placed him there.

> "It could not have been otherwise," said the prisoner. "All things have worked together as they have fallen out. It was the always-vain endeavour to discharge my poor mother's trust that first brought me near you [his wife and her father, Dr. Manette]. Good could never come of such evil, a happier end was not in nature to so unhappy a beginning. Be comforted, and forgive me." (3:11, 318)

But the heroes' acceptance of their own guilt is precisely the difference that saves them from the logic of an exact repetition. The "happier end" that Darnay cannot envision is possible; Clennam and Darnay marry the daughter of the man who has suffered at the hands of his son-in-law's family. The past is remade through love. Like David and Esther, Clennam and Darnay must experience death in order to come out into this new world. Clennam comes close to dying when in prison, while Darnay is sentenced to death. In *Our Mutual Friend,* just about everyone in the novel goes through a ritual "death by water," a dunk in the Thames that serves as a baptism into a new life.

All three novels present images of fruitless repetition, a mechanical reenactment of the past that does not recognize how re-presentation can afford new possibilities. Mr. Dorrit and Mrs. Clennam are utterly chained to the old repressive order, unable to adapt to any change in their circumstances. The revolutionaries in France are also unable to escape the bleak determinism of an obsession with the past. Madame Defarge's memory (her knitted register of past crimes to avenge) does not produce a new or better world. *A Tale of Two Cities* presents the Revolution as strictly just, as the harvested "seed" of an inhuman sowing (2:15, 253).[20] But strict justice is repudiated in the novel because its violence to the guilty only repeats the cruelty of the past.[21] A total faithfulness to the facts is not liberating and makes the Revolution a failure in its hopes to transform the world. In *Our Mutual Friend* all of contemporary London repeats itself endlessly and fruitlessly. Society offers an endless round of dull talk and dinner parties that fully justifies the "boredom" of Mortimer and Eugene Wrayburn, while London's economic life is represented as the continual reduction of everything to dust, with the dust then recycled into money and the whole absurd process begun again.

To break the past's hold requires an ability to see the world in a new way. Love provides that ability in each of these novels. By replacing the evil parent's (Clennam's mother, Darnay's and Harmon's father) enmity and greed with the good parent's (Clennam's father, Darnay's mother, and the Boffins as Harmon's substitute parents) wish to act justly, the hero breaks the cycle and remakes the world. The emotions and virtues Dickens has associated with fancy can have a profound impact on the real, and the reliance on love ensures the creation of a community (at the very least the community of the family formed by marriage) based on a shared vision.

The energy of imagination's vision, its ability to transform the world, is perhaps most strikingly illustrated in the chapter "The Dolls' Dressmaker Discovers a Word" in *Our Mutual Friend* (book 4, chap. 10). The fixation on an empty repetition is dramatized in Wrayburn's anguished repetition of Lizzie Hexam's name. Wrayburn, who hates the word *energy* above all others, cannot summon up the force necessary to move on to the next, and all-significant, word. Finally, the artist figure, Jenny Wren, supplies the magical word (*wife*)

20. Dickens presents the Revolution as a just outcome of the ancien régime's oppression, which fits the Carlylean logic of repressed "facts" returning to gain their revenge on those who ignore them. Dickens describes the French aristocracy as suffering from a "leprosy of unreality" (2:7, 100), while Carlyle, throughout *The French Revolution*, associates governments' downfalls with a failure to pay heed to reality. Thus, of the Girondins, Carlyle writes: "Reality will not translate into their formula; that they and their formula are incompatible with Reality; and, in its dark wrath, the Reality will extinguish it and them!" (*The Works of Thomas Carlyle*, 4:138). On the relation of *A Tale of Two Cities* to *The French Revolution*, see the essays collected in *DSA* 12 (1983), especially Michael Timko, "Splendid Impressions and Picturesque Means: Dickens, Carlyle, and *The French Revolution*," pp. 177–96; and Elliot L. Gilbert, " 'To Awake from History': Carlyle, Thackeray, and *A Tale of Two Cities*," pp. 247–66.

21. A Christian reading of the novel, which much of the book's own rhetoric about resurrection invites, would emphasize that justice is replaced by mercy in the "private" world of the Darnays, whereas the strict justice that reigns in the "public" world of the Revolution proves self-defeating. But I want to acknowledge, although without pursuing the point here, that *A Tale of Two Cities* presents serious difficulties to any straightforward Christian interpretation. William H. Marshall, "The Method of *A Tale of Two Cities*," *The Dickensian* 57 (1961): 183–89, presents a Christian reading of the novel, while Albert D. Hutter, "Nation and Generation in *A Tale of Two Cities*," *PMLA* 93 (1978): 449–62, and John Kucich, "The Purity of Violence: *A Tale of Two Cities*," *DSA* 8 (1980): 119–38, offer very different readings of the plot's dynamic transformations.

that frees him from the spell of the past. Imaginative vision embodies itself here in a word that, in renaming Lizzie, also remakes the world she and Wrayburn inhabit.

The aggression against the old world implicit in this creation of a new one is distanced from the heroes of *Little Dorrit, A Tale of Two Cities,* and *Our Mutual Friend.* The Clennam house is finally destroyed not by the son who repudiates his family, but by the mysterious Riguad-Blandois, who kills himself in the process of destroying the house. But, as Alexander Welsh has convincingly argued, Blandois must be recognized as Clennam's double, who undergoes the necessary death that accompanies the hero's break from his mother.[22] In *A Tale of Two Cities,* Darnay's escape from the past is merely personal since France remains in thrall to the violence started by the ancien régime. But even if only personally effective, Darnay's disavowal of the past must be paid for with the death of his double, Sydney Carton. The pattern of doubling continues in *Our Mutual Friend,* in which John Harmon becomes the mild-mannered Rokesmith, while the hideous characteristics of the elder Harmon are assumed by Boffin in order that Bella might fall in love with John for the right (transforming) reasons. Hatred of the elder Harmon is rendered harmless since it leads to the desired result—love—and the object of hatred (Boffin) is revealed to have been only playacting in any case. In the Wrayburn plot, Eugene's passivity saves him from any overt aggression, although he does "trifle quite ferociously with his dessert-knife" (1:2, 14) at the Veneerings' and tortures Bradley Headstone unmercifully. Wrayburn pays for his sins by almost dying, but just as Jenny Wren supplies the saving word for him, she also openly displays much of the aggression implicit in his situation and his actions. An ambiguous figure much like Carton, Jenny proves necessary to the tale even while not quite approved by it. Like Micawber, she embodies energies the tale cannot quite endorse.

Great Expectations addresses much more directly the aggression implied by representing the world according to one's own vision of it. Pip is hardly as passive as the other characters I have discussed, and his narrative explores the consequences of his attempt to shape the world to suit his needs. Unqualified by the happy, if somewhat disturbing, discovery that the past could be remade that informed *David Copperfield,* or by the pairing, in *Bleak House,* of the first-person narration with a more aggressive third-person narration, Pip's narration quickly exhibits an uneasiness with the imposition of selfish vision, an uneasiness that comes to dominate the whole novel. In the first few chapters, Pip's repudiation of his childhood world seems fully justified by the grotesque behavior of his sister, Pumblechook, and Wopsle. However, the fact that Pip takes it upon himself to repudiate that world fully makes his case different from the careful and limited repudiations practiced by Esther, Dar-

22. See Alexander Welsh, *The City of Dickens,* pp. 134–35.

nay, Clennam, and Harmon. Pip does benefit from having some of his aggression displaced onto minor characters. Thus, his obvious doubles, Orlick and Drummle, inflict physical pain on the two women—Mrs. Joe and Estella—who have caused Pip the most pain.[23] But that he writes his own story seems to place Pip more squarely at the center of his own life, and he takes responsibility for his destiny in a way the other heroes and heroines never do. And since that responsibility, from almost the very start, involves the guilt of self-assertion, Pip's story takes a very different turn. Alone among Dickens's young characters, Pip's attempt to break from the past is presented as unjustified. The world and self offered to him by Joe on the marshes is the best possible world.

In *David Copperfield,* David regrets having lost his mother and other portions of his past, but his act of memorial representation in his narrative allows him to recognize how his experiences have shaped him. In the end, he accepts the self his "personal history" leaves to him. Esther's narrative in *Bleak House* demonstrates her innocence and her right to happiness with Woodcourt. Pip's narrative repetition, however, does not (until the very end) emphasize the understanding of self and world he achieves in retrospect. Rather, Pip focuses on the future he had at one time imagined for himself; with his "great expectations," Pip is more like the Chancery suitors and third-person narrator in *Bleak House* than like Esther. What he finally learns is that the future created by his imagination was both less substantial and less desirable than the world from which he escaped. Pip's personal hopes are finally "molested," just as Rossetti's dream visions are, by a reality that proves more powerful than subjective fancies.[24]

Pip's own blindness and aggression offer a moral reason for the dashing of his hopes, but the novel also establishes an understanding of reality that eclipses the power of any individual vision. Pip discovers a world in which everyone he meets—Miss Havisham, Mr. Wemmick, Magwitch, even Herbert Pocket—tries to shape reality to suit the self's desires. Pip, of course, does the same. No single character, however, is successful. Instead, reality is formed by the interaction among competing wills. Miss Havisham's attempt to mold Estella does not work out as planned because the counterforce of Estella's will exerts its own influence on the final outcome. That the perceiving mind plays a role in making the world does not mean it can shape the world entirely as

23. For a discussion of Pip's relations to Orlick and Drummle, see John Kucich, *Excess and Restraint in the Novels of Charles Dickens* (Athens: University of Georgia Press, 1981), pp. 90–94.

24. My short discussion of *Great Expectations* is indebted to Edward Said's description of the novel in *Beginnings,* pp. 90–100. Said sees Pip's story as that of an individual who "appropriates" to himself the "authority" to create his own world and his own self, while the novel as a whole works to "molest" Pip's attempt by introducing a larger reality that defeats the self's grandiose ambitions.

it wishes—especially when the object of perception is another person. Used by Compeyson for his own ends, Miss Havisham and Magwitch want a similar control over the lives of Estella and Pip. But they cannot possibly achieve such control without generating a resentment that parallels their own feelings toward Compeyson. The result of their actions is quite different from what they expected. *Great Expectations* presents a Nietzschean world formed by the power struggles among various wills.

The thesis that reality is created through an intersubjective process, if pursued to its logical end, overcomes the dualism that separates mind (self) from world. The self is as much a social product as the world; the self's perceptions of (representations of) that world are not independently conceived, but socially produced. Similarly, the self's perceptions of itself are socially produced. Thus, the self's representations form part of the very process of social, intersubjective representation by which reality is formed. *Great Expectations* both accepts and rejects this collapse of the self into the real. Wemmick is a prime instance; that Wemmick's self is utterly different depending on whom he is with indicates that the self is socially produced. Wemmick at the office is a product of the necessity of resisting Jaggers's exploitation of all weakness. But we are also invited to sympathize with Wemmick's castle, with his attempt to preserve a private self that is untainted and uninfluenced by "Newgate cobwebs." Dickens has always associated moral rectitude with a self that maintains its integrity by standing apart from the public world of contemporary commercial society. Thus, when he accepts that the self and its desires are created through its involvement with others, Dickens can only envision the results as disastrous.

Pip's introduction to Estella and Miss Havisham provokes the loss of innocence that sets him on the wrong path. It never occurs to Pip that he has "coarse hands and . . . common boots" (8, 57) until Estella points it out. Once accountable to her standards, Pip can never rely on his own vision of himself. His character is now formed in relation to her criticisms. "What would it signify to me," Pip asks, "being coarse and common if nobody had told me so?" (17, 121). But the blame is not all Estella's. Pip cannot change his feelings despite his conviction that "it would have been much better" if he "could have settled down and been but half as fond of the forge as [he] was when [he] was little" (17, 121). He has made others' sentiments his own and must take responsibility for following these new impulses despite his uneasy sense that he is in the wrong. "How much of my ungracious condition of mind may have been my own fault, how much Miss Havisham's, how much my sister's, is now of no moment to me or to any one. The change was made in me; the thing was done. Well or ill done, excusably or inexcusably, it was done" (14, 100). Pip has been shaped by the world, and his desires and values reflect those of the world; he is as ungracious, aggressive, and self-serving as the other willful people who make up the world beyond the forge. The unity of that world and its values is demonstrated by its members all sharing a vital connection with Newgate and the criminals it lodges. Pip is not alone in being "encompassed by all this taint of prison and crime" (32, 249); that "stain" (32, 249) marks all the characters in the public world. The self, at least part of the novel demonstrates, has no separate existence; it is inhabited by all the others who have influenced its desires and perceptions. Thus, Pip can tell Estella: "You are part of my existence, part of myself. . . . The stones of which the strongest London buildings are made, are not more real, or more impossible to be displaced by your hands, than your presence and influence have been to me, there and everywhere, and will be. Estella, to the last hour of my life, you cannot choose but remain part of my character" (44, 345). Similarly, Estella's self carries the traces of her upbringing by Miss Havisham and her even more remote origins as the daughter of Magwitch and Jaggers's housekeeper.

Dickens, however, does not allow Pip to become totally absorbed in the fallen public world. Pip retains a "better self," a modicum of decency that is held aloof from the Nietzschean conflict of wills. Interestingly, goodness in the novel becomes associated with silence, as if representation has been completely tainted by its public nature, completely placed in the service of despicable desires. Certainly, naming something is a significant act in the novel, one that aims at establishing the self's priority over the thing named. Pip's naming of himself in the first chapter already suggests his attempts to forge his own destiny, while that name ironically later serves as the badge of his dependence on his unknown benefactor; he must keep the name *Pip* in order to maintain his great expectations. Even Joe's entrance into the world of representation is tainted by the egotism of his only being able to read his own name. Pip's only worthy actions are performed secretly. He sets up Herbert in business without Herbert knowing, and he keeps Magwitch from knowing that his fortune has been forfeited to the crown. Similarly, he does not express his discontent during the time he serves as Joe's apprentice. "I was quite as dejected on the first working-day of my apprenticeship as in that after-time; but I am glad to know that I never breathed a murmur to Joe while my indentures lasted. It is about the only thing I *am* glad to know of myself in that connection" (14, 100–101). Of course, Pip's narrative itself breaks that silence when confiding in the reader, which is another reason the narrative raises the issue of Pip's selfishness so acutely.

The only hope for a comic ending in *Great Expectations* comes, not from the articulation of an alternative vision (offered by fancy) as in the other novels, but in a silence that retains its separateness from the world's appropriation of everything—an appropriation that includes the shaping of the self's desires and the relegation of words to the task of furthering those desires. The comic ending that Dickens wrote for the novel at Bulwer-Lytton's request reveals the same resistance to expressing positive achievements in words. The words Pip and Estella exchange—"We are friends," says Pip, to which Estella responds "And will continue friends apart" (59, 460)—do not express the marriage that the last sentence of the new ending suggests. The submission of Pip's self and the words he uses to express that self to the public world leaves only a small, silent space for the values that engender a comic community. This almost complete triumph of the public, materialistic world explains Dickens's original plan to leave Pip, alone among his young protagonists, with an unhappy ending. The complete marriage of self to world in *Great Expectations* is envisioned as a total surrender of the comic values that retain some transforming power in the other novels.

Pip's position as exclusive narrator makes it difficult for Dickens to displace his hero's aggression onto minor characters who facilitate the creation of a new and better world. Pip is punished by discovering his inability to transform the social reality that has, instead, transformed him. Pip learns that his behavior mimics the social world's usual practices, and his story demonstrates that such behavior must be self-defeating. To assert his self in a context that places him so radically at the mercy of others can only prove futile. But the novel offers only the most minimal vision—represented by Joe and Biddy —of a comic alternative. The social reality that "molests" Pip must overwhelm all selves it subsumes; only existence beyond all representation (each man hidden away in his Walworth castle) provides some refuge from that reality. The difference between word and thing entails the speaker's attempt to alter that world for himself and for the other who hears the words he uses to describe reality. The changes in established fact that this difference can introduce are experienced as liberating in the other novels, but in *Great Expectations* Dickens finds these changes impossible to endorse.

6

The Development of George Eliot's Realism

George Eliot called her novels "realistic," but what she meant by "realism" and how successfully she practiced what she preached have been matters of controversy since her novels first appeared. In *George Eliot's Early Novels: The Limits of Realism,* U. C. Knoepflmacher offers the most extended consideration of Eliot's break with her own "realistic" dicta to present "ideal" characters shaped to serve the author's a priori moral concerns. For Knoepflmacher, realism, defined as a writer's presentation of the actual and commonplace, is still a possible undertaking; he only wishes to argue that George Eliot is not one of the writers who is most faithful to the task realism sets itself.[1]

More recently, critics have used George Eliot's failure to accomplish her self-proclaimed goal of writing realistic novels as evidence of the impossibility of the realistic undertaking itself. These critics view realism as a mistake, as a theory that loses sight of the inevitable transformation of the real when it is moved from life to art. It becomes a measure of Eliot's greatness that she transcends in her novels the limited critical ideology of her day, and her novels are used to "deconstruct" her own statements of her intentions and the possibility of a realistic literature in general.[2]

However, the question of George Eliot's realism cannot be sidestepped simply by proclaiming realism an impossible undertaking and thus arguing that her novels are not realistic. George Eliot was well aware that the work of art is not reality itself, and yet she still believed that something which she called realism was not only possible but was the proper goal of the serious artist. Writing of Ruskin, Eliot tells her readers: "The truth of infinite value that he teaches is *realism*—the doctrine that all truth and beauty are to be attained by a humble and faithful study of nature, and not by substituting vague forms, bred by imagination on the mists of feeling, in place of definite, substantial

1. *George Eliot's Early Novels: The Limits of Realism* (Berkeley: University of California Press, 1968). See the introduction and chap. 1 for Knoepflmacher's general definition of realism.
2. The most important "deconstructions" of Geroge Eliot's work are two essays by J. Hillis Miller: "Narrative and History," *ELH* 41 (1974): 455–73; and "Optic and Semiotic in *Middlemarch,*" in *The Worlds of Victorian Fiction,* ed. Jerome H. Buckley (Cambridge: Harvard University Press, 1975), pp. 125–45.

reality. The thorough acceptance of this doctrine would remould our life."[3] In an essay he wrote for the *Westminster Review* in 1858, George Lewes stated the principle of the difference between life and art clearly:

> Art is a Representation of Reality—a Representation which, inasmuch as it is not the thing itself, but only represents it, must necessarily be limited by the nature of its medium; . . . but while thus limited, while thus regulated by the necessities imposed on it by each medium of expression, Art always aims at the representation of Reality, i.e. of Truth; and no departure from truth is permissible, except such as inevitably lies in the nature of the medium itself. Realism is thus the basis of all Art, and its antithesis is not Idealism, but Falsism.[4]

George Eliot refers to this difference imposed by the medium, which includes the author's peculiar sensibility, when discussing her realism. "I undertake to exhibit nothing as it should be; I only try to exhibit some things as they have been or are, seen through such a medium as my own nature gives me."[5] In an early review of Ruskin (1854), Eliot had written, "The aim of Art, in depicting any natural object, is to produce in the mind analogous emotions to those produced by the object itself; but as with all our skill and care we cannot imitate it exactly, this aim is not attained by *transcribing*, but by *translating* it into the language of Art."[6] Later, of *Romola*, she will write, "Approximate truth is the only truth attainable, but at least one must strive for that, and not wade off into arbitrary falsehood,"[7] echoing the famous assertion in *Adam Bede* that the narrator will offer her readers no "arbitrary picture."[8] Lewes's and George Eliot's comments on the "translation" of life into art suggest a set of parameters for discussing issues of realism and representation in Eliot's novels. If the difference between the representative and the represented is understood, realism must focus on the nature and quality of representation. In Lewes's terms, realistic representation is "true," not "false." True representation has often been identified with resemblance or mimesis. Recent attacks on literary realism have, in many instances, called attention to the impossibility of resemblance between words and things. Lewes's and Eliot's statements reveal an awareness of the limits of mimesis; their notion of realism

3. *George Eliot: A Writer's Notebook, 1854–1879, and Uncollected Writings*, ed. Joseph Wiesenfarth (Charlottesville: University Press of Virginia, 1981), p. 273. (Henceforth referred to as *Notebooks.*) This passage comes from George Eliot's review of *Modern Painters III* in the *Westminster Review* of April 1856.

4. Unsigned review, "Realism in Art: Recent German Fiction," *Westminster Review* (American edition) 70 (1858): 273.

5. *The George Eliot Letters*, ed. Gordon S. Haight, 9 vols. (New Haven: Yale University Press, 1954–1978), 2:365. Henceforth referred to as *Letters.*

6. *Notebooks*, p. 240.

7. *Letters*, 4:43.

8. *Adam Bede*, ed. John Paterson, Riverside Edition (Boston: Houghton Mifflin, 1968), chap. 17.

does not require that the representative resemble the represented, only, to use Eliot's phrase, that the representative inspire an "analogous emotion" to that inspired by contact with the represented. They are concerned to prevent the representation from being "arbitrary." Realism is an art that is answerable to the facts. Much like Locke, Eliot insists that the word's link to the real must be strong and sure.

But how can a novelist be true to the facts when her works of fiction provide few, if any, statements about the actual world? To use Gottlob Frege's famous distinction, the statements in a novel make "sense" (the reader knows what it means to say that "Maggie is headstrong"), but those statements have no "reference" to any thing or one in the world.[9] Maggie does not exist, and is therefore neither headstrong nor docile. It would seem that a novelist is always "arbitrary," since she makes up characters and situations as she writes her tale and there appears no compulsion to make the character one thing rather than another.

To reduce literature to the "sense" function of language, for George Eliot, would assure its arbitrariness—and, hence, its triviality and its solipsism. She works to ground her novels in some reference to reality—either empirical or social—that transcends the self. Her realism is preoccupied with establishing the literary work's relation to the world and its power to denote, describe, and represent things and events in that world. I will argue that Eliot moves from a simple realism of matching words to world in *The Mill on the Floss* to a more complex realism, one that envisions a world and converts readers to that world's reality in her last two novels, *Middlemarch* and *Daniel Deronda*. The visionary realism of the later works reflects the earlier novel's inability to overcome the gap between mind's visions (as embodied in the words of imagination) and world, an inability that determines Maggie Tulliver's isolation from her society and her tragic end. *The Mill on the Floss* attempts to achieve a purely empiricist realism, one in which the mind passively receives impressions from a material world. But the awful price of passivity, particularly its inability to effect any change in the world as given, moves Eliot to a more romantic vision of mind's ability to influence the real world in which men find themselves.

In *Middlemarch* and *Daniel Deronda,* the novelist does not only denote a reality but also strives to create a context in which words that refer to invisible values and to an invisible (but possible) future can be understood. Experimenting with different ways of making "sense" in the imaginative space of fiction is not just arbitrary nonreferential "play" when the action of mind upon what it perceives is granted some influence over the forms reality takes.[10]

9. See "On Sense and Reference" in *Translations from the Philosophical Writings of Gottlob Frege,* ed. Peter Geach and Max Black (1st ed.; London: Basil Blackwell, 1952), pp. 56–78.
10. The "play" characteristic of much postmodernist literature stems, I think, from a

The crucial development of Eliot's realism is the shift from a world of objects inertly perceived to human interaction with that world as the "reality" to which words must "refer." My argument will be that we can explain this shift as a response to certain unresolved difficulties in *The Mill on the Floss*. My discussions of *Middlemarch* and *Daniel Deronda* will consider how the realism of the later novels works.

George Eliot's realism addresses the epistemological difficulties characteristic of the "modern" world described in Michel Foucault's *The Order of Things*. Foucault believes that, around 1800, the Enlightenment correlation of appearance with reality gave way to the romantic belief that the most important truths lie hidden beneath the surface. For example, in eighteenth-century biology, plants and animals were classified according to similarities between outward features, whereas in nineteenth-century biology, "life," a general term that designates sophistication of internal organization, becomes the means by which individual specimens are assigned to classes. If Foucault is right, the apprehension of reality becomes problematic after 1800, since it is no longer readily accessible to sight, but can only be discovered through an act of interpretation that reads and organizes external signs in order to grasp a hidden truth.[11] Words themselves undergo the same shift; they no longer carry their meaning on the surface, but now require interpretation because they refer to something that is absent (hidden). In other words, Foucault sees Saussure's division of the sign into the signifier (the sign's manifest appearance) and the signified (the meaning) as another example of the retreat of reality from the surface after 1800.

Realism can be understood as a response to this new complexity. It becomes important to stress language's referential abilities precisely because the link between word and referent has become a problem; a space has been opened up between the representative (signifier) which is present and the represented (signified) which is hidden. A recognition that hidden passions influence observable behavior informs George Eliot's realism from the start of her career; she never presents a world in which all that it is important to know can be perceived by the senses. But she has more difficulty in determining an appropriate status for the moods and emotions that must be searched out if our knowledge is to be complete. In George Eliot's fiction, "sympathy" becomes the crucial term that unites the epistemological, moral, and rhetorical levels.

---

complete loss of faith in mind's or imagination's ability to influence the course of a history that follows its own relentless, inhuman logic. The dualism that romanticism strives to overcome stands as the unalterable nature of things in much contemporary work, with art, as a mental construct, understood as occupying a realm of rather futile play that is completely unconnected to brute reality. For a fuller discussion of this issue, see my essay "A là Recherche du Temps Perdu in *One Hundred Years of Solitude*," *Modern Fiction Studies* 28 (1982–1983): 557–67.

11. See Foucault, *The Order of Things* (New York: Vintage Books, 1973), esp. chaps. 5–8.

Epistemologically, sympathy expresses the ability to plunge beneath the surface to recognize the passions that explain another's actions; morally, sympathy functions as the only escape from a solipsism that not only insures a limited knowledge of the world but also an inability to improve the life of others and oneself; rhetorically, the author requests our sympathy as she works to persuade us to accept her vision of the real and how our lot might be best endured and/or improved. Sympathy works to provide those links between surface and depth that have become so precarious. "The greatest benefit we owe to the artist . . . is the extension of our sympathies," and such extension can only be achieved by the strictest realism: "our social novels profess to represent people as they are, and the unreality of their representations are a grave evil. . . . Art is the nearest thing to life; it is a mode of amplifying experience and extending our contact with our fellow-men beyond the bounds of our personal lot. . . . Falsification here is far more pernicious than in the more artificial aspects of life."[12]

At first glance, *The Mill on the Floss* can be seen as portraying a lack of both epistemological and moral sympathy. St. Ogg's and Tom Tulliver fail to understand Maggie and they fail to tolerate her. The two failures coincide when they ostracize her for an act—the renunciation of Stephen Guest—that is actually Maggie's attempt to affirm her ties to Tom and her native town. But the novel is also an examination of Maggie's failings. Maggie is chastised throughout the novel for the shortcomings of her self-knowledge and her knowledge of the world, suggesting that her willfulness isolates her from satisfactory participation in the world. Yet when she finally comes to full knowledge at the point when she renounces Stephen, she is still subjected to her tragic end. This inconsistency in the novel's treatment of its main character points toward the novel's own epistemological problems, ones that will necessitate a recasting of George Eliot's understanding of realism. *The Mill on the Floss* is one of the few tragedies written by a major Victorian author. The Victorians were committed to achieving some kind of reconciliation between mind and world, some kind of comic accommodation. Matthew Arnold was so troubled by the pessimism of his tragic poem, *Empedocles on Etna,* that he decided not to reprint it in the second edition of his poems. Yeats's adoption of a tragic attitude marks one of his most significant differences from the Victorians.

Throughout most of the novel, Maggie's lack of knowledge is characterized as resulting from the conflict between her imagination (primarily literary) and the external world, and this conflict is presented as potentially tragic. "Everybody in the world seemed so hard and unkind to Maggie: there was

12. "The Natural History of German Life," in *Essays of George Eliot,* ed. Thomas Pinney (London: Routledge and Kegan Paul, 1963), pp. 270–71. Referred to in subsequent notes as *Essays.*

no indulgence, no fondness, such as she imagined when she fashioned the world afresh in her own thoughts. . . . The world outside the books was not a happy one, Maggie felt. . . . No wonder, when there is this contrast between the outward and the inward, that painful collisions come of it."[13] Maggie's imaginary world has no existing referent, and she will suffer because she continually acts as if the world of books and of her imagination does denote *the* world in which she lives, and because the fictional world "fashioned . . . in her own thoughts" is preferable to the actual world of the mill and St. Ogg's. Maggie's failure to grasp the fictional character of books—a failure she shares with Don Quixote—is best exemplified by the episode in which she runs away to the gypsies.[14] This incident points to a lesson Maggie will fail to learn again and again: the words of fictions do not accurately reflect the lived world that exists outside books and that serves as the referent of ordinary language.[15] *The Mill on the Floss* demonstrates its own "realism" by "molesting" the fanciful images of the world entertained by the protagonist.

The novel, however, cannot undermine Maggie's visions with a completely clear conscience because the plot leads us to sympathize with Maggie's perception that the world offered by fiction is better than the real world. Fiction makes its readers unhappy because it portrays a world preferable to the one experienced daily. *The Mill on the Floss* as a novel is, like its main character, torn between the desire to live in the beautiful world of literature and the sense that the frivolous dreams of imagination must be abandoned in favor of real life. *The Mill on the Floss* is a novel suspicious of books, ever wary of fiction as mere wish fulfillment that must be renounced, and that same renunciation is demanded of Maggie. Realism, at this stage in George Eliot's career, means the strict accountability of vision to the facts, even though Eliot understands those facts to be rather colorless, even bleak. The indulgence in fable of Eliot's next novel, *Silas Marner,* stems, I think, from this novel's stern renunciation of the imaginative.

The Mill on the Floss cannot endorse Maggie's imaginative reveries because they have no referent. The danger of such reveries is illustrated when desire is linked to imagination and fiction in the scene in which Philip Wakem offers Maggie a copy of Scott's *The Pirate.* Maggie (like Mary Ann Evans)

13. *The Mill on the Floss,* ed. Gordon S. Haight, Riverside Edition (Boston: Houghton Mifflin, 1961), bk. 3, chap. 5. Subsequent references are from this edition, with book and chapter numbers given parenthetically in the text.

14. At first glance, the novel that chastises one of its characters for forgetting the fictional nature of novels would seem to be pointing to its own fictionality. But it works the other way as well in both *Don Quixote* and *The Mill on the Floss.* By telling us that novels are fictional, the novel is telling us something "true" and is thus demonstrating its own veracity.

15. For two excellent readings of Maggie's imaginative extravagances and how they determine the novel's general shape, see Nina Auerbach, "The Power of Hunger: Demonism and Maggie Tulliver," *NCF* 30 (1975): 150–71; and Jonathan Arac, "Rhetoric and Realism in Nineteenth-Century Fiction: Hyperbole in *The Mill on the Floss,*" *ELH* 46 (1979): 673–92.

had once read part of the book, and it had awakened in her "for a long while" a longing for the Shetland Islands. Now Philip offers to lend her the book so she might finish it. But Maggie refuses, because if she reads it, she will "want too much" (5:1). The desires generated by imagination, because they have no reference to the real, are limitless. Haunted by a fear of endless desire, the novel checks the self's wishes by referring them to one's responsibilities to others and to the drastic consequences of wish-motivated action. Imagination's wishes, embodied in words and images cut loose from referential ties to the real, are dangerous because nothing governs their construction; they are completely "arbitrary," answerable only to themselves. To the modern reader, Maggie's love for Stephen might seem foolish, but hardly dangerous. But to George Eliot, that love typifies desire divorced from all reference to social context or one's ties (familial and affectionate) to others. Maggie has fallen into that romantic solipsism, a willingness to take the self's vision of reality as constituting the real, that many Victorians found the most objectionable feature of romanticism.

The only desires the novel can endorse, the only desires bounded by a relation to a reality that transcends the self, are the desires prompted by memory.[16] Ties to the world and to others, particularly Maggie's ties to Tom and Lucy, constitute memory, and the renunciations of Philip and Stephen are enacted in memory's name. Talking to Philip, Maggie insists, "I desire no future that will break the ties of the past" (6:10), and when she rejects Stephen, after a night spent floating free of her whole world, Maggie argues that their love "would rend me away from all that my past life has made dear and holy to me" (6:14). The past's reality primarily consists of the network of family relationships into which one is born, a social reality that, from the first, places the self in a situation where its own desires must be limited by the desires of those others with whom the self lives. In the renunciation of Stephen, Maggie achieves that clear knowledge of the real that the novel has held out as her goal. In the chapter entitled "Borne Away by the Tide," Maggie gives herself over to a "vision" of a life with Stephen, a vision that "excluded all realities" (6:13). But in the next chapter, entitled "Waking," she is disenchanted, recognizing that she has made herself "an outlawed soul with no guide but the wayward choice of her own passion" (6:14), and she uses the image of reality offered by memory to regain that

16. That the novel endorses Maggie's valuation of her past and the renunciation preached by Thomas à Kempis is, to say the least, a much debated point. I will not attempt to argue that point here, but refer the reader to John Hagan's essay "A Reinterpretation of *The Mill on the Floss*," *PMLA* 87 (1972): 53–63. Hagan summarizes the critical debate on this issue and gives what I find convincing arguments for the position I take here. For a good general discussion of George Eliot's allegiance to an ideal past, see Thomas Pinney, "The Authority of the Past in George Eliot's Novels," *NCF* 21 (1966): 131–47.

outward guide, to escape solipsism, and to place herself back into contact with the real. "If the past is not to bind us, where can duty lie?" Maggie asks Stephen, and concludes that "we should have no law but the inclination of the moment" if that past were abandoned (6:14). The social world, with the obligations it places on the self, serves in Eliot, as in Dickens, as the ultimate reality in the world of the novels.

Given this ascension by Maggie to clear knowledge, why is she denied a happy ending? To answer that question I must consider more closely the social reality that the novel establishes as the referent to which Maggie is bound. In fact, the novel presents two rather different versions of that reality, without ever explicitly acknowledging that these two versions are not one and the same. For convenience, I will call the two the "oppressive referent" and the "nostalgic referent." (The parallels to *David Copperfield*, and the significance of *The Mill on the Floss* as autobiography, become apparent here. David regrets the loss of those past things which inspire nostalgia while using the imagination to overcome those past things—like working in the blacking warehouse—that oppressed him. Maggie's situation is similar, although more complex because she feels nostalgic about, yet must struggle to overcome, the same experience: her relation to her brother Tom.) *The Mill on the Floss* fluctuates in its allegiance to the "oppressive" and "nostalgic" referents, and the result is the confusion at the core of the novel's tragedy that has troubled so many critics.[17] One cause for tragedy is simply the clash between the oppressively narrow (both words are the narrator's) world of St. Ogg's and the more extravagant claims of Maggie's imagination. This conflict, however, fails to explain completely Maggie's situation because it offers no reason for endorsing her acts of renunciation. If the novel blames Tom for being a prig, as it surely does, it also blames Maggie for having extravagant desires. If memory's only referent were the oppressive St. Ogg's, then the novel's praise of memory would be impossible to justify.

However, the novel offers another referent for memory, the "nostalgic referent." The past that Maggie holds sacred is a past separate from St. Ogg's, the childhood world characterized by a total absence of desire and by her perfect union with her brother. A conversation with Philip reveals this image of the past. Maggie speaks first.

17. For some discussions of the nature of the novel's confusion and some attempts to explain possible causes for that confusion, see F. R. Leavis, *The Great Tradition* (London: Chatto & Windus, 1962); Carol Christ, "Aggression and Providential Death in George Eliot's Fiction," *Novel* 9 (1976): 130–40; George Levine, "Intelligence as Deception: *The Mill on the Floss*," *PMLA* 80 (1965): 402–9; and Ian Adam, "The Ambivalence of *The Mill on the Floss*," in *George Eliot: A Centenary Tribute*, ed. Gordon S. Haight and Rosemary T. Vanarsdel (Totowa, N.J.: Barnes & Noble, 1982), pp. 122–36.

"O, it is quite impossible we can ever be more than friends—brother and sister in secret, as we have been. Let us give up thinking of everything else."

"No, Maggie, I can't give you up—unless you are deceiving me—unless you really only care for me as if I were your brother. Tell me the truth."

"Indeed, I do, Philip. What happiness have I ever had so great as being with you?—since I was a little girl—the days Tom was good to me." (5:4)

Philip's question makes clear that the brother-sister relationship signifies innocence and a lack of desire. Does Maggie care for him only in that way, have no sexual desire for him? Maggie's answer is that she will want no other type of union than the innocent and happy union she once knew with Tom. Later, the dream of Tom rowing past on the river without looking at Maggie (6:14) will inspire her renunciation of Stephen. The union with Tom predates passion, and the desire to regain that union, a desire fed by memory and used to effect the breaks with Stephen and Philip, is the only desire the novel allows Maggie to hold without chastisement.

Yet the novel contains much evidence to suggest that this endorsed desire is just as much an unjustified, "arbitrary" creation of Maggie's imagination as any of the other desires that she is chastised for holding. My description of the perfect childhood relies on Maggie's memories of it, not its presentation in the narrative, because the novel, from its earliest chapters, shows Maggie alienated from Tom, unable to win and keep his affection, just as she is alienated from the world around her. Nostalgia, of course, can only be generated by a consciousness of loss. But the novel only very dimly recognizes that it presents loss—the dualism of a self separated from participation with the larger world—as the inevitable human condition from the earliest moments of childhood. The famous opening chapter presents a nostalgic narrator/observer who is drawn toward a mystic union with the world, a union imagined as drowning in the Floss as its waters engulf the world. "I am in love with moistness, and envy the white ducks that are dipping their heads far into the water here among the withes, unmindful of the awkward appearance they make in the drier world above" (1:1). The narrator lives in that "drier world" but the narrative refuses to accept absolutely that condition. The narrative will, at times, insist on the reality of Maggie's image of her childhood, even if unable to portray that perfect union with Tom in actuality. And, of course, the novel indulges its mystic desires in its watery ending.

Maggie's happy memories of her early union with Tom are hardly justified by our view of their childhood. The experience of separation from Tom, in fact, is the source of her passionate desire for union, for love, the desire that is identified as "the strongest need in poor Maggie's nature" (1:5). From the start, Maggie is a creature of the desires generated by her separation from the world, desires seemingly beyond her ability to satisfy. There seems little reason for the novel to endorse the desire for Tom while other desires (including ones much more likely to be fulfilled) are ruled out. The privileging of images of familial union might be explained by their priority in time or their sexual innocence, but more important for my purposes here is the recognition that Eliot cannot quite manage to give over all belief in the "reality" of a primitive and completely satisfying union of the self with another. Such a reality would offer the ground that her earliest and most simple understanding of realism requires. But in *The Mill on the Floss* that reality becomes as transcendentally inaccessible as the divine is for Carlyle and Ruskin.

The Mill on the Floss, then, offers two explicit reasons for Maggie's tragedy: her incompatibility with the narrow world of St. Ogg's, and her growth away from the perfect world of her childhood. The first reason locates the cause of the tragedy in the nature of the two combatants; the second reason locates the cause in the changes wrought by time.[18] Either cause might be sufficient, but the novel's identification of two referents leads to its presenting both. The novel appeals to time's distancing Maggie from her childhood when it affirms the reality of the "nostalgic referent"; the novel's appeals to Maggie's conflict with her environment when demonstrating imagination's divorce from the real. The two reasons, while existing side by side in the novel, are never explicitly combined because, while the novel sends Maggie to her tragic end, it tries to evade the more sweeping tragic conclusion that mind and world, desire and reality, are necessarily irreconcilable. (Rossetti reaches that more sweeping conclusion in despair, while Yeats will make the defiant pronouncement of the tragic impasse the basis of much of his poetry.) To maintain the possibility of a world in which the words and images of imagination can find a correlative in reality, the novel must cling to its insistence that the dream of union can actually be achieved, must cling to its insistence that Maggie's perfect childhood did exist, that she is right to preserve its image in memory as her proper "guide." Admittedly, the novel cannot find its way back to that perfect union; it can only be approximately achieved in the pyrrhic ending of the flood, but the possibility of union in the real world must be asserted.

18. The conjunction of these two causes is reflected in Knoepflmacher's reading of the novel in *George Eliot's Early Novels.* The chapter on *The Mill on the Floss* is entitled "Tragedy and the Flux," but the reason for tragedy most often cited by Knoepflmacher is Tom's and Maggie's "opposing temperaments" (183), the fate which has made Tom take after the Dodsons and Maggie after the Tullivers. "In Tom, the Dodson strain has been magnified; in Maggie, the 'richer blood' of the Tullivers is dominant. . . . Tom embraces the reality of St. Ogg's; Maggie yields to the fantasy life that was her father's destruction" (210). But how does this cause of Maggie's tragic end relate to the "flux" mentioned in the chapter's title? Knoepflmacher identifies the two causes offered by the novel for its tragic ending, but does not seem to recognize that either cause should be sufficient and that the need to present two causes points to important confusions in the novel's structure and aims. For Knoepflmacher's more recent thoughts on the novel's ending, including a response to some of the points raised here, see "Genre and the Integrations of Gender: Wordsworth to George Eliot to Virginia Woolf," in *Victorian Literature and Society: Essays Presented to Richard D. Altick,* ed. James R. Kincaid and Albert J. Kuhn (Columbus: Ohio State University Press, 1984), pp. 94–118.

The Mill on the Floss, however, tacitly recognizes that the "nostalgic referent" is a human construction since the novel gives the reader the means by which to understand that the perfect childhood is open to the same kind of criticism as Maggie's notions about the gypsies. George Eliot, at this point in her career (and, I would assume, at this point in her meditations about her own past), is not quite ready to abandon that image of an ideal past in which reality was adequate to desire, in which imagination was not forced to construct a world in which to live. The explicit belief in *The Mill on the Floss* that such a past existed means that any fictional construct must be rejected in favor of the reality itself. Thus, the narrator rejects the indirection of metaphoric and figurative language in favor of a plain style that names things directly. "O Aristotle! if you had had the advantage of being 'the freshest modern' instead of the greatest ancient, would you not have mingled your praise of metaphorical speech, as a sign of high intelligence, with a lamentation that intelligence so rarely shows itself in speech without metaphor,—that we can so seldom declare what a thing is, except by saying it is something else?" (2:1). *The Mill on the Floss,* being modern, laments the loss of the ability to "declare what a thing is" directly.

When explicit about her preferences, the narrator of *The Mill on the Floss* (like *David Copperfield*'s narrator) opts for a Lockean plain speaking. The real is revealed in memories closely bound to actual experience and by words that denote a thing exactly. Unable to find any benefit in the present words and images that refer to a lost past, *The Mill on the Floss* is condemned by nostalgia to tragedy. The novel's realism insists there was a referent in the past that served as the "thing" language denotes, but now that referent is gone, and language, floating free of that past, keeps saying "something else," except when restrained by the strongest efforts of memory. Unlike David, Maggie cannot accept the substitutes (Philip and Stephen) that time offers her for the original object of desire. Unable to assert that imagination's wishes and words find a home in the present, the novel locates that home in the past, and then laments its exile from that past.

This exile can be tied to the novel's allegiance to what Umberto Eco has termed a "metaphysics of the referent," a phrase that describes those theories of meaning which hold that the word's significance is dependent on its standing for some locatable real thing that the word designates.[19] In "correspondence" theories of meaning the only recognizable referents are actually existing things, and the meaning of a word is guaranteed by its correspondence to something that exists. Such theories have usually been put forward by empiricist or positivist philosophers, as the emphasis on concrete existing particulars would lead us to expect.

In *A Theory of Semiotics,* Eco presents his case against correspondence

---

19. *A Theory of Semiotics* (Bloomington: Indiana University Press, 1976), p. 70.

theories. Eco does not deny that words can name, or "mention," things, but he insists that their meaning is in no way dependent on this ability. Rather, he argues that the meaning of words is essentially cultural, since the "codes" that establish significance are conventional and are social creations. Two important points undermine the insistence that language's relation to real things is the source of its ability to signify. First, words used to lie still succeed in conveying a message, although the state of affairs the lie designates does not exist; second, the meaning of "a sign can only be explained through another sign." "The semiotic object of a semantics is the *content,* not the *referent,* and the content has to be defined as a *cultural unit.* "[20] Contents are human constructions; in a fully Kantian sense, then, the "real things" referred to by language are representations generated by the way men perceive the world. (The representational Locke had already raised many of these issues, but the Locke who is the father of a faith in direct perception of real things also serves as the father of correspondence theories of meaning.) Eco's rejection of any appeal to a direct, nonmediated apprehension of a real thing that serves as the referent of speech is clearly indicated by his redefinition of Frege's distinction between "sense" ("*Sinn*") and "reference" ("*Bedeutung*"). "To say that Walter Scott and the author of *Waverley* are two expressions that have the same *Bedeutung* but two *Sinn* concerns a theory of sign-function only insofar as: (i) the *Bedeutung* is intended as the definition of an historical entity that a culture recognizes as a single person, and is therefore a denoted content; (ii) the *Sinn* is a particular way of considering a given content, according to other cultural conventions."[21] By denying any appeal to real things as referents, Eco places both the referential and sense functions of language entirely within the system of the human production of meaning. For Eco, the mind always shapes the world it engages; his account of language joins hands with Coleridge's rejection of the passive reception of external impressions found in empiricism.

In *The Mill on the Floss,* George Eliot has come close to the romantic recognition that referents are constructed entities, that they are "contents" in Eco's sense. But the novel backs away from this knowledge in favor of a desire for a perfect world that will be revealed to a passive, receiving self. Such revelation (in keeping with the novel's hints at mysticism) is desired because a reality that the self plays no role in creating seems more real than any human construction could be. (This odd conjunction between mysticism and empiricist realism not only reminds us of the religious bases of much Victorian realism—the desire to perceive a world created by God—but also indicates that empiricism is equally devoted to perceiving a world not created by men, even if the empiricist replaces God with transcendent, preexisting laws of nature.)

20. Ibid., p. 61.
21. Ibid., pp. 61–62.

The Mill on the Floss must end tragically because George Eliot is torn between her insistence that the nostalgic referent exists even while she cannot imagine how to gain access to it, and her unacknowledged understanding that the image of a perfect childhood is only a creation of Maggie's desires. The impasse reached in *The Mill on the Floss* marks the bankruptcy of a simple realism where words denote an actual world. From this autobiographical novel, George Eliot turns to historical novels that attempt to describe the temporal and social processes by which cultural contents are created. The novelist's response to the problems encountered in *The Mill on the Floss* is to explore the way in which the Maggies of the world create their visions of reality, and to consider how that vision might be communicated to others so that a community might act upon it. The impotence dictated by a "metaphysics of the referent," by a belief in a preexisting, unalterable reality proves intolerable.

Here is George Eliot's equivalent to Dickens's "fancy," to the powerful "imagination" celebrated by the romantics. Like Dickens, she will work to make sure that the constructs of imagination truly transcend the self, and will find a new possibility for comedy in this interaction between mind and reality that offers a chance to alter the world to better suit human needs. George Eliot's historical novels work from the premise that the grounds of human life, the final referents of our speech, are humanly constructed, with the fact that those grounds change from one historical period to another taken as one important proof that they are man-made. The later novels examine both how referents are constructed and how individuals are to judge correctly the social conditions (and the possible behavior allowed by those conditions) of their particular time. The novels remain "realistic," although the identity of the referent to which they are bound changes radically. That referent is now the interaction between selves that generates social reality and the interaction between mind and world that establishes the conditions of life. My discussion of *Middlemarch* will, I trust, make the import of these generalizations clear, while my discussion of *Daniel Deronda* will consider how Eliot carefully limits the individual imagination's power to remake the world.

The historical vision in *Middlemarch* commits George Eliot to a more complicated understanding of the relation of words to world than is found in *The Mill on the Floss*. If Foucault is right in claiming "reality" is hidden in the nineteenth century, then the theory of evolution remains a primary example of that hiddenness.[22] The thing is never only what it is now, but is also

22. In keeping with Eco's insistence that referents are culturally produced, we should note that Foucault claims reality "hides" itself, not because reality itself changes after 1800, but because the way culture organizes its knowledge about reality changes. The theory of evolution, for Foucault, would be one example of a general movement away from explanations of reality by surface characteristics to explanations that search out data and connections not immediately available to perception. George Levine, *The Realistic Imagination*, p. 148, discusses the effect of

the history of what it has been and the potential of what it will be. Names are inadequate; only narratives can fully describe an object. A knowledge of the thing as it appears now is not enough; we must view a thing's history. Of Lydgate, the narrator of *Middlemarch* writes:

> He was at a starting-point which makes many a man's career a fine subject for betting, if there were any gentlemen given to that amusement who could appreciate the complicated probabilities of an arduous purpose, with all the possible thwartings and furtherings of circumstance, all the niceties of inward balance, by which a man swims and makes his point or else is carried headlong. The risk would remain, even with close knowledge of Lydgate's character; for character too is a process and an unfolding. The man was still in the making.[23]

The novelist will show the "process" and "unfolding" that reveals, over time, the referent of the name *Lydgate*. A referent is not simply an object out there that is named, but an object always in process, always being created by virtue of its interaction with others in the whole context we call society and history. Realism must not only be flexible enough to record the object's changes but must also denote the process of change itself, catch the object in the middle of its march from one condition to another.

The novel's plot explores the consequences of the interaction between character (nature or potential) and environment. Lydgate and Dorothea Brooke are understandable only in the context of Middlemarch. There are no "things in themselves" in the novel. The thing is always in relation to other things, and its nature is constituted by those relations, among which is included the crucial fact of how something is perceived by various other members of the community. The part can be differentiated from the whole, can be given a distinctive name, but the part is only fully known when seen in relation to the whole. This epistemological holism is the foundation of George Eliot's conception of "form," developed in the late 1860s. She writes:

> As knowledge continues to grow by its alternating processes of distinction & combination, seeing smaller & smaller unlikenesses & grouping or associating these under a common likeness, it arrives at the conception of wholes composed of parts more & more absolutely bound together by various conditions of common likeness and mutual dependence. And the fullest example of such a whole is the highest example of Form: in other words, the relation of multiplex interdependent parts to a whole which is itself in the most varied & therefore the fullest relation to other wholes.[24]

---

the Darwinian revolution on plot and character in mid-Victorian fiction.

23. *Middlemarch,* ed. Gordon S. Haight, Riverside Edition (Boston: Houghton Mifflin, 1956), bk. 2, chap. 15. Subsequent references are to this edition, with book and chapter numbers given parenthetically in the text.

24. "Notes on Form in Art," in *Essays,* p. 433.

One example of the adherence in *Middlemarch* to this recognition that parts cannot be divorced from the whole occurs during the negotiations surrounding the appointment of a hospital chaplain. "Thus it happened that on this occasion Bulstrode became identified with Lydgate, and Lydgate with Tyke; and owing to this variety of interchangeable names for the chaplaincy question, diverse minds were able to form the same judgment concerning it" (2:18). In a world in which names become "interchangeable," clear knowledge results, not just from the proper assignment of names, but also from designating the processes by which names slide and come to stand for one another.

Furthermore, names give an illusion of separateness, an illusion that sometimes serves to aid the desire to deny the intimate connections between certain entities. Lydgate distinguishes between the pleasure he feels in Rosamond's company and "love," but the narrator comments, "Our passions do not live apart in locked chambers, but, dressed in their small wardrobe of notions, bring their provisions to a common table and mess together, feeding out of the common store according to their appetite" (2:16). The "feeding" metaphor points to that communion in which separate things take part, that interdependence of dissimilars that Eliot calls "form," and apart from which the dissimilars cannot be understood. The novelist must maintain the tension between individual and context, between separate identity and definition by interaction. That tension is "form" and is the pattern all knowledge must assume. The object is always modified by its environment, the meaning of a word is always dependent on the words with which it appears, and the object's reality is influenced by the manner in which it is perceived. Realism must take these interactions into account.

Middlemarch, while abandoning a "metaphysics of the referent," is still a realistic novel in its attempt to designate the process by which referents ("contents" in Eco's terms) are culturally produced. Eliot's early realism aimed for a direct revelation of the existing world to her readers. Her later realism understands that such direct presentation is not possible and takes as its subject those very processes by which the world is produced. The referent in *Middlemarch* is the process of cultural representation (the "form" that human knowledge takes in a given historical setting), with a secondary referent being the problems individuals face in properly recognizing their historical period's method of organizing signification. (George Eliot's understanding of history shares some common ground with Carlyle's theory of transient cultural forms in *Sartor Resartus* and Ruskin's presentation of radically different historical eras. But in *Middlemarch* Eliot is much closer to a complete historicism than either Carlyle and Ruskin; that is, she is more willing to accept that each historical age creates its own reality, independent of any transcendent reality that will apocalyptically destroy aberrations from its standards. Eliot's ethics, however, do not allow her to forgo all appeals to transcendent principles, and I will argue that when she must face the consequences of historicism more squarely in *Daniel Deronda,* Eliot retreats to belief in a transcendent reality.) The novel's realism is assured not by its individual words actually referring to existent things, but by its accurate portrayal of how meanings are created. The novel's particular created form would be recognized as distinct from social forms prevailing in contemporary society, but as contiguous to those forms (related to them metonymically). The given "whole" of the novel could then be related, in a further act of knowledge, to the "other wholes" discovered in experience, as outlined in the "Notes on Form."

The cultural production of referents is illustrated in Lydgate's story; the doctor's fate springs from the union between his personality—revealed in the tale of his passion for the French actress—and the attitudes and actions of Rosamond and Middlemarch toward him. The story of Dorothea is more concerned with the problems an individual encounters in her attempt to understand how society "codes" the world, and how it creates those codes. Dorothea, like Maggie Tulliver, is given the task of working from a position of ignorance (her complete misjudging of Casaubon) toward the knowledge enjoyed by the narrator.

The first obstacle to knowledge lies in the limited perspective of the self, a perspective further hampered by the tendency of desire to influence perception. The limitation of a single point of view is a constant theme in George Eliot's novels, a limitation that is overcome by determined acts of sympathy. In *Middlemarch* the narrator performs a singular act of self-humiliation to demonstrate her overcoming such limitation. "One morning, some weeks after her arrival at Lowick, Dorothea—but why always Dorothea? Was her point of view the only possible one with respect to this marriage? I protest against all our interest, all our effort at understanding, being given to the young. . . . Mr. Casaubon had an intense consciousness within him, and was spiritually a-hungered like the rest of us" (3:29). Only by portraying both sides of the relationship can the narrator present its full reality. An extension of sympathy permits the narrator's presentation of another's point of view. The visible switch in point of view is an indication to the reader of the narrator's good faith, as well as a demonstration of the novel's interaction thesis. The narrator's flexibility follows the flexibility of a world in which subjects acting with and reacting against one another create the world of social experience. Yet this switch in point of view also raises serious questions about the possibility of gaining adequate knowledge of that created world. The switch is a staged renunciation, a point when the narrator, despite her desire to do otherwise, will extend her sympathy to Casaubon. This renunciation is absolutely necessary to the novel's realism. To define the real, the referent of speech, as the product of the interaction of people through time is to define that referent as both radically beyond the reach of individual actions and radically affected by individual action. As long as the individual is limited to his own point of view, he must always fail to know fully or accurately his society and his world. Yet, since the individual is involved in the construction of that society and that world, his every action, however limited, alters that world. In this last notion, we find one reason for Eliot's argument for "minute causes," for the eventual effect of actions that now seem trivial.

The epistemological problem posed by this interaction theory of the referent is acute, and it is on this point that J. Hillis Miller focuses in his deconstruction of *Middlemarch*. [25] Miller argues that the novel presents all knowledge as partial (i.e., governed by individual desires and limited to individual perspectives) and that all acts of knowledge (interpretations) change the thing known in the very act of coming to know it. The novel's narrator is in "bad faith" insofar as she claims to transcend the limitations of a particular point of view, especially since her novel demonstrates the impossibility of such transcendence. (And, of course, once a possible knowledge of something transcending the self is denied, then realism as shared public knowledge becomes impossible.) The referents of speech are created by an intersubjective process, but are viewed by individuals from subjective stances. As a result, the novel is full of characters who miss the actual significance of the people and events they encounter. Dorothea misinterprets the intentions and characters of Sir James and Mr. Casaubon; Middlemarch does not understand Lydgate or the necessity for reform; the novel's scholars, Casaubon and Lydgate, fail in their efforts. The complexity of social reality dooms these individual attempts to comprehend it, and surely Miller is right to question the narrator's mastery of that complexity when the novel only portrays characters who cannot master it.

I want to argue, however, that the social reality which functions as the referent in *Middlemarch* is, while complex, not necessarily unknowable. We must remember that individual acts of understanding are socially mediated as much as individual attempts to create social reality are. In other words, Lydgate's story (like Pip's in *Great Expectations)* demonstrates that a man does not simply create himself and cannot simply impose his will on a particular society, shaping it to conform to his vision of how things should be. Similarly, individual acts of comprehension are not purely individualistic. The individual must use categories, concepts, and words given to him by society and its language. Thus Dorothea's early aspirations can be tied to certain "codes" of religious piety, while Rosamond's ideas come, in part, from novels. This sharing of codes already provides the common ground that allows one self to understand and sympathize with another. Thus, in her point-of-view switch,

25. Miller's reading of *Middlemarch* is offered in the two essays cited in note 2 to this chapter.

the narrator stresses Casaubon's similarity to other people: he "was spiritually a-hungered like the rest of us." In stressing the cultural construction of the language we share, extreme individualism is overcome. What Eliot portrays in *Middlemarch* is not the imprisoning of each self in a solipsistic universe, but the fragmentation of a modern world that offers the individual so many different and partial ways to understand his experiences. The characters' misinterpretations are not tied to any absolute necessity of misreading, but to there being "no coherent social faith and order which could perform *the function of knowledge* for the ardently willing soul" (Prelude, my emphasis). The narrator working in this world of multiple "codes" is master of them all, and can show us how two people working out of different "social faiths" misunderstand one another.[26] Social codes, because social, are available to the individual even while their creation and existence are independent of his will. The social nature of language affords, for George Eliot as for Dickens, the possibility of comedy.

Can a "coherent social faith and order" be reestablished? George Eliot sees all the difficulties of the task, but also comes to think that such reestablishment is the proper task of the novelist and the justification of realism. But the realism demanded by this goal is quite different from the realism of *The Mill on the Floss*. The historical novels demonstrate that social reality keeps changing, and the novelist who would adequately describe that reality must adapt her language to those changes. A plain style is not adequate because its meanings lag behind the changes taking place in the world; such language seems doomed to a nostalgic naming of things that are no longer there. In a world of change, language should aim to mirror the process of change in its own processes; language must create novelties as the novelties of the world are created. In other words, the vision of reality found in *Middlemarch* calls for a metaphoric language that introduces new concepts and images into the social world in which language is used.

Metaphor, no matter how strikingly new, is always social insofar as speakers of the language can understand it. If not understandable, it is not metaphor, but nonsense. Metaphoric speech does not, however, "refer" to the world as ordinary "plain" speech does, a point underlined by recalling the description of metaphor in *The Mill on the Floss*: metaphor declares "what a thing is . . . by saying it is something else." A metaphor, since it applies the word in a way that violates its dictionary meaning, only makes sense if the audience is able to adjust its understanding of the word to accommodate its novel use. If a metaphor does succeed in making sense, it functions as a dynamic

26. We know that George Eliot set out to master different social "languages," especially the scientific, to write *Middlemarch*. For discussions of her research and how it comes to be used in the novel, see W. J. Harvey, "The Intellectual Background of the Novel: Casaubon and Lydgate," in *"Middlemarch": Critical Approaches to the Novel*, ed. Barbara Hardy (New York: Oxford University Press, 1967), pp. 25–37; and Robert A. Greenberg, "Plexuses and Ganglia: Scientific Allusion in *Middlemarch*," *NCF* 30 (1975): 33–52.

enactment of the cultural production of meaning that *Middlemarch* has taken as its referent. Since George Eliot, in the historical novels, is interested primarily in how socially held meanings are created, a new interest in visionary or metaphoric language, the direct means by which new meanings are introduced, appears inevitable.[27] Ladislaw's call for a "vague" language as opposed to mimetic painting points toward the change in George Eliot's own attitudes toward language since she wrote *The Mill on the Floss:* "Language gives a fuller image, which is all the better for being vague. After all, the true seeing is within; and painting stares at you with an insistent imperfection. I feel that especially about representations of women. As if a woman were a mere coloured superficies! You must wait for movement and tone. There is a difference in their very breathing: they change from moment to moment" (2:19). The static pictorial image or the word that simply designates an object is not adequate to a reality that "changes from moment to moment."

Middlemarch has many characters who wish to win their fellow citizens over to their particular vision of society and of the future. Mr. Brooke, Bulstrode, Ladislaw, and Lydgate all have a cause to promote. They want to persuade the village to see things in a new way. All of them, with the possible exception of Ladislaw, fail, but that failure does not mean that Eliot disapproves of the attempt.[28] The centrality of politics in her historical novels—and the disheartening fact of political chaos in modern times—can be directly linked to the lack of a "coherent social faith." The realism of *Middlemarch* is based on the belief that men can understand what they make; in Eliot's historical novels, politics is a crucial field of human making. And politics, as practiced by Savonarola, Felix Holt, and Ladislaw, is primarily the linguistic art of persuasion. The politician prepares for novelty by preaching those novelties, by using words to say new things. Ladislaw is a poet before he is a politician, and despite many readers' dissatisfaction with him as a character, I think the novelist sees him as the right husband for her heroine and wants to suggest that Dorothea and Will take up the proper task when they work to further Will's career in political persuasion.

27. My discussion of metaphor here is greatly influenced by Paul Ricoeur's *The Rule of Metaphor,* trans. Robert Czerny (Toronto: University of Toronto Press, 1977). For a short summary of Ricoeur's work on metaphor, see his essay "The Metaphorical Process as Cognition, Imagination and Feeling," *Critical Inquiry* 5 (1978): 143–59. U. C. Knoepflmacher's excellent essay "Fusing Fact and Myth: The New Reality of *Middlemarch,*" in *This Particular Web: Essays on "Middlemarch,"* ed. Ian Adam (Toronto: University of Toronto Press, 1975), pp. 43–72, discusses, in ways that obviously parallel my argument here, George Eliot's more complex vision of reality in *Middlemarch* and the consequent need to develop a more "fluid," metaphoric language.

28. The reasons for their failures and the lessons such failures are meant to teach others who might pursue the same task are outside the scope of my discussion here. It seems characteristic of George Eliot's fiction that she demonstrates the complexity of certain undertakings by portraying characters who fail where she hopes to succeed.

The distinction between plain language and metaphoric language, and the way in which the latter might be seen as more "realistic," can be considered once more by discussing the relative positions of Mary Garth and Dorothea Brooke in *Middlemarch*. (Interestingly, the two characters are kept apart, never meeting in the course of the narrative.) *Middlemarch* is not entirely free of the nostalgia we found in *The Mill on the Floss*. There was a time when Theresas were aided by a coherent social faith. There was a time when epic was possible. As long as the writer cherishes a past to which her characters and the modern world cannot return, her historical novels will be burdened by a protest against their very subject: the fact and necessity of change. Mary Garth is allowed to live in the nostalgic and unchanged world of childhood in a way Maggie Tulliver was not. Significantly, Mary explains her constancy to Fred Vincy in terms of adherence to a familiar language. "It would make too great a difference [not to love one another]—like seeing all the old places altered, and changing the name for everything" (8:86). The old names are adequate because Mary is granted immunity from the very fact of change that the novel demonstrates is inevitable.

Yet Dorothea, although denied Mary's peaceful ending and sent into exile from her native town, is more central to the novel; and Dorothea's heroism, her acceptance of modernity (with its constant change and its lack of a coherent social faith), indicates that *Middlemarch,* unlike *The Mill on the Floss,* is more concerned with looking forward than with looking back. The whole novel is based on the premise that the provincial world it describes is dead (killed by the Reform Bill and the railroad), and that world is examined to find the indications of its descendant's birth. While Mary is concerned to keep the same name for everything, Dorothea is attempting to find new names for things. Mrs. Cadawallader expresses the opinion of Middlemarch when she tells Dorothea, "We have all got to exert ourselves a little to keep sane, and call things by the same name as other people call them by." To which Dorothea retorts, "I have never called everything by the same name that all the people about me did" (6:54).

This independence is both Dorothea's strength and her weakness, a measure of her distance from the common and of her modernity. Dorothea's use of her own names for things, her indulgence of her imagination, will not be punished as Maggie's similar traits were. *Middlemarch* fully admits the limitations of the world's Mrs. Cadawalladers, and finds in imaginations like Dorothea's new contents. George Eliot would like everyone to call things by the same names, but not by the names Mrs. Cadawallader and Middlemarch would use. The historical novels indicate the complexities of the process by which things acquire names. Only metaphoric language, which mimics that process, can offer us access to the ways in which social reality is constituted. And this metaphoric language of art, in its presentation of the foundations of thought and of codemaking, carries with it the possibility of generating a future society in which human needs are better served than at present.

George Eliot's later novels hold, as their rhetorical (read "political" or "moral") purpose, the desire to create that "coherent social faith" by which the social realities of the future, the new referents of speech, might be constructed and understood. The novelist cannot produce these changes herself, which is why her novels (like Dickens's) are addressed to the society that must join her in building this envisioned future. The Victorian unwillingness to grant the individual power to remake the world makes Dorothea and Will's apparent failure no surprise; even while completely sympathetic with their undertaking, Eliot finds it extremely difficult to envision its success.

In *Daniel Deronda* the hero not only steps out of the world of everyday England, but even discovers a concrete alternative to that world. The process of discovery requires an exercise of sympathetic imagination and gains Deronda participation in a new community that offers a fuller and more satisfying life. Deronda, like Dorothea, is not bound by the names the whole world uses, in contrast to Gwendolen Harleth, who is fatally limited by "not being one of the exceptional persons who have a parching thirst for a perfection undemanded by their neighbours."[29] At issue in the novel are the means by which such "perfection" can be known.

Daniel Deronda has certainly elicited more complaints from readers than any other major nineteenth-century novel.[30] Its author's grand ambitions and mature command of her art make the novel impossible to ignore (as *Romola,* or even *Felix Holt,* are ignored), but few have been satisfied by the triumph granted to Deronda and withheld from Gwendolen. I will argue here that this dissatisfaction results from Eliot's final refusal to grant the imagination autonomy; in *Middlemarch* she could suggest that men create their world because a concrete description of that new creation does not fall within the compass of the novel. In *Daniel Deronda,* however, Eliot falls back on a preexisting reality that knowledge uncovers as opposed to a new world that imagination creates. The novel proceeds as if the issue is the development of a new human

29. *Daniel Deronda,* ed. Barbara Hardy (Baltimore: Penguin Books, 1967), bk. 1, chap. 6. Subsequent references are to this edition, with book and chapter numbers given parenthetically in the text.

30. Leavis's complaint in *The Great Tradition* is, of course, famous; Henry James, quite ingeniously, pays tribute to Eliot's intelligence and good intentions, while also raising the same complaints as Leavis plus some, by couching his discussion of the novel in dialogue form. See "*Daniel Deronda:* A Conversation," in *George Eliot: A Collection of Critical Essays,* ed. George R. Creeger (Englewood Cliffs, N.J.: Prentice-Hall, 1970), pp. 161–76. More recent complaints include Cynthia Chase's deconstruction of the novel, "The Decomposition of the Elephants: Double-Reading *Daniel Deronda,*" *PMLA* 93 (1978): 215–27, and Nancy Pell's excellent feminist reading in "The Fathers' Daughters in *Daniel Deronda,*" *NCF* 36 (1982): 424–51. Chase faults the novel for making Daniel's desire to be Jewish "cause" the fact of his Jewishness, while Pell probes Eliot's inability to grant Gwendolen the happy ending given to Deronda.

vision, but then the terms are radically altered as an independent and transcendent reality is revealed to the hero. Both Deronda and Gwendolen are "molested" by this greater reality, Deronda positively in having his true identity and vocation revealed to him, Gwendolen negatively in the discovery that her narrow vision has left her vulnerable to truths of which she was unaware. In order to gain knowledge of reality, the novel finally relies on direct knowledge, in violation of the narrative's general reliance on mediated knowledge.

The doctrine that knowledge is always mediated derives from the novel's insistence that knowledge is a social product. From the very beginning, Gwendolen's understanding of herself is always based on how the world reacts to her. Her limited understanding results, in large part, from her having been exposed to such a narrow set of observers. With the exception of her brief encounter with Daniel at the gaming tables, Gwendolen's interview with Klesmer is her "first experience of being taken on some other ground than that of her social rank and her beauty" (3:23). She is unable, however, to accommodate herself to Daniel's and Klesmer's more exacting standards; she only wants to know those things about herself that gratify her vanity. Only after her marriage will she become more open to that valuable source of information: the disapproval of others. "No chemical process shows a more wonderful activity than the transforming influence of the thoughts we imagine to be going on in another. Changes in theory, religion, admirations, may begin with asuspicion of dissent or disapproval, even when the grounds of disapproval are but matter of searching conjecture" (5:35). The vital necessity is to transcend one's own settled point of view in order to learn something new; whether the stimulus to such transcendence is real hardly matters.

Thus Daniel is led by another (his tutor) to reconsider his own position in the world, to think about how he might be viewed by others. The results of Daniel's meditations, while factually false, are highly beneficial because he develops the habit of contemplating an event from the possible perspective of another. He comes to possess "a subdued fervour of sympathy, an activity of imagination on behalf of others" (2:16). The word *sympathy* becomes associated with Daniel; almost every major description of him in the novel includes that term. And sympathy becomes the point where knowledge and morality meet when Daniel lectures Gwendolen on directing her life according to an awareness of needs beyond her own. "Some real knowledge would give you an interest in the world beyond the small drama of personal desires. It is the curse of your life—forgive me—of so many lives, that all passion is spent in that narrow round, for want of ideas and sympathies to make a larger home for it" (5:36).

In this joining of morality with knowledge Eliot must limit the autonomy of the imagination. The practice of sympathetically enlarging one's view of the world in no way determines the kind of new knowledge gained. One's knowledge (like Gwendolen's) will be largely determined by the company one keeps. Access to new people will provide new contents. But Eliot wants to insist that some kinds of knowledge are both more real and more moral than other kinds. She seeks to establish the necessity of possessing certain kinds of knowledge (primarily the knowledge of one's own relative insignificance and of the importance of sympathy) and to establish a hierarchical distinction between lower and higher kinds of knowledge. If we are merely required to be open to new experiences and to others' perspectives, no criteria exist for valuing Daniel's thoughts over Sir Hugo Mallinger's. But Eliot's morality requires her to blame Gwendolen for heeding her neighbors' opinions while failing to confront the diminished image of herself provided by Klesmer's and Daniel's judgments. In presenting the Eliot philosophy of sympathy to Gwendolen, Daniel defines such transcendence of self as the entry point to "the higher, the religious life, which holds an enthusiasm for something more than our own appetites and vanities" (5:36).

Eliot is only entitled to such a distinction between higher and lower realms of experience if she assumes an ordering of creation independent of men and their knowledge. Knowledge gained through social processes of mediation cannot yield such a distinction. Like all the Victorians, Eliot sees no way to retain morality if she abandons the notion of a prior order to which knowledge and action must conform. In *Middlemarch,* Eliot had gone much further than most of her Victorian contemporaries in declaring the ability of imagination to fashion a world, but in *Daniel Deronda* she retreats in front of the full consequences of such imaginative potency. She becomes almost Carlylean in her pronouncements about a reality that will overwhelm mere human constructions, and she returns to an epistemology of revelation to explain how we know the preordained nature of the world.[31] If "the truth seems highly improbable," that is because it is "different from the habitual lazy combinations begotten by our wishes" (3:22). Our attempts to evade the hard facts can only succeed temporally. In the long run, none can "escape suffering from the pressure of that unaccommodating Actual, which has never consulted our taste and is entirely unselect" (4:33). Our failure to know the "Actual" stems from the reprehensible blindness that characterizes egotism. "The most obstinate beliefs that mortals entertain about themselves are such as they have no evidence for beyond a constant, spontaneous pulsing of their self-satisfaction —as it were a hidden seed of madness, a confidence that they can move the world without precise notion of standing-place or lever" (3:23).

31. Mary Wilson Carpenter, "The Apocalypse of the Old Testament: *Daniel Deronda* and the Interpretation of Interpretation," *PMLA* 99 (1984): 56–71, argues much more strongly than I do here for considering *Daniel Deronda* an apocalyptic novel. Certainly Eliot's desire for a revelation that will transform the world of present-day England has become so strong by the time she writes her last novel that she adopts a more completely biblical and apocalyptic rhetoric (reminiscent of Carlyle and Ruskin) than in any of her previous novels.

This appeal to reality moves Eliot away from the belief that the real is created by social construct. Gwendolen has a "better self" (3:23)—an essential being that does not need to be created and to which she should pay heed. Her interaction with Deronda will not forge that self, but merely act to reveal it to her. Gwendolen wonders if Deronda "had some way of looking at things which might be a new footing for her," and the narrator goes on to comment, "It is one of the secrets in that change of mental poise which has been fitly named conversion, that to many among us neither heaven nor earth has any revelation till some personality touches theirs with a peculiar influence, subduing them into receptiveness" (5:35). While making great claims for the difference contact with another can make, this passage stops short of envisioning the creation of new realities. Instead, the passivity of "receptiveness" (a state into which the misled self must be "subdued") emphasizes that existing facts can be revealed to the self through another's ability to shift its habitual point of view. By retaining a model of revelation here, Eliot greatly reduces the power granted to imagination. Reality exists prior to any act of imagination, which is limited to generating new modes of perceiving the real.

What has bothered critics of the novel is that Eliot seems prepared to make far greater claims for the imagination, only to lose her nerve in the end.[32] The historical novels, as I have argued, present history as the field of human making, and *Daniel Deronda* quite explicitly takes up the question of how to create a suitable future. In the visionary Mordecai we are given a portrait of the romantic seer, a man who is reaching beyond the boundaries of the known to bring new contents into human life. Like a Carlylean poet-hero, Mordecai widens perception beyond the normal "formulas." "Were not men of ardent zeal and far-reaching hope everywhere exceptional?—the men who had the visions which . . . were the creators and feeders of the world—moulding and feeding the more passive life which without them would dwindle and shrivel into the narrow tenacity of insects, unshaken by thoughts beyond the reaches of their antennae" (7:55). But Eliot, like Carlyle, attributes these "visions" to the poet's seeing further into reality than other men, not to the poet's genera-

32. Cynthia Chase has outlined most completely the reversal at the end of the novel in which the future that Daniel has been creating for himself through imagination suddenly becomes a historical fact (his Jewish identity) that has always been true. I want to suggest that Eliot is drawn to the idea of a creative imagination but that she must, finally, repudiate such creativity because she cannot tolerate the possibility of "arbitrary" constructions, unanswerable to preexistent "facts." Peter Dale has written the most intelligent recent defense of the novel. In "Symbolic Representation and the Means of Revolution in *Daniel Deronda,*" *Victorian Newsletter* 59 (1981): 25–31, Dale argues that Eliot's last two novels move away from a "positivistic" desire to link words to things and toward a presentation of "the image . . . not as a sign for something else, but as a simple concentration of spiritual energy that exerts a force on another consciousness" (28). By focusing on the image's rhetorical power, its ability to influence the behavior of others, Dale is able to sidestep the issue of Eliot's need to have the image also stand for something real. But, certainly, Dale's sympathetic reading does suggest what Eliot was trying to accomplish in her later work.

ting a new world. The imagination in *Daniel Deronda* does not create novelties, but uncovers (reveals) deep truths that for various reasons (primarily, egotism) have remained hidden.

The world of the novel is Platonic; things and people have an essential, preexisting identity that knowledge must strive to seek out. Gwendolen is blamed for not discovering her "better self," acting instead on a false egotistic notion of her identity; Daniel is rewarded for so persistently refusing to act until his true identity is revealed to him. As Alan Mintz writes, "Deronda's transcendence puts him beyond the problem of vocation . . . unlike Lydgate, Deronda *is* his vocation."[33] Given this Platonic structure, it is inevitable that Daniel's investigations should lead him into the past (his preexistent identity) even as he strives to envision a future. The future's difference from the present will only rest on a new understanding of what has always been real, not on some new fact. The novel even shares the Platonic antitheatrical prejudice. Since one's essential identity carries with it certain obligations (the grounds for one's proper vocation), the self often willfully evades recognizing that identity. Play-acting, in the case of Gwendolen, Daniel's mother, and Hans Meyrick, takes on such an evasive function, while Mirah's virtue is proved by her being such a poor actress. Her lack of talent is attributed to her having "no notion of being anybody but herself" (3:20).

Imagination in *Daniel Deronda,* then, plays essentially the same role as it does in *Sartor Resartus.* Mordecai, as a man of vision, offers an insight into a reality most men cannot perceive. And, as in Carlyle and Ruskin, the visionary's perceptions of those further reaches are hardly clear. "Mordecai's mind wrought so constantly in images, that his coherent trains of thought often resembled the significant dreams attributed to sleepers by waking persons in their most inventive moments; nay, they often resembled genuine dreams in their way of breaking off the passage from the known to the unknown" (5:38). The images in which Mordecai thinks are valiant efforts to represent a world most difficult to grasp; they are the manifestations of "the passionate current of an ideal life striving to embody itself" (5:38). The struggle to find a place for the "ideal" components of thought and imagination within the material world in which they must be embodied dominates *Daniel Deronda* as it does *The Mill on the Floss,* but in the later novel a larger space for the contents of imagination is opened up in the world of experience.

In her endorsement of Mordecai's images as clues to the highest and most important reality, George Eliot has left her early positivist leanings far behind. Imagination becomes the crucial means by which reality makes its fullest appearance. Maggie Tulliver's departures from direct perception and actual memories to indulge her imaginative fancies cannot compare in extravagance

33. *George Eliot and the Novel of Vocation* (Cambridge: Harvard University Press, 1978), p. 163.

to Daniel's and Mordecai's visions. But Eliot is willing to defend her later heroes and to allow the world to accommodate their fondest hopes in ways unsuited to the prevailing ethos of *The Mill on the Floss*. Since all our representations of the world are potentially mistaken, the narrator in *Daniel Deronda* argues, there is no reason to privilege scientific reasoning over passionate imagining. "No formulas for thinking will save us mortals from mistake in our imperfect apprehension of the matter to be thought about. And since the unemotional intellect may carry us into a mathematical dreamland where nothing is but what is not, perhaps an emotional intellect may have absorbed into its passionate vision of possibilities some truth of what will be. . . . At any rate, presumptions to the contrary are not to be trusted" (6:41).

Needless to say, the epistemological agnosticism of the preceding statement reflects Eliot's recognition of the limited claims to which logic entitles her, not her actual sentiments. She believes imagination can open up new visions of the real, visions that might allow a more general sharing in Daniel's earned ability to experience one of "those rare moments when our yearnings and our acts can be completely one" (8:63). And Eliot also believes we can know when imagination's visions have revealed actual possibilities, and when its visions offer deluded hopes that could never be realized. The ability to distinguish between the two opens the way for a possible successful marriage between mind and world. Daniel's commonsensical insistence that some things must be accepted as unalterable while others should be changed by human action surely represents the author's sentiments, although we must note that he is hardly specific about which things belong to which category. "There will still remain the degrees of inevitableness in relation to our own will and acts, and the degrees of wisdom in hastening or retarding; there will still remain the danger of mistaking a tendency which should be resisted for an inevitable law that we must adjust ourselves to" (6:42).

Imagination affords that power to adjust which makes change for the better possible. But to insure that change is neither willful nor random Eliot must locate it within a larger structure of determinate reality, that "degree of inevitableness" no human act or wish can overcome. Her need to submit her most passionate visions to that reality links Eliot to the other writers I discuss in this book.

7

Of Truth and Lies in Browning's Poetry

I've told my lie
And seen truth follow, marvels none of mine
("Mr. Sludge, 'The Medium' ")

A short discussion of Browning's poetry can serve as a last overview of Victorian attitudes toward issues of representation and truth before considering the ways in which Yeats's work both derives from and differs from that of the Victorians. Browning shares with Dickens and George Eliot a vision of social reality that limits the validity of the individual's point of view by placing it in a larger intersubjective context. But Browning also feels a need for the more spiritual vision of reality that is found in the work of Rossetti, Carlyle, and Ruskin. In the dramatic monologues Browning develops a species of irony that allows him to point toward higher truths without ever stating them directly; the monologues stand as perhaps the most brilliant and sustained use of indirection within the Victorian period. But Browning is less capable of accepting the rigorous abstention from certain knowledge imposed by irony when he writes his longer poems. *The Ring and the Book* both uses and transcends the ironic perspective that governs the monologues. The poet finally relies on revealed truth to legitimize condemnation of the murderer, Count Guido Franceschini, and establish beyond reasonable doubt the purity of his murdered wife, Pompilia.

Browning's monologues plunge us into a world in which no words are trustworthy. "My first thought was, he lied in every word"[1]—so begins "Childe Roland to the Dark Tower Came," and the suspicion of the "hoary cripple" manifested by the poem's speaker is a suspicion the reader would do well to adopt in evaluating any of Browning's speakers. Lies are language used by a speaker to further his own purposes, words which, unconnected to any true state of affairs, are constructions of that speaker's imagination. The undetected lie is never called a lie; undetected, the lie passes as another example of ordinary language, as referring to some fact about the world. The lie finds its name only when the listener discerns that the speaker's words are shaped

---

1. All passages from the shorter poems are taken from *Robert Browning: The Poems,* vol. 1, ed. John Pettigrew and Thomas J. Collins (New Haven: Yale University Press, 1981). Passages from *The Ring and the Book* are from *The Ring and the Book,* ed. Richard D. Altick (New Haven: Yale University Press, 1981). Line numbers for the shorter poems, and book and line numbers for *The Ring and the Book,* are given parenthetically in the text.

according to the speaker's needs and not in relation to some real existent conditions.

To the liar, both the listener and reality are a threat. Either one, and especially the two in conjunction, threaten the success of the lie. The lie aspires to completeness, a self-sufficiency of words to themselves that is "molested" by reference to a reality beyond words as a standard to assess their truth value. In Browning's dramatic monologues, the speaker is often a liar. Even where the word *liar* might seem too strong, the speaker is often attempting to use words to alter radically his listener's perception of and attitude toward certain things, most notably the speaker himself. The speaker hopes that the world presented by his words will be taken as "real," just as the liar wants his words to be taken as "true." The success of Browning's speakers is limited, however. The monologues, while allowing their speakers a certain amount of control over language and its shaping of a world that suits the speakers' purposes, almost always contain some principle by which the speaker's control can be "molested," his altering of facts for his own ends detected.

Mastery over language and the transformation of life into art afford the speakers in many Browning poems a stay against the chaos of a world that acts independently of individual desire. The need behind the lies in these poems is the need for control, and we often first encounter Browning's characters in positions where their control is threatened, where they need something from the person they are addressing. (Various independent realities in the world will prove resistant to control, with social reality—the fact of other people who possess their own individual wills—an important factor, but not the only one.) Andrea Del Sarto wants his wife to spend the evening with him; Fra Lippo Lippi needs to persuade the guard to keep his nocturnal excursion a secret; Blougram tries to win over his young critic; Mr. Sludge has to placate his patron. The listener possesses a certain power since he can deny the speaker something the speaker wants. The listener must be won over, must be made to see the world as the speaker does, and thus fall in line with the speaker's wishes. The poems are presented as acts of persuasion;[2] an argument is put forward, usually with a fairly clear goal, and the reader, like the supposed listener, is expected to pass judgment.[3]

"Fra Lippo Lippi" is fairly straightforward in this respect. The painter offers the circumstances of his induction into the monastery as his excuse for not adhering strictly to the rules of his order. He also appeals to the same

2. On strategies of presentation in Browning, see W. David Shaw, *The Dialectical Temper* (Ithaca: Cornell University Press, 1968). Robert F. Garrat, in "Browning's Dramatic Monologue: The Strategy of the Double Mask," *VP* 11 (1973): 115–26, offers an extended discussion of how Browning's speakers adopt a mask in relation to their particular situations and listeners.

3. Robert Langbaum, in *The Poetry of Experience* (New York: W. W. Norton, 1963), chap. 2, introduced the concept of "judgment" as a key definitive feature of the dramatic monologue.

childhood experiences to defend his "realistic" art, which has been criticized by his superiors. (We feel this second argument is addressed more to the readers of the poem than to the night watchmen of Florence.) The friar's success is fairly complete; the watchmen will keep his secret, and the reader, in general, approves of both the man and his aesthetic. The style of the poem approaches the colloquial, and this mitigates our suspicion that the friar's language is crafted with a calculated effort to mold his audience. A plain style proves, paradoxically, a good rhetorical strategy; words that do not seem carefully shaped to persuade often prove the most persuasive.

This last paradox must inform any reading of "My Last Duchess." Our admiration of the duke's rhetorical genius is based on two elements not present in "Fra Lippo Lippi." The duke can tell his story indirectly, and the duke can make his rhetorical point indirectly. The second indirection depends on the first. The story of the previous wife's death is told through the painting; the whole point—the duke's expectations of his next wife—is conveyed through the story of the last duchess. The duke is in complete control of each phrase he uses. (Much of our pleasure when reading the poem is recognizing and appreciating that control.) His language is able to say exactly what he wants to say without ever descending to the crudity of actually stating that meaning outright.[4] Yet, and we come back to the paradox here, such absolute control puts the listener on guard. The duke's subtlety makes the listener and the reader look for hidden motives and purposes in a way that Fra Lippo Lippi's directness does not. The duke's great care about what he says suggests that there exists something behind speech that he is determined not to reveal. And the assumption is that what is hidden must be hidden for a reason.

The duke's care with words, calling for an equal attention to those words on the listener's part, places a new stress on interpretation. Language must be examined and studied to uncover the meanings it carries. Browning's obsession with language's function as the medium of interaction between men links him to the Victorian novelists; a world independent of the speaker is created in the process in which his words are interpreted by others, often in ways he never intended. The confrontation between selves implied by such a process is never far from the surface in the dramatic monologues. The auditor is a threat because he might break through the words offered by the duke to an interpretation that locates the duke's attitudes and actions within an entirely different context. The duke's monologue creates a world, like the lie, in which everything is ordered completely in relation to the sensibility and desires of the speaker. But the listener might not accept that offered world as valid. The speaker must placate and persuade the listener, must locate his audience as well within that world being created in speech.

4. Of course, the duke does say "I choose never to stoop" outright, but generally is able to avoid such directness, as in the famous "I gave commands; / Then all smiles stopped together."

Browning's speakers manifest a veiled hostility toward their listeners. This other, who must be carefully managed, may refuse to play his or her assigned role. Both Mr. Sludge and Andrea Del Sarto alternately debase themselves in front of their audience and attack that audience as the source of their troubles. Sludge justifies his own lies and his manipulation of his patron as a response to the patron's attempts to use the medium. "You used me? / Have not I used you, taken full revenge" (583–84). The clash of wills is almost Nietzschean here, as befits a world in which the self attempts to manipulate all realities (including other people) to serve his own needs. Andrea's wife wins out over the painter, while the battle between Sludge and his patron is not resolved within the limits of the poem. As we would expect, Sludge is full of contempt for lesser wills, deriding the "fools" who have been taken in by his table-rappings. At the same time, he fears and hates his patron, who seems to be emerging from his former gullibility and now refuses to be taken in entirely by Sludge's monologue.

The poem ends with Sludge plotting his revenge, yet aware that he must leave his patron's hometown. The medium consoles himself with the thought that his patron can be fooled and, if not, the world is full of other fools. The refusal to grant the other an ability to think and plan, the reduction of others to fools, implies the denial of their full reality. Sludge recognizes that some such process of dehumanization has occurred to him—he has been "treated," he says, "as a showman's ape" (600)—and part of his revenge is his reversal of that process. Sludge declares himself the only reality in the world.

> What do I know or care about your world
> Which either is or seems to be? This snap
> O' my fingers, sir! My care is for myself;
> Myself am whole and sole reality
> Inside a raree-show and a market-mob
> Gathered about it: that's the use of things. (906–11)

The Ring and the Book, with its more direct statement of Browning's principles, makes the more immediate fallacy of Mr. Sludge's viewpoint clear. Even as a strategy for deceiving others, forgetting their humanity will not serve the villain well. The Pope comments on Count Guido's failed plan to trick Pompilia's "parents": "Thus schemes / Guido, and thus would carry out his scheme: / But when an obstacle first blocks the path, / When he finds none may boast monopoly / Of lies and trick i' the tricking lying world" (10.-572–76). Failure to remember that the other can plot and scheme independently of our scheming can only insure defeat. The final result stems from the interaction between Guido's schemes and those of Pompilia's parents.

The attempt to evade the reality of the other as an active agent in the world recurs throughout the monologues. "My Last Duchess" offers a prime example. The duchess's vitality, that "spot of joy" on her cheek that offends the duke so much when she is alive, makes her portrait a striking one. The duke can enjoy the blush when it exists within his control (only he grants access to the painting). The static thing, the work of art, can be controlled in a way the living person cannot be. The logic of dehumanization is, ultimately, the logic of murder. The other who cannot be manipulated must be murdered or else that other will destroy the world the speaker has constructed. The only way to keep reality totally within one's power, to prevent its creation by an intersubjective process that transcends the self, is to be alone in the world, or to surround oneself with completely passive others. "Porphyria's Lover" murders Porphyria because he believes that her future actions will destroy this perfect moment they enjoy now.

But the speaker, even while viewing the other as a threat, needs the other. The speaker's constructed world lacks substance if others are not witnesses to it. A total escape from social reality is unsatisfying. Browning's speakers want a world that is entirely self-made but is also peopled. The murdered duchess remains in the duke's world as a portrait, as a semblance of another who shares that world with him. Similarly, Porphyria's lover still sits with the body of his beloved and will continue to sit with her until someone from the outside world arrives. But we assume that the satisfaction offered by the painting or the corpse cannot last long. We learn of the last duchess and her fate during the duke's search for a new duchess, a new witness to his world. In the context of the duke's monologue, the portrait of the late duchess functions as both an example and a warning, an example insofar as the new wife should be like the portrait (a dead thing) in offering no resistance to the duke's whims, a warning insofar as the new wife will be, like her predecessor, reduced to a portrait if she does not act like one. The duke needs a living witness to his world, even while fearing one, and his monologue is aimed at protecting himself before-hand from too much vitality in that witness. This self-protective motive parallels the self-protection already implicit in his mastery of language. The poem's auditor, the envoy from the bride's father, is also a witness to the duke's world, one whom the duke treats most carefully. The self's lack of power, its inability to create reality entirely on its own, is obliquely acknowledged in this fear of the other.

"Andrea Del Sarto" presents the other side of this attempt to control the other. Andrea has painted his wife countless times, but still cannot make her be what he wants her to be. Looking at her, he wishes he could turn her into a work of art. "Let my hands frame your face in your hair's gold, / You beautiful Lucrezia that are mine!" (175–76). But the poem reveals how little Lucrezia is his, how she keeps stepping out of the frame within which he would enclose her. Andrea, whose art is perfect, must face up to the messiness of life. He knows his art is "lifeless" precisely because its perfection never hints at the disorder, the lack of clarity, of the real. The perfection of his art suppresses the excesses, the resistance to form and order, that characterize the "otherness" of other people and of that reality that stands against our desires. Reality is larger than any individual human attempt to comprehend it (for Browning), so that Andrea's seeming mastery of reality must be shallow, must reflect an inability to abandon himself to the incalculable world beyond himself.

Andrea's artistic failure is tied to his having chosen to live life, not art. He has married the Madonna of his paintings, and the implication is that art has become for him a retreat from the chaos of living into a world of sterile order and perfection. The more exalted art of Raphael and Michelangelo, in contrast, displays an activity in which form struggles with chaos. Andrea is, finally, humble in the face of his inability to control the other, his wife, who thwarts his desires. He feels he has gotten what he deserves. "Yes, / You loved me quite enough, it seems to-night" (257–58). His fate justly reflects his crimes (stealing Francois's money, letting his parents die in poverty), his lack of artistic vision, and, most of all, his attempt to bring the order and perfection of art into life (by marrying his model), instead of infusing art with some of the vital disorder of life. The poem ends with Andrea's wife walking out of the world the artist has tried to construct in his monologue. He has not succeeded in getting her to play the role he has assigned to her.

Both "My Last Duchess" and "Andrea Del Sarto" revolve around the attempt to control the other and reality itself by transforming life into art. Again and again in Browning's poems, art and life are presented as distinct, with art seen as a willful human construction in contrast to a reality that transcends individual control. That reality, as in *Great Expectations* and *Middlemarch*, is, at times, portrayed as the social world created by the interaction of men with one another. But certain "facts" about the world, as well as confrontation with an other, can also explode the pretense to self-sufficiency of Browning's speakers.

Browning uses the nineteenth-century "discovery of time" as one example of reality's following laws that do not necessarily coincide with human wishes. The fact that reality inevitably changes necessitates changes in our views of the world.[5] Yet the visions of control entertained by the speakers are almost always static. The constructed worlds of art and of the lie are presented as if they manifest what will always be the case. Reality proves threatening because contact with it might require altering or abandoning the constructions of imagination. "The Statue and the Bust" offers a perfect example of characters unwilling to test their vision of reality against reality itself. Perhaps their

---

5. The best discussion of Browning's attitudes toward time, a discussion to which I am indebted here, is J. W. Harper's " 'Eternity Our Due': Time in the Poetry of Robert Browning," in *Victorian Poetry*, Stratford-upon-Avon Studies no. 15 (London: Edward Arnold, 1972), pp. 59–87.

love affair would not be the joy they imagine it would be, so the lovers never act upon their fantasies. Instead, as a logical consequence of their actions (or, more properly, their failure to act), they have themselves made into works of art, the statue and the bust, frozen in the static position of entertaining eternally a desire that never changes, yet is never acted upon. We might say these lovers not only see the other as a threat, but themselves as well. They guard against the possibility of their feelings ever changing by existing in the same anticipatory moment for years.

Reality finally breaks in at the moment when they each, seeing their own reflections, realize they have grown old, a realization that inspires their decision to make themselves eternal in art. Art achieves a completion that the moment in time never enjoys, since the moment's location in a sequence that contains other moments shows that one moment does not contain everything in itself. Art not only freezes the instant, but also extracts it from time and concentrates all that is presented of the thing into that one manifestation. Thus, all we have of the duchess is the portrait, all we have of the lovers is the statue and the bust. The bishop of St. Praxed's is so concerned about his tomb because he knows that the tomb is the form he will assume for eternity. Whatever is not expressed in the tomb, he will not be. The temptation of art is the artist's power to choose what aspect of a thing will be presented, what the representation will express, and what aspects and interpretations will be suppressed.

So many of Browning's speakers are artists—Andrea Del Sarto, Fra Lippo Lippi, Cleon, the various musicians—that the reader is bound to consider the monologues as meditations on the status and nature of art.[6] These speakers who turn the other into an artifact are also packaging themselves. They not only select what to present, but also present it as if it were all that can be said on the subject. The artist organizes and presents meaning, and the artist who wishes to control his audience and its interpretations of the world will attempt to govern completely what meanings the audience derives from his work. In the monologues, Browning works to undermine his speakers' control over the interpretation of their words, and this undermining functions, as we shall see, as a crucial element in establishing the reader's relation to Browning's own art. The speaker who so actively strives to shape the world and his listener's perception of the world must finally be rendered passive— at the mercy of the listener and of reality. Browning's speakers often offer instances of the romantic imagination gone mad; they impute to themselves a power to create the world that the poet finally denies to them.

6. I have found Harold Bloom's numerous discussions of the status of art and the artist in Browning's work the most thought-provoking treatments of this subject. See *The Ringers in the Tower* (Chicago: University of Chicago Press, 1971), pp. 157–68; *A Map of Misreading* (New York: Oxford University Press, 1975); and *Poetry and Repression* (New Haven: Yale University Press, 1976), pp. 175–204. For an excellent discussion of Browning's views of art's proper function, see David J. DeLaura, "The Context of Browning's Painter Poems: Aesthetics, Polemics, Historics," *PMLA* 95 (1980): 367–88.

The social nature of language offers the first limit to the speaker's control. To take the extreme example of the lie again, the lie only works (i.e., is not called a lie) so long as the listener takes the utterance to be what the speaker intends him to take it to be, namely a supposed statement of fact. When the listener apprehends the lie in some other way, he has eluded the stance the speaker intended him to take. The monologues, on several levels, illustrate the rule that words, once spoken, take up a public existence that is to some extent independent of their originating speaker. Words attract a scrutiny over which the speaker has limited control. The same holds true for the work of art. It is viewed and judged by an audience that can think for itself.

Examples of the speaker's language revealing more than or something other than what the speaker intended to reveal occur throughout the monologues. Fra Lippo Lippi's three references to the prior's niece point to an infatuation he never makes explicit; the bishop of St. Praxed's opening invocation—"Vanity, saith the preacher, vanity!"—reads as an unintended pun. More generally, several of the poems function as wholes to convey meanings beyond the speaker's control. In other words, and this is no new thought, the structure of the monologues is ironic.[7] Reading "My Last Duchess," "The Bishop Orders His Tomb," "Johannes Agricola in Meditation," and other Browning poems, the reader is able to derive a sense of the speaker's personality that is independent of the image the speaker intends to project. Andrea Del Sarto states this principle simply when he says, "I am judged" (78). The speaker's words, like Andrea's paintings, exist in the world, open to criticism. And, of course, the similarity between the speaker and works of art is heightened by the fact that Browning's speakers are artifacts; they exist within poems. In the process of judgment that follows the presentations, the artist or speaker is likely to be surprised to discover what his work reveals. The reader "knows" the bishop of St. Praxed's or Johannes Agricola in a way they do not know themselves.

The ironic structure of the monologues is built primarily on a strict notion of overdetermination, but opens out to a more mystical acknowledgment of indeterminacy. In relying on a notion of overdetermination, Browning's irony is akin to George Eliot's (although with the vast difference that Eliot's narrators usually express their ironic understanding of a situation directly whereas Browning's irony is always only implied). Just as George Eliot allows the reader to see the many causes of a character's behavior that the character himself cannot see (Casaubon and Lydgate are but two obvious examples), Browning directs us as readers toward uncovering a finite set of

7. The best general discussion of the ironic structure of dramatic monologues is Alan Sinfield, *Dramatic Monologue* (London: Methuen, 1977), chaps. 1–3. For more specific discussions of irony in Browning, see Michael Mason, "Browning and the Dramatic Monologue," in *Robert Browning,* ed. Isobel Armstrong (Athens: Ohio University Press, 1975), pp. 231–66; and F. E. L. Priestly, "Some Aspects of Browning's Irony," in *Browning's Mind and Art,* ed. Clarence Tracy (London: Oliver and Boyd, 1968), pp. 123–42.

causes that determine the speaker's words and actions.[8] The assumption is that the speaker himself can never be in control of or aware of all these causes, and that the listener or reader will, at times, recognize causes the speaker cannot or does not wish to acknowledge.[9] The irony here is close to dramatic irony; the audience (reader) enjoys a position of superior knowledge relative to the actor (speaker). While the speaker is not entirely in control of the meaning of his actions and utterances, there is a true meaning to those actions, a meaning that is accessible to another.

Fra Lippo Lippi's belief in realistic portrayal is a perfect example of overdetermination. The painter offers a genetic explanation (his childhood in the streets), a religious justification (the goodness and beauty of all things created by God), and an intellectual argument (art serves to awaken us to the beauty of the ordinary) to explain his artistic practices. But his whole speech and situation offer the reader two other causes for his aesthetic: the painter's carnality and his need to rebel against the superiors who would suppress that carnality. The friar is aware of his sensual nature—"I'm a beast, I know" (270) —and, although less explicit about it, certainly knows that he dislikes the prior, but he never links these facts to his art; that link is left to the reader to supply. Similarly, various reasons for the duke of Ferrara's love of art can be offered, but an explanation of that love as a response to the threat of the other can only be supplied by the reader. Overdetermination, however, is by no means the same thing as indeterminancy; in this limited setting, irony is a reliable, even precise, means of knowledge. In uncovering a set of determinate, finite causes to the reader, irony indicates the limits of individual knowledge, blinded as it is by self-love, but not the impossibility of knowledge itself. (The parallel with the narrator's ability in *Middlemarch* to avoid the errors her characters commit in ignorance is almost exact.)

The poems supply the means by which causes that are unknown to the speaker can be uncovered. Thus we feel able to talk of Browning's attitudes toward his speakers or toward certain positions they adopt. The presumption is that the poet has "planted" various details that "tell." The speaker's attempt to construct a world that totally encloses himself and his listener has been a failure; as readers we are able to take up a stance outside that world and judge it. But that stance is afforded us by the grace of the poet, so our first inclination

8. Browning also wrote what can be called "positive" monologues, such as "Rabbi Ben Ezra," in which the speaker is almost a lyrical persona, voicing sentiments close to the poet's own.

9. W. David Shaw, "Victorian Poetry and Repression: The Use and Abuse of Masks," *ELH* 46 (1979): 468–94, offers a theory of reading, which he applies to Victorian poetry, that assumes a "necessary indirection" (476) and locates in the reader the ability to detect the repressed material the poet cannot recognize. Obviously, my model for reading the monologues is very similar to Shaw's, although I will argue that Browning is more in control of his poetry than Shaw's essay allows. Even there, however, we are not so far apart since Shaw sees in "Childe Roland" an "honest confrontation" of the repressed (472–73).

is to say that Browning succeeds where his characters fail. We do not accept the "truth" of the duke's world, or of the bishop's, or of Porphyria's lover's. We reject them as egotists to the point of solipsism at best, and as insane at worst. But we do accept that the poem itself in each case has presented the "truth" of these characters. Having read "The Bishop Orders His Tomb" we feel we know exactly who the bishop is, that we can list the various factors that determine his personality. The poems are organized by the poet to make a point, to reveal a truth. They make that point indirectly, but nonetheless forcefully. Among various men who (like the speakers in the poem) try to gain control over language and over others, the poet is "the town's true master, if the town but knew" ("How It Strikes a Contemporary," 40).

The poet, it would seem, is a successful liar. But I want to argue that Browning recognizes the similarity of his position to that of his speakers, that he works to undermine his own constructions as he does theirs, and that the self-consciousness of his undermining marks the essential difference between his lies and the lies of his speakers. Like Rossetti and Carlyle, Browning finally devalues his own art in the face of a reality that overwhelms it. Browning's determinate irony yields to a larger, more encompassing irony—a romantic irony similar to Carlyle's. Just as that master rhetorician, the duke of Ferrara, cannot totally enclose the living duchess in his world, so Browning continually confronts (and tries to bring, through indirection, into his poetry) a vital, living reality that eludes his best efforts to include it in his artistic universe. Reality, like Andrea Del Sarto's wife, keeps walking out of Browning's art. The poet's lies, his fictions, his created situations and characters, are most successful when they call up, in Mr. Sludge's formula, a subsequent truth, with marvels not of the poet's creation. With the arrival of truth, the poet's lies are annihilated, just as any lie is destroyed once it is measured against the reality it failed to acknowledge. However, to call truth in, these lies are necessary, and as such they are not to be scorned even while recognized as fictions.

"Mr. Sludge, 'The Medium' " offers one of Browning's fullest considerations of the function of lies in relation to that "truth" and "reality" to which the poet owes allegiance. Mr. Sludge is a lesser artist, not merely because he is a cheat and a scoundrel, but because his use of lies is not self-conscious and not primarily directed (by the road of indirection) to uncovering the truth. The medium's description of how "truth" overwhelmed him in the midst of his fraudulent practices makes it obvious that he has no clear understanding of what is happening in those moments, and thus he can only respond by trying to see how he can turn those moments to his own advantage. Browning's poems are full of corrupt artists; in The Ring and the Book, both Guido's fatuous lawyer and Guido himself are portrayed as artists. Like Carlyle and George Eliot, who deride fiction in works of fiction, or like Ruskin in his effort to distinguish between "noble" and "ignoble" mystery, Browning needs to differentiate the misuse of art and its power from its correct use. Misuse of art, as we have seen, follows from emphasizing its separation from the world and its subordination to the whims of the creating artist. Art must open out toward others and the real. Guido thinks of his murder of Pompilia as a work of art —a work that was undone by "Artistry's haunting curse, the Incomplete!" "Being incomplete, my act escaped success" (11.586).

For Browning, only such radical incompleteness can guarantee art's integrity. Irony functions to indicate at all times the incompleteness, the lack of self-sufficiency, of the artwork. But art is not simply to be dismissed. Browning finds art absolutely necessary because he believes the truth is ineffable. The vital and the real always escape all efforts to capture them in language or in art; all representations of the truth are lies insofar as they are only, and will always be only, approximations. Browning's irony, like Carlyle's, ultimately derives from the conviction that all representatives are inadequate. The poet's irony, the incompleteness of his poems, points us toward the truth that no words can ever successfully utter, but that is the ultimate object of knowledge. In the "Essay on Shelley" Browning states the law of "approximate" representation: "An absolute vision is not for this world, but we are permitted an approximation to it, every degree of which in the individual, provided it exceed the attainment of the masses, must procure him a clear advantage."[10]

The poet, then, tries to find those approximations that "exceed the attainment of the masses" (some lies are better than others) *and* continually lets us know that his poems are not the truth but only ways of trying to reach the truth. (Browning's position, then, is very similar to Ruskin's. Ruskin recommends that we pay attention to the great artist, since the master will have greater insight into the truth, but Ruskin also wants the master's images— clouds—to function as representatives of the limits of representation even while providing some vision of God's light.) "Abt Vogler" and "Two in the Campagna" are two of the more familiar examples of Browning's discussing the difficulty of incorporating life's most important, vital, and intractable truths into art. The organist, through his music, approaches the "ineffable Name" (65) that is the goal of his "extemporizing," but can only conclude that his "failure here" (81) reveals the inevitable distance of man from God in this world. In "Two in the Campagna" the speaker is able to "touch" a "thought" (6) that seems to offer an understanding of love, of the true nature of the other, but the thought cannot be articulated and thus it fades. Reality, the artist's subject, lies just beyond speech, as something we approach through words but never quite attain.[11]

10. *Robert Browning: The Poems,* 1:1005.
11. This description of the "reality" that lies just beyond speech in Browning is influenced by J. Hillis Miller's chapter on Browning in *The Disappearance of God* (Cambridge: Harvard University Press, 1963). Miller sees Browning's poetry as dominated by a "philosophy of

In the shorter monologues, Browning almost always retains the strategy of indirection. Not only does he not state openly the truths that he claims cannot be stated, but he also only suggests his epistemological and aesthetic stance indirectly. Such, however, is not the case in *The Ring and the Book*. In the long poem, Browning describes why the lies of poetry are necessary and do serve an important function. Even more significantly, the poem does not abide by the aesthetic it announces. In *The Ring and the Book*, Browning falls back on revelation and on the direct statement of revealed truth. As Ian Jack writes, "In spite of all the talk about the 'stereoscopic' and 'relativist' elements in *The Ring and the Book*, one is driven to the conclusion that the complexity of its technique is more apparent than real, and the poem is inspired by a vision of life that is simpler and more naive than that which informs the great short poems of the 1840s and 1850s."[12] Like all the writers discussed in this book, Browning at times displays an impatience with indirection that leads to his reliance on simpler ways of perceiving the real.

In many respects, *The Ring and the Book* is set up to protect an adherence to indirection. The truth at issue is only a human truth (the facts of a murder case), so it would seem that Browning would not be risking cosmic anarchy if he exposed our inability to know for certain the guilt or innocence of the involved parties. And, certainly, the poem's interest and structure depends on its demonstrating how different the facts appear when viewed by different people. In this lower, human world "how else know we save by worth of word" (1.835), and words' inadequacy must mean our knowledge will remain less than complete. That inadequacy defines our fallen condition:

> the barren words
> Which, more than any deed, characterize
> Man as made subject to a curse: no speech—
> That still bursts o'er some lie which lurks inside,
> As the split skin across the coppery snake,
> And most denotes man. (10.348–53)

The lie (the limits of representation) is always mixed with the truth in any human utterance.

---

incompleteness" because the poet can never approach God directly (99). W. David Shaw, in "Victorian Poetry and Repression," takes "reality" as the great unspoken in all Victorian poetry. "Reality," Shaw writes, "can never enter a text without complicated mediation and disguise" (469). In "Browning's Monologues and the Development of the Soul," *ELH* 47 (1980): 772–87, David Bergman considers the effect on the shorter poems of Browning's mysticism. Herbert F. Tucker, Jr., in "Browning's Lyric Intentions," *Critical Inquiry* 7 (1980): 275–96, discusses the ineffable in Browning entirely within a secular framework. For Tucker, the characters in the monologues experience "the friction of their inarticulate intentions against the hard surface of words in which they would frame those intentions" (281).

12. *Browning's Major Poetry* (Oxford: Clarendon Press, 1973), p. 298.

The inevitability of such a mixture of truth and lie means that poetry's "white lies," its "make-believe" (1.456–57) are not blameworthy. But in defending poetry against the complaints of the "British Public," Browning goes far beyond explaining that all human speech partakes of lying, i. e., conceals as well as reveals in the way Carlyle attributes to the symbol. Instead, in the key metaphor of the ring, Browning insists that poetry's lies work to reveal the truth. As I read the ring metaphor, Browning has moved from associating poetry's lies with the necessary inadequacy of all human speech to a much simpler notion of lies as the fictions the poet invents.[13] The poet admits that he has put words into his characters' mouths, words they never actually spoke, words that depart from the "pure crude fact" (1.34) that can be found in the book that is the poem's source. Although the poet's fictions, like the goldsmith's alloy, are necessary for the formation of the tale, they can be separated out again at the end of the process, leaving the pure unmixed truth. The lie is no longer the irredeemable condition of fallen man but merely a heuristic device by which the truth, which can be perceived directly and purely, is uncovered. In describing how the poem works to reveal the truth, Browning comes close to Mr. Sludge's formula. The poet's "motions" call forth a "gold" that is not the poet's. And the ring metaphor allows Browning to claim that the "truth," which is the only "good," is neither corrupted or compromised by its (brief) association with lies.

> there's nothing in nor out o' the world
> Good except truth: yet this, the something else,
> What's this then, which proves good yet seems untrue?
> This that I mixed with truth, motions of mine
> That quickened, made the inertness malleolable
> O' the gold was not mine,—what's your name for this?
> Are means to the end, themselves in part the end?
> Is fiction which makes fact alive, fact too? (1.698–706)

In *The Ring and the Book,* Browning's answer to the last question is yes. Words reveal the truth, without words' fallen (lying) nature altering the quality of the truths revealed. By the end of the poem, Browning has so overcome his mistrust of words that he can talk of "speaking truth": "it is the glory and good of Art, / That Art remains the one way possible / Of speaking truth, to mouths like mine at least" (12.839–40).

13. See Richard D. Altick and James F. Loucks, *Browning's Roman Murder Story: A Reading of "The Ring and the Book"* (Chicago: University of Chicago Press, 1968), pp. 22–28, for a very helpful discussion of the ring metaphor. Altick and Loucks recognize how the metaphor is used to establish that the poet does not alter the truth in representing it in his poem and discuss Browning's need to make such a claim in relation to both positivist and romantic theories of imagination and perception.

This ability to speak truth depends on a direct apprehension of truth. The poem offers two means by which truth is revealed, one active and one passive, but both ultimately dependent on a notion of divine revelation. Actively, through the use of imagination and thought, men can attain to some degree of insight into a reality that already exists, waiting for men to apprehend it. The discussion here fully deserves the name *Neo-Platonic,* with its description of men who struggle to recover a "good" of which the individual "soul" offers intimations. Man is "formed to rise, reach at, if not grasp and gain / The good beyond him" (1.714–15). He "creates, no, but resuscitates, perhaps" (1.718) that good by "project[ing] his surplusage of soul" (1.722), thus animating a world that would lay dormant without man's revivifying touch. But Browning is careful to insist that this imaginative activity only "resuscitates"; it does not create.

The epistemological and moral consequences of this position become evident in the Pope's monologue. Morally, since man has been "formed" by God to know the good, "life's business" (10.1237) becomes to "find the truth, dispart the shine from shade" (10.1242). Protestations of the necessary ignorance of our fallen condition cannot be allowed to justify the actions of the wicked. In this poem, at least, Browning's need for a criteria on which to base moral judgments does not allow him to portray a world in which the truth remains radically unknowable.

Epistemologically, this active use of imagination to seek out the good and the true must be dependent on God's having created a species that is capable of such activity. God is responsible for the capabilities of thought that allow the truth—and God—to be revealed to men.

> Man's mind, what is it but a convex glass
> Wherin are gathered all the scattered points
> Picked out of the immensity of sky,
> To reunite there, be our heaven for earth,
> Our known unknown, our God revealed to man? (10.1310–14)

Thus, the Pope, although admitting that no human knowledge is certain, still judges the murder case, untroubled by doubt. And certainly the reader is expected to endorse the Pope's verdict. Characteristically, when insisting on the certainty of his knowledge the Pope uses a visual metaphor. "So do I see, pronounce on all . . . / Grouped for my judgment now,—profess no doubt / While I pronounce: dark, difficult enough / The human sphere, yet eyes grow sharp by use" (10.1238–41).

The more passive method by which truth is received is illustrated in the experiences of the priest, Giuseppe Caponsacchi, and of Pompilia. In their case, another person serves as the vehicle of revelation. The priest's description of the effect Pompilia has on him uses many of the metaphors of classic mysticism. He is carried outside of himself, his life utterly transformed, by this "invasion" which renders him "passive" and which he describes as a "death."

> By the invasion I lay passive to,
> In rushed new things, the old were rapt away;
> Alike abolished—the imprisonment
> Of the outside air, the inside weight o' the world
> That pulled me down. Death meant, to spurn the ground,
> Soar to the sky,—die well and you do that.
> The very immolation made the bliss;
> Death was the heart of life, and all the harm
> My folly had crouched to avoid, now proved a veil
> Hiding all gain my wisdom strove to grasp (6.932–41)

The priest identifies Pompilia's word with God's (6.998), and obedience to that word reveals his proper course of action to him. Similarly, Pompilia cites her knowledge of the priest as the only trustworthy guide offered to her in a dark world. Through another, we can learn the truth. "Through such souls alone / God stooping shows sufficient of his light / For us i' the dark to rise by" (7.1826–28).

Throughout her monologue, Pompilia, who has had the advantage of this more direct revelation, expresses her mistrust of words. The truthful priest can "read" her innocence correctly, but "printing" serves as a metaphor for the ways truth is obscured. Caponsacchi has

> a sense
> That reads, as only such can read, the mark
> God sets on woman, signifying so
> She should—shall peradventure—be divine;
> Yet 'ware the while, how weakness mars the print
> And makes confusion, leaves the thing men see. (7.1482–87)

Words involve her in the world's perversions of the truth; only an appeal to God, "Truth's self," can get her beyond the doubt to which all words are submitted in this world.

> why, what was all I said, but truth,
> Even when I found that such as are untrue
> Could only take the truth in through a lie?
> Now—I am speaking truth to the Truth's self:
> God will lend credit to my words this time. (7.1184–88)

Pompilia, "perfect in whiteness" (10.1004), will not even condescend to speak lies to those who can apprehend the truth no other way. She refuses to partake in the use of this world's imperfect representations. At the end of her monologue, she rejects earthly marriage because it is so inadequate an image of the heavenly marriage it is meant to suggest. "Marriage on earth seems such a counterfeit, / Mere imitation of the inimitable: / In heaven we have the real and true and sure" (7.1807–9). Against the false images offered by words, Pompilia holds fast to her vision of the priest's face, to that presence through which God's light shines.

> Thus I know
> All your report of Caponsacchi false,
> Folly or dreaming: I have seen so much
> By that adventure at the spectacle,
> The face I fronted that one first, last time:
> He would belie it by such words and thoughts.
> Therefore while you profess to show him me,
> I ever see his own face. Get you gone! (7.1168–75)

Pompilia, undoubtedly, is too pure to live in this world, but she articulates the poet's most extreme protest against the very tools of his trade. Living in this world, the poet must keep speaking, but he must also continually let his readers know that words are not all there is, in fact are not really even the truth. Browning's ambivalence toward the poetic word can only be overcome by asserting poetry can speak truth (as at the end of *The Ring and the Book)* or by constructing his poems in such a way that they direct the reader beyond the words toward a reality that cannot be expressed but which he insists exists. (His ambivalence also surfaces in his continual need to present fraudulent artists.) The lie apes completion, seems self-sufficient, but is in fact radically insubstantial. Its completion is only achieved by exclusion, of the other and of reality. The poet continually breaks open the apparent completeness of his poems by bringing back in that which his language has excluded. Just as the speakers in the monologues have their worlds collapsed by the other (listener, reader, poet) and by an appeal to reality, so the forces of reality, of life and death, appear in various poems to "molest" the constructions of the poet. "Cleon" presents a poet who sees his work as futile since it has kept him writing when he should have been living and is now powerless to keep off death. "A Grammarian's Funeral" presents a similar vision: a life spent studying how to live and how to use words is a life spent out of contact with life. If nothing else brings such scholarly recluses back into contact with life, death will. The constructions of the poet will be revealed as lies at death, even if their insubstantiality has been unrecognized up to that point.

Yet in most of the monologues, as distinct from *The Ring and the Book,* Browning accepts that indirection is the condition of human life. Whatever contact with reality we can have must be through words, lies though those words may be. And the fact of those words being lies necessarily means our knowledge is far from complete. Here we find a reading of "Childe Roland to the Dark Tower Came."[14] Knowing the hoary cripple lies, the speaker follows his directions anyway. All we have are lies to point us on our way. The path Roland (an image of the poet) takes shows that all previous questers have only approached the tower, never reached it. All have failed to return and describe it to the world completely and accurately, yet the tower is that indeterminate something that generates the whole quest.

Granted a vision of that reality, the speaker can only die. Browning cannot imagine the apocalyptic moment within the confines of this life. The dark tower is the reality and truth that, for Browning, exist just beyond language, a reality that can never be brought into language and that is the subject our lying words attempt to articulate. There is the suggestion here that the continuation of this dualistic gap between words and reality is necessary for survival. The false poet—the duke of Ferrara or the bishop of St. Praxed's —tries to deny that gap exists by making his words the only reality, but his constructed world is eventually undermined by the other and by reality. The true poet also constructs fictional worlds out of words, but undermines those worlds himself as a way of indicating their failure to reflect or represent faithfully the truth that transcends language. Irony is the inevitable mode of all speech when the most important subjects of concern cannot be brought into language. And irony allows Browning to continue using representatives even while declaring their inadequacy. As a rhetorical strategy, irony enables Browning to write poetry and, if the consequences of Roland's direct vision hold for the poet, enables Browning to live.

14. Both Shaw, "Victorian Poetry and Repression," and Garrat, "Browning's Dramatic Monologue," find in "Childe Roland" the mask employed in all the dramatic monologues, but used in this case to break through to some kind of higher vision. They both suggest that in this poem the strategy of indirection leads the poet further into the heart of the mystery than in the other monologues.

8

Yeats: Poverty and the Tragic Vision

And through the mansion of the spirit rove
My dreams round thoughts of plenty

. . . it may be the arts are founded on the life beyond the world, and that
they must cry in the ears of our penury until the world has been consumed
and become a vision.

It may be that in a few years Fable, who changes mortalities to
immortalities in her cauldron, will have changed Mary Hynes and Raftery
to perfect symbols of the sorrow of beauty and of the magnificence and
penury of dreams.

Throughout his career, Yeats's "dreams" circle "round thoughts of
plenty."[1] But everywhere he turns, he only finds poverty. He adopts various
strategies that he hopes will yield that plenty he seeks, only to conclude in the
end that poverty is the inescapable human condition. In certain respects Yeats's
work is quite different from that of the Victorians, most notably, perhaps, in
his final despair that the gap between mind and world, desire and reality, can
ever be overcome through the marriage found in apocalyptic romantic visions
or the comic ending of most major Victorian novels. But despite Yeats's
difference from the Victorians, I think his basic aims and his final adoption of
a tragic vision can be illuminated by reading his work in terms of the issues
raised in this book.

Yeats's effort to escape poverty takes the form of an attempt to locate
or create a reality that will satisfy desire. One part of Yeats hopes and argues
that poetry—and, in particular, the poetic symbol or image—can grant access
to that full life. The essays on poetry written in the 1890s present this hope

1. All references to Yeats's works have been taken from the editions listed below. The
source of each reference is noted parenthetically in the text according to the abbreviation listed
in front of each work. (CP) *The Collected Poems of W. B. Yeats* (New York: Macmillan, 1970).
(E&I) *Essays and Introductions* (New York: Collier Books, 1968). (M) *Mythologies* (New York:
Collier Books, 1969). (E) *Explorations* (New York: Collier Books, 1973). (A) *The Autobiography of William Butler Yeats* (New York: Macmillan, 1953). (L) *Letters on Poetry from W. B. Yeats
to Dorothy Wellesley* (Oxford: Oxford University Press, 1964). (Letters) *The Letters of W. B.
Yeats*, ed. Allan Wade (London: Rupert Hart-Davis, 1954). (V) *A Vision* (New York: Collier
Books, 1966). My two prose epigraphs are from E&I, 184, and M, 30. The two lines of poetry
are from the "The Seeker," one of Yeats's earliest published poems (1885). This poem is
reprinted in *The Variorum Edition of the Poems of W. B. Yeats*, ed. Peter Allt and Russell K.
Alspach (New York: Macmillan, 1966), pp. 681–86.

most fully. Another part of Yeats, however, can never quite believe that poetry enjoys a bounty the world itself lacks. Yeats struggles to insure the poetic word's reality, but also works to reveal the word's "penury." Faced with both the world's and the word's poverty, Yeats is left with his tragic vision of men who desire what they can never have. The ability to assert this vision, however, offers the important consolation that the poet has identified the nature of reality. By tracing through Yeats's efforts to combat poverty and his final acceptance of it, we will be able to see how Yeats continues, in some ways, the efforts of the Victorians, while also identifying certain features of the modernist turning away from the Victorians.

Throughout his career, Yeats is adamant in his rejection of the materialistic modern world represented by "Carolus Durand, Bastien-Lepage, Huxley and Tindall" (A, 167), a world of "sterile complication" (A, 93) and "abstraction" (A, 167), characterized by "wheel biting upon wheel, a roar of steel or iron tackle, a mill of argument grinding all things down to mediocrity" (A, 140). Like Carlyle, and the romantics to whom Carlyle and Yeats both are indebted, Yeats strives to prove the existence of another "reality," a spiritual world that can be revealed by art.[2] But unlike Carlyle or any of the other Victorians, Yeats feels no need to glorify the word *fact* and finds no benefits that would recommend either silence or a plain style. Yeats's romanticism displays almost none of the empiricist tempering that characterizes most Victorian adaptations of romantic strategies.

Yeats does, however, reveal a Victorian fear of the "arbitrary" or solipsistic. He wants to insure that his imaginative words do have a referent beyond the self. His words, quite clearly, refer to nothing in this impoverished world, so the poet searches for another world, demonstrably independent of himself, that can serve as the referent of his visionary words. During the nineties, Yeats is usually vague about the exact nature of this other world, but does write a number of essays that insist that symbolic poetry grants access to a reality beyond the mundane empirical world. The essays work to define the proper content of poetry, by contrast (explicit or implicit) to the material world, and argue that poetry can contain that bounty the ordinary world so obviously lacks.

> All art that is not mere story-telling, or mere portraiture, is symbolic, and has the purpose of those symbolic talismans which mediaeval magicians made with complex colours and forms, and bade their patients ponder over daily, and guard with holy secrecy; for it entangles, in complex colours and forms, a part

2. That Yeats divides reality into two realms, one spiritual and one material, is apparent from the most casual reading of his work. The critics have covered this topic thoroughly, and I have no wish to retrace that discussion here. See, for example, Alex Zwerdling, "W. B. Yeats: Variations on the Visionary Quest," in *Yeats: A Collection of Critical Essays,* ed. John Unterecker (Englewood Cliffs: Prentice-Hall, 1963), pp. 80–92.

of the Divine Essence. A person or a landscape that is part of a story or a portrait, evokes but so much emotion as the story or the portrait can permit without loosening the bonds that make it a story or a portrait; but if you liberate a person or a landscape from the bonds of motives and their actions, causes and their effects, and from all bonds but the bonds of your love, it will change under your eyes, and become a symbol of infinite emotion, a perfected emotion, a part of the Divine Essence; for we love nothing but the perfect, and our dreams make all things perfect, that we may love them. . . . religious and visionary thought is thought about perfection and the way to perfection; and symbols are the only things free enough from all bonds to speak of perfection. (E&I, 148–49)

This praise of the symbol, in typical Yeatsian fashion, is set up in contrast to that "mere story-telling, or mere portraiture" that defines a realistic, non-symbolic art that is bound to the reality it would portray. His symbol, cut loose from any such ties, partakes of the "Divine Essence," thus offering a liberation from the ordinary and access to the ideal.

What Yeats wants the symbol to accomplish is clear enough, but this passage raises some doubts about the symbol's effectiveness. The symbols point to the "Divine Essence," yet are generated by desire, in particular that love of perfection that Yeats identifies as our only love. It is "our dreams" that make "all things perfect," and the passage suggests that these images or symbols of perfection are manufactured by the dreaming self as a negation of the less-than-perfect world it inhabits. Such doubts raise the whole problem of reference. The words of "mere story-telling" refer (are "bound," to use Yeats's term) to the world they portray. Are the symbols similarly bound to the eternal, essential realm? Yeats wants to avoid the suggestion of any one-to-one correspondence between the symbol and some reality, no matter how ethereal, to which it refers. Rather, he wants to establish that the symbol (in Coleridgean fashion) partakes of the Divine Essence; the symbol enacts or embodies the very reality it evokes.

Denis Donoghue has identified a dramatic principle of enactment as the key element of Yeats's understanding of poetry, but I think we must recognize that Yeats wants two things here, only one of which is satisfied by dramatism.[3] The poem is to be the enactment of a certain vision of perfection, but Yeats also wants to ground the poem in a reality that insures the symbol is not arbitrary. To satisfy this second desire Yeats must rely on the notion of

3. Denis Donoghue, *William Butler Yeats* (New York: Viking Press, 1971), p. 5, writes: "He thought of experience as, potentially, a dramatic poem: circumstance the matter, conflict and imagination the instruments, poetry the end. As for truth itself, he believed that it could not be stated, could not be known, but might be enacted. Truth lives in the mode of action, not of knowledge; it is enacted in the temporal form of the play, and only that form is true." I will make use of this insight into the essentially "dramatistic" quality of Yeats's work, but I also want to stress that Yeats is never reconciled to accepting that truth cannot be known. Dramatic conflict is the "instrument," but poetry is never the sole end. Yeats never abandons the search for truth and, indeed, even claims to have found it at times in his career.

reference even while trying to avoid it. Yeats has no desire to write "pure poetry," if that term is taken to mean poetry whose words have no meaning or function beyond their use in the poem. Yeats's poetry quite deliberately points to issues and ideas beyond itself. The symbol, for Yeats, only works because there really does exist the divine realm from which the symbol draws its meaning. Yeats's understanding of that divine realm's nature changes over the course of his career, but he retains his belief that the symbol is worthless if that reality beyond sense does not exist. Yeats is as dependent as the Victorians on the notion of a reality that validates the words of art. He portrays the symbol's relation to that reality as a mysterious thing, but still would say that symbols are not perfection themselves, but "speak of perfection," a position that requires some notion of reference to explain how the speaking is done. The symbol's enactment is always representative, pointing away from itself to something else.

Throughout his essays of the nineties, Yeats tries to grant the symbol as much freedom as possible while still preserving its ability to refer. He explains the "new" art of Ibsen and Maeterlinck (an unlikely pair) as based on

> vague symbols that set the mind wandering from idea to idea, emotion to emotion. Indeed all the great masters have understood that there cannot be great art without the little limited life of the fable, which is always the better the simpler it is, and the rich far-wandering, many-imaged life of the half-seen world beyond it. There are some who understand that the simple unmysterious things living as in a clear noon light are of the nature of the sun, and that vague, many-imaged things have in them the strength of the moon. (E&I, 216)

Yeats's preference for the things of the moon is clear; he wants his symbols to suggest "innumerable meanings, . . . casting lights and shadows of an indefinable wisdom on what seemed before, it may be, but sterility and noisy violence" (E&I, 161). That this wisdom is "indefinable" hardly seems to bother Yeats. The symbol, however vague, remains "indeed the only possible expression of some invisible essence, a transparent lamp around a spiritual flame" (E&I, 116). The symbol (and poetry that is symbolic) is the one true way.

Yeats has none of Carlyle's, Ruskin's, or Browning's belief that the symbol conceals as much as it reveals, in part because Yeats has taken great pains to distinguish the symbol as a special example of language, one quite different from the words of ordinary speech. As a "transparent lamp," Yeats's symbol is totally adequate to the task given it. Browning expresses the desire for such a poetic language in the metaphor of the ring at the beginning of *The Ring and the Book,* but his dramatic monologues demonstrate language's opacity, not its transparency. Yeats's faith in words never quite deserts him, even when he comes to question the worth of those things words can give us, and even when he begins to chastise the word for some of its inevitable limitations. The word in Yeats remains the only way possible to express certain crucial truths of the ideal world and of the heart. Unlike the Victorians, Yeats seldom abandons the word for more direct forms of knowledge. Even in *A Vision,* knowledge comes through words, not sight (despite the book's title), and that knowledge is finally to be used to provide "metaphors for poetry" (V, 8).

For all his praise of vagueness, Yeats does nail down the referent, although he usually hammers timidly for fear of offending readers with too bold a statement of his belief in an eternal realm.[4] He remains vague about details, but the central premise remains: his symbols are tied to a reality beyond sense. The essay entitled "Magic" offers Yeats's most explicit public statement of his beliefs. He argues that symbols come from the "Great Mind" or the "Great Memory"; he offers several narratives of magical experiments to prove his contention that symbols are not products of the self. The similarity of Yeats's belief in a "Great Mind" to Jung's notions of a "collective unconscious" and "archetypes" has often been noted; this belief allows Yeats to overcome the persistent Victorian fear that the poet's visions and images are purely self-generated. Reference to the "Great Mind" assures that the symbols are not arbitrary. And Yeats spent a fair amount of time collecting the time-honored symbols of Ireland, with the goal of bringing them back into common currency in his work. In 1913, Yeats looks back on this project as an attempt to overcome the threat of solipsism. "I sought some symbolic language reaching far into the past and associated with familiar names and conspicuous hills that I might not be alone amid the obscure impressions of the senses" (E&I, 349).

For Yeats, then, as for so many Victorians, a thing's reality is demonstrated by its being public, by its being perceived by many people. Since that something exists "out there" to be perceived, the perceiver necessarily adopts a passive, receptive attitude toward it. So we find Yeats, in his own way, repeating the passive descriptions of perception found in a writer like Ruskin, although the world perceived in Yeats's essays is always an invisible world that is "seen" only through representative "images," never directly. "Every visionary knows that the mind's eye comes to see a capricious and variable world, which the will cannot shape or change, though it can call it up and banish it again" (E&I, 151). The will's lack of control over the vision proves it is not self-created.

Juxtaposed with this notion of a passive intelligence are, however, passages in which Yeats insists on poetry's power: "poets and painters . . . are continually making and unmaking the world" (E&I, 157). In the "Magic" essay, this movement from passivity to activity occurs within one sentence.

---

4. Richard Ellman, *Yeats: The Man and the Masks* (New York: E. P. Dutton, 1948), pp. 150–51, discusses Yeats's timidity in both his prose and his poetry and his habit of presenting his most cherished beliefs in questions or as suppositions rather than as assertions.

"We should rewrite our histories, for all men, certainly all imaginative men, must be forever casting forth enchantments, glamours, illusions; and all men, especially tranquil men who have no strong egotistic life, must be continually passing under their power" (E&I, 40). Is it "all men" who cast forth enchantments, or is the world divided into two kinds of men, the passive recipients and the "egotistic" enchanters? While this sentence begins by making "all men" active, the very next sentence makes all men passive: "Our most elaborate thoughts, elaborate purposes, precise emotions, are often, as I think, not really ours, but have on a sudden come up, as it were, out of Hell or down out of Heaven" (E&I, 40). Are men the sources of glamours, or do glamours come from the unearthly reaches of Heaven and Hell? Do men impose their "illusions" on others, or are we all possessed by powers divine and/or satanic?

The confusion can only be explained by Yeats's contradictory desires here. Yeats wants to confirm the imagination's power, but can hardly grant that power to the poet's lone voice. Thus he grounds imagination in a realm beyond the poet. Imagination remakes the world, but only according to the dictates of the Great Mind. The poet is the most powerful of men, while he is the most helpless of puppets. And even this limited claim for the imagination is made in the most tentative fashion, placed in questions that apologize for their boldness at the end of the "Magic" essay: "And surely, at whatever risk, we must cry out that imagination is always seeking to remake the world according to the impulses and patterns in that Great Mind, and that Great Memory? Can there be anything so important as to cry out that what we call romance, poetry, intellectual beauty, is the only signal that the supreme Enchanter, or some one in His councils, is speaking of what has been, and shall be again, in the consummation of time?" (E&I, 52).

Yeats's sense of the poet's and imagination's power is reminiscent of similar comments in Carlyle. Both writers share the same problem: how to explain the ways in which art can grant us access to a spiritual realm (that they want to call "real") that other forms of discourse do not reveal. Like George Eliot and Browning, as well as Carlyle, Yeats, when making use of the romantic imagination, talks of imagination "calling" the world into human view, but works to guarantee that imagination is not understood as creating that world it allows to be seen. But Yeats's imagination is not as tangled in the obscure forms of this world as the imagination found in the Victorians. As we have seen, the Yeatsian symbol is exempt from the frustrating concealment the Victorians identified in representatives. And by reviving the romantic distinction between "imagination" and "fancy" (which Yeats, significantly enough, calls "fantasy"), Yeats also grants imagination some immunity from the problems of fallen knowledge that plague its functioning in the texts of the Victorians. Yeats believes imagination can pierce through the mere appear-

ances of the ordinary world to apprehend "the imperishable beings and substances" that lie beyond sense.

> If 'the world of imagination' was the 'world of eternity,' as this doctrine
> [of Blake's] implied, it was of less importance to know men and nature than
> to distinguish the beings and substances of imagination from those of a more
> perishable kind, created by the fantasy, in uninspired moments, out of memory
> and whim; and this could best be done by purifying one's mind, as with a flame,
> in study of the works of the great masters, who were great because they had
> been granted by divine favour a vision of the unfallen world from which others
> are kept apart by the flaming sword that turns every way; and by flying from
> the painters who studied 'the vegetable glass' [of nature] for its own sake, and
> not to discover there the shadows of imperishable beings and substances. (E&I,
> 117)

The "great masters," by virtue of imagination, are allowed "a vision of
the unfallen world" that all men seek. The great artist's power rests on his
ability to transmit that vision in his art. While Browning's poet fails to convey
adequately the vision, Yeats's ideal poet has the symbol. Dickens and George
Eliot downplay the power of the individual with a strong imagination by
placing that individual (Dorothea Brooke is the perfect example) in a social
context that limits her effectiveness. For the two novelists, imagination's vision
has power only insofar as society takes it up and its images pass into common
parlance. Here again Yeats defies exact categorization. Like the Victorians,
Yeats wanted the poet's vision to have practical public consequences and felt
the need for the social endorsement of poetic values. Yet, pessimistically certain
from the start that the modern commercial world is hostile to the visions of
imagination, Yeats is careful to avoid tying the symbol's effectiveness to the
response of a particular audience. His poetry is still valid, still indicates universal truths, even if modern life continues to empty most men's lives of any
contact with the symbolic or the imaginative. Yeats did not allow the oddity
of claiming the "universality" of certain truths that only a few can perceive
bother him overmuch. The poet's greatness is determined not by his ability to
persuade men to share his vision, but by his having had the vision and his
having made it available to others by putting it into words. Unlike Browning,
Dickens, or George Eliot, Yeats has very little interest in the social processes
by which others hear and judge one's words.

Yeats's theory of the symbol holds that the symbol is the only way certain
realities can ever be brought into human awareness. "A symbol is indeed the
only possible expression of some invisible essence" (E&I, 116). Poetry's power
rests on its being absolutely necessary for the expression of that invisible
essence, and its triumph is not significantly marred if only a few understand

it. By stripping the symbol of its dependence on an endorsing audience, and by seeing it as unambiguous, as completely revelatory, Yeats grants the poet, the master of symbols, greater powers than any Victorian does. The poet/mage possesses the secret of the "only possible expression" of the truth. "It is not possible to separate an emotion or a spiritual state from the image that calls it up and gives it expression. Michelangelo's *Moses,* Velasquez's *Philip the Second,* the color purple, a crucifix, call into life an emotion or state that vanishes with them because they are its only possible expression, and that is why no mind is more valuable than the images it contains" (E&I, 286).

The poet's power might be stated most radically as follows: the eternal realities do not exist *for men* until the poet gives them expression. For Yeats, the truth only comes into a position from which it can be perceived at the moment the poet finds the appropriate expression. That truth is not the poet's creation, but he is responsible for its entrance into the human world. Since the symbol is the form truth takes in the human world, the symbol is the way truth exists for men. "Vision" in Yeats is never direct, but always of "images" rather than of "things-in-themselves." Thus Yeats, unlike the Victorians, rarely appeals to some direct source of knowledge apart from mediated forms. "Images" are to vision what "symbols" are to language, the privileged, but still mediate, forms in which the highest truths are given to us. The two terms—*image* and *symbol*—are almost equivalent in Yeats, although *image* more usually refers to the process of gaining knowledge or insight, while *symbol* refers to the embodiment of that knowledge in art.

Because Yeats accepts the adequacy of images and symbols, the issue of mediate forms as "lies" or "concealments" does not arise for him. There is only good poetry and bad poetry, just as there is "imagination" and "fantasy." Good poetry contains symbols that make reading the poem a revelation; bad poetry only reveals its lack of vision, its failure to present symbols that give "dumb things voices, and bodiless things bodies" (E&I, 147). From this reliance on the word to uncover the truth comes Yeats's devotion to absolute precision in his writing. Since the symbol or image governs the very process of coming to know, finding the correct representative means finding the truth (the following passage also indicates the intimate connection between *image* and *symbol* for Yeats): "I believed that the truth I sought would come to me like the subject of a poem, from some moment of passionate experience. . . . That passionate experience would never come—of that I was certain—until I had found the right image or right images" (A, 162–63). Representation and revelation are not as distinct for Yeats as they are for the Victorians. Since Yeats (at least in his essays) believes in totally adequate representatives (images or symbols), he believes, in a way the Victorians cannot, that representatives can be revelatory.

The poetic word, for Yeats, is not impoverished when it embodies a spiritual realm the poet claims exists. Symbolism is justified by the contention that symbols reveal that spiritual realm. But to move away from the essay's claims about poetry to the poems themselves is to risk great disappointment. The poetry, with few exceptions, is torn between its attempt to body forth the spiritual realm and the suspicion that the words of poetry are impoverished in the sense of being mere phantasms of desire. The essays present a program for poetry that the poems themselves never quite enact. That Yeats, when writing the poems, quite consciously places his belief in the spiritual within a context that qualifies that belief is made clear by a revealing comment in his essay "Symbolism in Painting": "The systematic mystic is not the greatest of artists, because his imagination is too great to be bounded by a picture or a song, and because only imperfection in a mirror of perfection, or perfection in a mirror of imperfection, delights our frailty" (E&I, 150). Too great an imagination, too clear a vision of the spiritual, is disastrous to art. The characteristic Yeatsian juxtaposition of the ideal and the ordinary is stated here as a basic condition of art, a few years (the comment dates from 1898) before Yeats expands his ideas about opposition into the theory of the mask. The essays present Yeats's understanding of how the poet might achieve a "vision of perfection." But that vision must not be brought into poetry, unless reflected in a "mirror of imperfection."

The first poem in Yeats's *Collected Poems*, "The Song of the Happy Shepherd" (CP, 7–8), shows the poet torn between asserting the poetic word's "plenty" and its poverty.

> Of old the world on dreaming fed;
> Grey Truth is now her painted toy;
> Yet still she turns her restless head:
> But O, sick children of the world,
> Of all the many changing things
> In the dreary dancing past us whirled,
> To the cracked time that Chronos sings,
> Words alone are certain good.

The poet distinguishes between a world of "dream" and a world of "Grey Truth." The world of "dream" is relegated to the past and cannot be revived even when the inability of "Grey Truth" to satisfy the "restless" imagination is recognized. Dreams, we learn in the next stanza, fade as surely as facts, and the poet justifies his praise of words by claiming that they alone outface "cracked time." The "glory" of the past's "warring kings" now all depends on the "idle word" of some "entangled story." The moral is:

> Then nowise worship dusty deeds,
> Nor seek, for this is also sooth,
> To hunger fiercely after truth,

> Lest all thy toiling only breeds
> New dreams, new dreams; there is no truth
> Saving in thine own heart.

Dreams are used here as an image of futility; work which "only breeds new dreams" would be wasted. What we desire is "truth," and the poet tells us such truth is only found in one's "own heart." Yet the picture offered of the man who follows this advice and searches into his own heart is hardly enticing.

> Go gather by the humming sea
> Some twisted, echo-harbouring shell,
> And to its lips thy story tell,
> And they thy comforters will be,
> Rewording in melodious guile
> Thy fretful words a little while,
> Till they shall singing fade in ruth,
> And die a pearly brotherhood;
> For words alone are certain good;
> Sing, then, for this is also sooth.

Each man will be his own poet, but will only have the shell for an audience. The result is a debilitating isolation in which the words of the poet's "story" fail to connect him to the world or to others. Not surprisingly, this poet's words "fade" and "die." A faith in "words alone" leads the singer into a narcissistic reverie from which no escape is apparent. At this point the poem's speaker, our teacher, leaves us to visit the grave of an old friend, the fawn.

> His shouting days with mirth were crowned;
> And still I dream he treads the lawn,
> Walking ghostly in the dew,
> Pierced by my glad singing through,
> My songs of old earth's dreamy youth:
> But ah! she dreams not now; dream thou!
> For fair are poppies on the brow:
> Dream, dream, for this is also sooth.

The speaker, the "happy shepherd," dreams as a defense against death, as a way of reviving his dead friend. Similarly, he sings of "earth's dreamy youth," even though the first two stanzas have argued that we should not turn back to that dreamy past or expect it to comfort us. The singer returns to that earlier argument when he recognizes that his songs are out of place because the world does not dream now. But his only suggestion for restoring poetry is to restore dreaming as well.

Obviously, the poem's argument is not very coherent, and I can justify this extended treatment only by indicating that its inconsistencies are illuminating. The words *dream* and *truth* carry two quite different meanings in the poem, and it only begins to make sense if we distinguish between the two.[5] *Dream* is for the most part synonymous with imagination, but in the one line "Lest all thy toiling only breeds / New dreams" the word stands for images so divorced from reality that they have no substance, no effectiveness. The sudden use of the word in this way reveals Yeats's unspoken fear that the products of imagination, while beautiful, have their own distinctive poverty as fantasies that do not touch upon the real.

Truth is used even less consistently. "Grey Truth" refers to an empty realism, a positivistic allegiance to the empirically demonstrable. This impoverished world is the great enemy of the poetic vision, an enemy Yeats combats throughout his career. But *truth* in the poem also takes on its more usual meaning as the reality outside self that validates or substantiates the self's understanding of the world. In this use of the word, *truth* is contrasted to *dream,* and the reader is instructed to search out the truth. Yet, if truth is superior to dream, how do we explain the poem's final advice that we dream? Since the truth is to be found in "thine own heart," we might say that the only truth the poet acknowledges are the heart's dreams, and thus reconcile the seeming contradiction here. But this answer ignores the poem's rejection of *both* truth and dream in favor of words, which "alone are certain good."

Yeats's point here, apparently, is that words allow a union of dream and truth that transcends the limits of both. Truth is limited by its being bound to fact, by its lack of new contents. Dream is limited by its lack of substance. Words can allow expression to the images of the heart's desires, thus bringing those images into the real world. "Grey Truth" can be enriched by this interjection of imagination's vision through words. While desire and reality might not be reconciled, at least both can take up their place in poetry. This ideal of a poetry that presents fully both dream and brute fact manifests itself throughout Yeats's career; I will discuss further examples as I move through the poetry.

But the poem does not fully justify such an optimistic reading. The word's position on the threshold through which the thoughts of night enter the light of day is an uneasy one, and the description of the man who whispers his dream into a shell suggests the word might not be up to the task it has been given. The ordinary world will, very likely, not be receptive to the dreamer's words. The dreamer will be condemned to utter his cry in isolation; this abstract, materialistic world is so set against the "heart's truths" that it will afford them no place. The dreamer makes no significant impact on the world.

The implications of Yeats's portrait of the dreamer's plight extend further than just rejection by a positivistic world. Floating behind that picture is the

5. Frank Hughes Murphy, *Yeats's Early Poetry* (Baton Rouge: Louisiana State University Press, 1975), pp. 11–17, also discusses how "truth" carries two different meanings in "The Happy Shepherd," although Murphy's discussion is aimed in a rather different direction than mine.

secondary meaning of *dream* as unconnected to the real world; the words that convey the dream desires may be afflicted by the dream's unreality. The melancholy isolated dreamer talking to a shell suggests Yeats's lack of faith in the dreamer's ability to break out of his imaginative, self-enclosed visions and actually make contact with the world. The dreamer's words do not establish the desired contact between dream and truth, but turn back upon themselves (quite literally in their being echoed by the shell), caught up in fruitless self-communion. Yeats has taken this Pre-Raphaelite image for art and has clearly seen how it holds within it all the deepest terrors of Rossetti. (The melancholy dreamer of this poem certainly seems a figure from a Pre-Raphaelite painting.) Yeats tells us words alone are certain good, but his poem suggests the Victorian fear that poetry and its words are not real, since they are purely personal and finally insubstantial. When he can guarantee that the poet's words are tied to some transcendent, nonpersonal spiritual realm, Yeats is willing to affirm the poetic symbol more fully than any Victorian does. But his stated faith in words is part bluster, since Yeats is hardly free from doubts that the world built of words is somehow untrue, only a dream.

When we turn to the poems of the nineties to find examples of symbols that are tied to the spiritual realm, that "speak of perfection," and are "the only possible expression" of some hitherto unrevealed truth, the search is, more often than not, unrewarded. Of course, Yeats's magical (we might say "mystical") symbolism calls on poetry to perform astounding miracles, so a failure to achieve the art the essays describe need not surprise us greatly. The poems do reflect an aesthetic that relies on words to bring into existence certain emotions and to sustain those emotions over and against the power of what this mundane world offers to knowledge. "The Lover Tells of the Rose in His Heart" (CP, 54) is fairly typical.

> All things uncomely and broken, all things worn out and old,
> The cry of a child by the roadway, the creak of a lumbering cart,
> The heavy steps of the ploughman, splashing the wintry mould,
> Are wronging your image that blossoms a rose in the deeps of my heart.
>
> The wrong of unshapely things is a wrong too great to be told;
> I hunger to build them anew and sit on a green knoll apart,
> With the earth and the sky and the water, remade, like a casket of gold
> For my dreams of your image that blossoms a rose in the deeps of my
> heart.

My choice might seem unfair since the images of everyday life, in their vividness, overwhelm the rather weak "image that blossoms a rose" in the speaker's heart. Other poems, for example "To Some I Have Talked with by the Fire" (CP, 49), devote more attention to the visionary images, less to the quotidian ones. However, whether more or less is offered of the visionary, the power of the early symbols to battle successfully the mundane world is always quite limited. Yeats's early poetry might be characterized as the attempt to revive the integrating symbol found in the great romantic poets by a poet afflicted by Victorian doubt. Yeats's early reaching out toward the spiritual seems "in all things Pre-Raphaelite" (A, 70), as Yeats would later characterize his youthful ideas. His fragile and rather thin-blooded symbols hardly seem capable of bearing all the metaphysical weight they are asked to carry.

In the poem just quoted, the rose, as in its other frequent appearances in Yeats's early poetry, is meant to act as that "talisman" that calls our attention to the "Divine Essence." The image gains its power for Yeats from its various traditional meanings (both in poetry such as Dante's and in occult practices such as those of the Rosicrucians) and from its negation of the impoverished world. Held in the heart, this image signifies a rejection of the mundane, a "hunger" for a "green knoll apart." But the speaker's "remaking" of the world is clearly set in the future tense. The image promises a world apart, a world yet to be fashioned, but does not offer in this poem (as it does in the essays) any clear indication that such a world exists. Even in the poems in which Yeats relates actual visions of the spiritual realm mentioned so often in the essays, he never claims to have begun to bring these truths to bear on the ordinary world. If the arts are to "cry in the ears of our penury until the world has been consumed and become a vision," Yeats's poetry is more involved in announcing our present poverty than in constructing the new world that will arise once the familiar one is consumed.

My judgment of the early poetry would be unjustifiably harsh if it were not for the high claims Yeats makes for poetry in the essays of the nineties, claims the poetry simply does not justify. Furthermore, Yeats himself is rather harsh on his early work in later appraisals of it. The image's actual genesis, the later Yeats will claim, is the "hunger" of the poet, not any supernatural truth. The poverty of the world causes the poet's recourse to symbols and his dream of another world. "Man made up the whole, / Made lock, stock and barrel / Out of his bitter soul" (CP, 196). Words alone are certain good for the young poet because they, unlike the world, can satisfy dreams of plenty. But after the nineties Yeats becomes more suspicious of the satisfactions offered by the word, more prone to look behind the consolatory images offered by poetry to uncover the "bitterness" that pushes the poet to seek refuge in his art.

That the later Yeats still wants and needs an eternal realm that serves as the referent for his symbols is amply demonstrated by A Vision; his attempt to guarantee the validity of his work by an appeal to the supernatural is never fully abandoned. But after the nineties he becomes more willing to discuss openly, and use as a poetic subject, the inability of words and of poetry to give man what he wants. The poems of the nineties, as I have suggested, quite consciously place images of poetic perfection in conflict with imperfect realities, but only inadvertently do the early poems work to question the word's reality. The later essays and poems more directly consider how the word reveals its own distinctive poverty.

The savagery with which Yeats attacks dreams in poems like "Nineteen Hundred and Nineteen," and his inability to recover a realm—either social or spiritual—that can finally substantiate poetry's images, links him to the "suspicious" pair, Nietzsche and Freud, who strip away the illusion that human words represent any "truth" beyond the desiring self.[6] Yeats feels both the insufferableness of the world he is given and the need to dismantle the compensations devised by imagination almost in the very instant they are constructed.

The "suspicious" Yeats repudiates much of his early poetry because it has avoided admitting the existence of the "foul rag-and-bone shop of the heart" (CP, 336). The symbol has afforded Yeats not only an escape from the empirical world, but also an avoidance of desire's sufferings. The goal of the nineties was an "imagination that neither desires nor hates, because it has done with time, and only wishes to gaze upon some reality, some beauty" (E&I, 163). Poetry will afford Yeats an eternal perspective above the conflict between the ideal and the real. The position he wishes to occupy is described in "To the Rose Upon the Rood of Time" (CP, 31).[7] "No more blinded by man's fate," the speaker finds in "all poor foolish things that live a day, / Eternal beauty."

The Yeats who questions the efficacy of his early poetry denies the possibility of an imagination that neither "desires nor hates," and takes passion as his central theme. Poetry's power lies not in its contemplation of the world from an eternal perspective or even in its bringing eternal truths into time, but in its passionate reaching out from a position of poverty toward that which men desire. The referent of the symbol or image is human need. An early poem like "The Lover Tells of the Rose in His Heart" can be reread as an expression of passion, no longer an indication that the image in the heart intimates the existence of an otherworldly realm. Passion becomes a prominent theme in

6. Paul Ricoeur, *Freud and Philosophy: An Essay in Interpretation,* trans. Denis Savage (New Haven: Yale University Press, 1970), pp. 20–36, distinguishes between interpretation "as recollection of meaning" and "interpretation as exercise of suspicion," citing Marx, Freud, and Nietzsche as the primary exemplars of the second mode. In Yeats's movement away from symbolism to the theory of the mask, we can identify a movement from one mode of interpretation (recollection of meaning) to the other. Yeats's reading of Nietzsche surely had some influence on this shift. For the fullest discussion of Yeats's reading of Nietzsche and its impact on his work, see Otto Bohlmann, *Yeats and Nietzsche* (London: Macmillan, 1982).

7. "To the Rose Upon the Rood of Time" has attracted much critical attention. See Murphy, *Yeats's Early Poetry,* pp. 39–41, and Robert O'Driscoll, *Symbolism and Some Implications of the Symbolic Approach: W. B. Yeats During the Eighteen-Nineties* (Dublin: Dolmen Press, 1975), pp. 50–53, for longer readings of the poem that make essentially the same point I wish to stress here: the poet's desire to occupy a position between or beyond the material and the ideal, observing both but a partisan of neither.

Yeats's work in the early part of this century. The slim volume (fourteen poems) entitled *In the Seven Woods* (published in 1904) and the essay entitled "Discoveries" (1906) present Yeats's new emphasis, with the essay contrasting his new views with his older ones in a passage that deserves quotation in full.[8]

> Without knowing it, I had come to care for nothing but impersonal beauty. I had set out on life with the thought of putting my very self into poetry, and had understood this as a representation of my own visions and an attempt to cut away the non-essential, but as I imagined visions outside myself my imagination became full of decorative landscape and of still life. I thought of myself as something unmoving and silent living in the middle of my own mind and body, a grain of sand in Bloomsbury or in Connacht that Satan's watch-fiends cannot find. Then one day I understood quite suddenly, as the way is, that I was seeking something unchanging and unmixed and always outside myself, a Stone or an Elixir that was always out of reach, and that I myself was the fleeting thing that held out its hand. The more I tried to make my art deliberately beautiful, the more did I follow the opposite of myself, for deliberate beauty is like a woman always desiring man's desire. Presently I found that I entered into myself and pictured myself and not some essence when I was not seeking beauty at all, but merely to lighten the mind of some burden of love or bitterness thrown upon it by the events of life. We are only permitted to desire life, and all the rest should be our complaints or our praise of that exacting mistress who can awake our lips into song with her kisses. (E&I, 271–72)

The reversal here is almost complete. The poet should seek himself, "not some essence" or "vision" outside of himself, but his own "fleeting" nature. The doctrine of the mask, which Yeats develops around this time, allows him to reinterpret his early poetry, finding in its lack of desire the very proof of its creator's passionate needs. If Yeats as symbolist has imagined himself about to grasp the "unchanging and unmixed," Yeats as master of masks sees through the symbolist pose to the "fleeting thing that held out its hand" to grasp the unchanging. And that reaching hand is most fully evident not when the poet is "seeking beauty," but when he is merely trying to "lighten the mind of some burden of love or bitterness." The poet will now find his subject in the confrontation of the self with "life," not in a search for an eternal sphere removed from any such passion.

The conversion to passion, with a new emphasis on desire and on the forces that thwart desire, becomes quite evident when we move from *The*

8. The suggestion that Yeats's poetry changes dramatically in the early years of this century is hardly new. See O'Driscoll, *Symbolism and Some Implications of the Symbolic Approach*, p. 76, and Richard Ellman, *The Identity of Yeats* (New York: Oxford University Press, 1954), pp. 127–31. In 1904, Yeats declares "the subject of all art is passion" (E, 155), and "passion" remains a favorite word with him throughout the rest of his career. As with all such divisions between "early" and "late," caution against overstatement must be exercised, and I will devote attention to describing some of the continuities in Yeats's work as well as the changes.

Wind Among the Reeds (1899) to *In the Seven Woods* (1904). (Between the two books comes the marriage of Maud Gonne, the annihilation of a dream particularly dear to Yeats.) "The Folly of Being Comforted" (CP, 76) strikes the new note, with its focusing on the persistence of desire in the face of both its frustration and the recognition that the desired woman is unworthy of the speaker's passion. Although time has changed the woman so that she is not even faithful to the image he had of her, only the real woman, changed though she be, can satisfy the speaker's "heart." Desire craves not the image, but the real thing that it is "emblem of" (CP, 336), and the heart refuses to be "comforted" by any thing but the thing itself. Furthermore, in a stance that will become increasingly characteristic in Yeats, the heart clings to its desire despite the knowledge that no satisfaction can (ever) be found. The "kind" friend who offers solace is a tempter who must be resisted. As Richard Ellman writes, "Maud Gonne seems essential to Yeats's view of things; some overwhelming defeated passion is needed to agitate the mind to its extremities."[9] Where the image created by desire might not find a correspondent existing reality and where the reality that does exist might never satisfy the heart's desires, passion itself becomes the content of poetry.[10]

The new emphasis on passion determines the tragic vision found in much of the later poetry. Tragedy results from the incompatibility between desire and the nature of things. Nietzsche describes "the tragedy at the heart of things" as the "contrariety at the center of the universe, . . . an interpenetration of several worlds, as for instance a divine and a human, each individually in the right but each, as it encroaches upon the other, having to suffer for its individuality. The individual, in the course of his heroic striving toward universality, de-individuation, comes up against that primal contradiction and learns both to sin and to suffer."[11] Nietzsche's description of the individual

9. *Eminent Domain* (New York: Oxford University Press, 1967), p. 122.

10. The focus of Yeats's poetry, especially his later poems, on a passion that fails to find its object and that, as a result, must find its justification in its own vitality and energy has been the subject of much excellent work. Harold Bloom, *Yeats* (New York: Oxford University Press, 1970), has inspired much debate by finding the tragic poses in the later poetry "inhumane nonsense" (438), and by concluding that the real despair in Yeats is not the result of some cosmic tragic failure of desire to find its object, but the poet's recognition "that his concern was not with the content of the poetic vision, as Blake's was, but with his relation as poet to his own vision" (457). In other words, Yeats's poetry, according to Bloom, is self-referential in a way Yeats hoped to escape, but the poet is finally honest enough to admit that passion itself, and personal passion at that, has been the subject of his poetry, not some vision of the nature of reality. Obviously, Bloom's conclusion is only possible if he calls Yeats's notions of tragedy, which serve as the poet's statement about the nature of reality, "nonsense." For discussions and defenses of tragedy's role in the later poetry, see Robert S. Ryf, "Yeats's Major Metaphysical Poems," *Journal of Modern Literature* 4 (1975): 610–24, and Claire Hahn, "The Moral Center of Yeats's 'Last Poems,'" *Thought* 50(1975): 301–11.

11. *The Birth of Tragedy*, trans. Francis Golffing (Garden City, N.J.: Doubleday, 1956), p. 64.

who struggles to achieve a unity that ever eludes him speaks directly to some of Yeats's deepest concerns. ("Unity of Being" is the highest good in *A Vision.)* The poet's own descriptions of tragedy emphasize the impossibility of desire's being satisfied. "Some Frenchman has said that farce is the struggle against a ridiculous object, comedy against a movable object, tragedy against an immovable; and because the will, or energy, is greatest in tragedy, tragedy is more noble; but I add that 'will or energy is eternal delight,' and when its limit is reached it may become a pure, aimless joy" (E, 449). "The poet finds and makes his mask in disappointment, the hero in defeat. The desire that is satisfied is not a great desire, nor has the shoulder used all its might that an unbreakable gate has never strained" (M, 337). Tragedy describes "great" desires, those that set themselves against an "immovable" object and that are invariably not satisfied.

The adoption of a tragic vision yields certain benefits, most notably that "aimless joy" of human energy fully expended (the influence of Nietzsche is clearly seen in this notion) and the conviction that the poet has come into contact with reality. Those forces that thwart desire come from beyond the self; the dramatic conflict between passion and that which frustrates it must reveal the true nature of the universe. Seen in this context, *A Vision,* despite its odd terminology and charts, should not surprise the reader of Victorian poetry. Yeats wants to insist that his tragic vision derives not from personal experience, but also states the metaphysical truth about reality. *A Vision* plays the same role in Yeats's later poetry that the "Great Mind" and "imperishable beings" play in the essays of the nineties. His individual poems will still be grounded in an understanding of the ultimate nature of reality.

I hardly intend to attempt an exhaustive account of *A Vision* here (presuming I was capable of any such thing), but I hope it will be readily seen that the book offers a basically tragic understanding of the universe.[12] Two forces, the primary and the antithetical, are always at work in the world, and all life arises out of the conflict between them. (Significantly, Yeats gives the name *primary* to that which is most distasteful to him, that which serves to stifle the individual imagination, implicitly admitting, in Victorian fashion, the primacy of the real over the secondary products of the imagination.) Where there is no conflict, there is no life. Since the two forces have opposite aims, the chances for effective compromise are nonexistent outside the mysterious Thirteenth Cone.[13] Even if compromise were achieved, the cessation of con-

12. The fullest, and I think best, available discussion of *A Vision* is Bloom's, in chaps. 14 and 15 of *Yeats.* Bloom is especially good on how the system replaces the "God of the Christians" with "what Martin Buber grimly calls the 'composite god' of the historicists and Gnostics, the god of process, a dehumanizing divinity" (220). And Bloom recognizes that this deified process is also endless, offering no resolution or possible fulfillment: "the man of *A Vision* . . . can attain knowledge of process, but no freedom from the labyrinth process makes" (209).
13. The Thirteenth Cone is mysterious because it is unattainable, but also because it is

flict would only be temporary since time is always moving men toward a future in which the relative power of the two forces is different than at present. Life, Yeats tells us, gives us one thing (the Fated Image), while passion aims for another (the Chosen Image). "Without this continual Discord through Deception there would be no conscience, no activity; Deception is a technical term of my teachers and may be substituted for 'desire.' Life is an endeavour, made vain by the four sails of its mill, to come to a double contemplation, that of the chosen Image, that of the fated Image" (V, 94). In Yeats's system there is no chance of an eventual Dantean resolution—"In his will, our peace" —since there is no presiding single will. The Victorians always finally subordinate the individual will to a larger reality—either God in Carlyle, Ruskin, and Browning, or society in Dickens and George Eliot—even when, as in the case of Ruskin, the individual's difference from the larger force is preserved in order to maintain a space for human life. In Yeats, however, as in Nietzsche, both reality (or the divine) and the human (or the individual) are "in the right." Each suffers "as it encroaches on the other" but there is no way to choose one over the other; the conflict between them constitutes life and is seemingly endless. Victorian tragedy, as in *The Mill on the Floss,* and Victorian irony, as in *Sartor Resartus* or Browning's dramatic monologues, is recognizably influenced by Christian thought even when not orthodox, since the "lack" is always in fallen man, the limit always located in human knowledge and human words. Man can be reconciled to the world, the romantic marriage can be achieved, when he overcomes the deficiencies in himself. In Victorian literature every individual perspective, every individual expression, must be finally recognized as partial; tragedy results from the mistake of taking the partial for the whole.[14] Maggie Tulliver is misled by taking the words of human desire as her only guide. The Victorians work to reveal that individual perspectives are inadequate understandings of the whole truth; this revelation,

---

hard to gauge how seriously Yeats takes it. Is Yeats's claim to substitute the Thirteenth Cone for God made earnestly? "Berkeley in the *Commonplace Book* thought that 'we perceive' and are passive whereas God creates in perceiving. I substitute for God the Thirteenth Cone; the Thirteenth Cone therefore creates our perceptions—all the visible world—as held in common by our wheel" (E, 320). Yeats calls the possibility of union between the human and the Thirteenth Cone "unthinkable" since "all thought, all perception" would be "extinguished" (E, 307).

14. The subjection of any individual perspective to correction follows the description of irony in Kenneth Burke's *A Grammar of Motives.* Burke writes, "Irony arises when one tries, by the interaction of terms upon one another, to produce a *development* which uses all the terms. Hence from the standpoint of this total form (this 'perspective of perspectives'), none of the participating 'sub-perspectives' can be treated as either precisely right or precisely wrong. They are all voices, or personalities, or positions, integrally effecting one another" (512). Burke calls the interaction of these "sub-perspectives" dramatism; we can add that the drama is a tragedy when the "sub-perspectives" are so incompatible that no union of them into a "total form" is possible. A poem like "The Tower" strives for dialectical resolution, but tragic incompatability is more characteristic of Yeats's work.

often accomplished through the use of irony, requires that the author speak from a more universal perspective than the individuals presented in the text. The Victorian writers hold out the hope that the fuller comprehension of the real enjoyed by the writer can also be achieved by the reader. The dualistic separation of mind and world is not inevitable. Better (more supple) knowledge will bring men and reality into accord. Man's fallen condition, while annoying, is only temporary and need not be irredeemably debilitating. The "concealment" of words and the "veils" that frustrate knowledge do make full understanding difficult, but do not make conflict between man and world inevitable.

In Yeats, however, tragedy does not result from misunderstandings generated by faulty words or faulty knowledge; irony for him is not linguistic or epistemological but cosmic. Words—whether used to express desire or used to portray the conflict between desire and the real—state fully and accurately the nature of the world. The poet's knowledge is not partial or clouded. What he knows is that man exists in endless conflict with the world he must live in. Tragedy is *the* nature of experience, not a temporary disaster caused by some failure in the individual that can be overcome. In Yeats's tragic art, the poet detaches himself from the individual far enough to allow the presentation of the total context in which particular actions and their necessary failure can be recognized. In this respect, "Lapis Lazuli" is not so different from "To the Rose Upon the Rood of Time." Both poems show the poet adopting a position that places him above the conflict he describes. But, unlike the Victorian writers when they adopt a perspective above the fray in their works, Yeats does not suggest his characters' fates could have been any different.

Yeats's confidence that tragedy is real and that his poetic words can fully state his understanding of that reality leads once again to the mixture of activity and passivity found in his work. Insofar as tragic reality exists prior to poetry, as something to be perceived by men, the poet presents himself as passive. But since it is human desire, pushed to its most energetic expression, that uncovers the "immovable" tragic object, a poetry about tragedy deals with man at his most active. A famous passage in the *Autobiography* affords an example of this mixture.

> As life goes on we discover that certain thoughts sustain us in defeat, or give us victory, whether over ourselves or others, and it is these thoughts, tested by passion, that we call convictions. Among subjective men (in all those, that is, who must spin a web out of their own bowels) the victory is an intellectual daily recreation of all that exterior fate snatches away, and so that fate's antithesis; while what I have called "the Mask" is an emotional antithesis to all that comes out of their internal nature. We begin to live when we have conceived life as tragedy. (A, 116)

Tragedy accepts the existence of a power (called "fate" here) beyond man that frustrates desire, but, at the same time, insists on the validity and nobility of that desire. Man actively asserts his desire in the face of a reality before which he stands defiant, but helpless. To say "we begin to live when we have conceived life as tragedy" is to place the moment of conception, of creation, in man's hands. Yet that very power is exercised alongside an acknowledgment of reality's power over us. The active energies in men can achieve the "victory" of spinning "out of their own bowels" those images or "thoughts" that represent all that "fate" has snatched away.

The "Discoveries" essay shows that Yeats was aware that his change in tone and subject at the beginning of the century was both drastic and consistent. The antithesis between mundane reality and desire is still at the heart of his poetry. However, in the nineties, desire for Yeats often seemed a neo–Platonic "intimation" that another world existed, one that could fulfill desire. In the later poetry, the passionate wish becomes the essentially human, that *cri de coeur* of a creature who knows "the folly of being comforted." The symbol, which Yeats tried to distance from desire, offered access to another world, but passion forms its image of an "other" out of a clear statement of its own lack. Yeats now describes art as offering " 'a hollow image of fulfilled desire.' All happy art seems to me that hollow image, but when its lineaments express also the poverty or the exasperation that set its maker to work, we call it tragic art" (M, 329). Art can offer an image of passion fulfilled, but that image is "hollow" because the fulfillment occurs in art, not life. Tragic art reminds us the image is hollow, reminds us of the "poverty and exasperation" that prompted the artistic creation of the image. Poetry's cry cannot disguise the essential "poverty" of the images of fulfillment it has to offer. We can imagine desire satisfied, but cannot experience that satisfaction outside of art. The poverty of words is apparent in their inability to alter the nature of the real.

Active and passive poems, ones that present an "image of fulfilled desire" and ones that "molest" that image by indicating its "hollowness," alternate throughout the later poetry. The volume entitled *The Tower* (1923) offers a good example. The first poem is "Sailing to Byzantium" (CP, 191), in which the poet creates through art a refuge for himself from the world of the "dying generations." But Yeats, characteristically, cannot rest content with getting "out of nature," and the next poem, "The Tower," considers how the poet might succeed in bringing imagination to bear on this world. After this attempted compromise between poet and the real comes the Civil War poems ("Meditations in Time of Civil War" and "Nineteen Hundred and Nineteen") with their brutal insistence that the dreams of imagination are completely ineffectual and unreal. I will discuss these poems more fully in a moment, but first want to consider how the activity and passivity in Yeats compare to that of the Victorians.

The active Yeats, with his reliance on art to create a new and better world, seems more modern than Victorian. But, as I have tried to demonstrate, the Victorians do use imagination to help bring forth a better future. The romantic effort to bring imagination to bear upon the world is far from completely absent in Victorian literature, even if the Victorians limit imagination's autonomy. Yeats is more willing to affirm the constructions of imagination than many Victorians, but he only does so in a context that also insures that imagination's ineffectiveness. In Yeats are displayed the first hints of a distinctive and peculiar feature of much modern literature: the combination of a powerful conception of imagination with the insistence on the absolute separation between art and life. The result, contrary to expectation, is an imagination that actually influences life less than the comparatively weak imagination described by the Victorians. I would argue that the Victorians are much more careful to limit imagination's power because they take its ability to change the world much more seriously than many of the modernists.[15]

On the other hand, Yeats's passivity seems at first glance more Victorian. The passive poems undermine (or "molest") the dreams of desire in the name of a reality that contradicts images of fulfillment. But the savagery of Yeats's attacks on illusion links him to those creators of the twentieth century—Marx, Freud, and Nietzsche—more than to the Victorians. In Victorian literature, the writers show a deeper sympathy for characters who struggle to know the real and who mistake their own desires for reality. Characters like Maggie Tulliver and Dickens's Pip, even though they are punished for their failings, are hardly villains since their authors find illusion and confusion perfectly understandable in this fallen world, even if disastrous. The difference in tone between Browning's poetry, even when he is dealing with obvious rascals like the duke of Ferrara and the bishop of St. Praxed's, and Yeats's poems points to this same distinction. Free from many of the epistemological doubts of the Victorians, Yeats displays much less patience with a lack of clear sight. In part, this exasperation is directed against himself, as the Civil War poems indicate, but the crucial point is that for Yeats the necessity of mediation in perception or in language does not also involve inevitable limitations to knowledge.

The most negative poems in *The Tower*, "Meditations in Time of Civil War" (CP, 198–204) and "Nineteen Hundred and Nineteen" (CP, 204–8), completely deny that imagination has any power in the face of reality. Furthermore, reality in these poems is not simply a cosmic tragic force that frustrates human wishes, but is human nature itself, the kind of wishes men have. Men

15. The modernist's conviction that art cannot influence the world is expressed by Auden's claim that poetry "makes nothing happen." In *The Dehumanization of Art* (Princeton: Princeton University Press, 1968), Jose Ortega y Gassett discusses at length this modernist insistence that "art is a thing of no consequence" (49). Auden's statement is too knowing and cynical to be called despairing, but still expresses a wish that poetry did make a difference. The artists Ortega describes value art precisely because it is "of no transcendent importance" (49).

are a certain way, these poems conclude, and the social order reflects that given human nature. Any dream of change is only a dream. The first stanza of the "Meditations" imagines a rich, full life, described through the metaphor of an overflowing fountain. But the second stanza considers whether this imagined fullness can be realized.

> Mere dreams, mere dreams! Yet Homer had not sung
> Had he not found it certain beyond dreams
> That out of life's own self-delight had sprung
> The abounding glittering jet; though now it seems
> As if some marvellous empty sea-shell flung
> Out of the obscure dark of the rich streams,
> And not a fountain, were the symbol which
> Shadows the inherited glory of the rich. (CP, 198)

The hope that life might become "rich" is a "mere dream," but a dream that reading Homer fosters. For Homer, the development of life in poetry was not separated from the life society as a whole led. "Life's own self-delight" is a truth, a fact "certain beyond dreams," and Homer's poetry is based on the recognition of that truth. But modern poetry ("it seems"), while true to this vision of "life's self-delight," cannot connect to the society it addresses. The image of the seashell returns, replacing the fountain as the proper "symbol" for that life which is expressed in poetry and the houses of the rich. (Yeats, as a lover of the aristocracy and the enemy of poverty, puns shamelessly on the word *rich* in the poem.) The seashell folds in upon itself; it does not overflow as the fountain does, but protects its fragile beauty by turning inward. The other poems of the "Meditations," as well as "Nineteen Hundred and Nineteen," explore the strategy of "solitude" as a way for the poet to protect his vision in a hostile world. His era's violence inspires the poet's love of the unchanging and his melancholy fear that nothing he values can survive. "But is there any comfort to be found? / Man is in love and loves what vanishes, / What more is there to say?" (CP, 205).

Human nature itself explains the violence, and the only possible comfort is that, in response to these times, the poet will be moved (out of opposition) to create great art: "only an aching heart / Conceives a changeless work of art" (CP, 200). The poet's desire for the changeless indicates his difference from the general rule of human nature. This difference is the specific focus of the Civil War poems: the poet finds in himself a vision and desires that are incompatible with what appears to be the vision of most men. The poems mix defiance and despair. Yeats will continue to be true to his vision; he will set his poems up against the dominant vision (and violence) of his time. But he sees clearly that all power has passed from the poet. The solitary poet can claim "triumph can but mar our solitude" (CP, 206), but the acceptance of solitude is the acceptance that triumph cannot be his. Poetry vainly cherishes ideals most men will never heed or hold.

> I turn away and shut the door, and on the stair
> Wonder how many times I could have proved my worth
> In something that all others understand or share;
> But O! ambitious heart, had such a proof drawn forth
> A company of friends, a conscience set at ease,
> It had but made us pine the more. The abstract joy,
> The half-read wisdom of daemonic images,
> Suffice the ageing man as once the growing boy. (CP, 204)

Yeats, facing the failure of his poetry to sway the world, considers what his life would have been like if he had been involved in matters "all others understand." His "ambitious heart," which we well know craved such persuasive authority over others, might have been satisfied, the uneasy conscience that accompanies his failure to make the world a better place might have been assuaged. Yet such practical success, Yeats suggests, would have been even more frustrated by its inability to alter the course of events, to prevent the war. As a politician his voice would have been no more heeded than his poetry. The powerlessness of all words, all visions, seems absolute to Yeats at this point. And if a clear connection with the world would have meant involvement in this violence, Yeats can only be thankful for his solitude. "The abstract joy," abstract because never realized in this world but only in poetry, will have to be enough. This last sentence carries a suggestion of prayer, asking "abstract joy" to "suffice the ageing man as once the growing boy." The prayer is necessary because we sense that the "ageing man," with his vision of evil, is much less capable than the growing boy of losing himself in the solace of abstract joy.

"Nineteen Hundred and Nineteen" is even more brutal than the "Meditations" in its acceptance that poetry (as Auden says in his elegy for Yeats) "changes nothing."[16]

> O but we dreamed to mend
> Whatever mischief seemed
> To afflict mankind, but now
> The winds of winter blow
> Learn that we were crack-pated when we dreamed. (CP, 206)

16. Bloom's discussion (in Yeats) of the Civil War poems is, I think, brilliant, and underlines the hopelessness of Auden's comment on poetry's futility. Of "Nineteen Hundred and Nineteen" Bloom writes: "Loss of civilization, personal loss, cannot be converted into imaginative gain, as they are by Wordsworth, Coleridge, sometimes Keats, working through a compensatory and sympathetic imagination. Loss in Yeats, at his finest, . . . is more than the Body of Fate of the poet at Stage 17; it must be accepted for its own sake. . . . It belongs to experience, and experience, by its nature, cannot be redeemed" (358).

The poem goes on to "mock" all those who thought their individual actions, their visions of a possible future for Ireland, could shape that future. There is a force in events (which Yeats could link to his gyres when he wanted to be specific) that mocks human efforts to control history.[17] The poverty of dreams and the words in which they are embodied is absolute; visions in no way influence the shapes assumed by reality. The images of these two poems only indicate the extent to which the world resists all human visions of order and peace.

Yeats's savagery against dreamers in "Nineteen Hundred and Nineteen" is directed against himself as well as others. The visionary Yeats, the creator of Byzantium and other residences of the imagination, is so familiar to us that it seems odd to find him asserting that poetry and its dreams are worthless and ineffectual. The pattern of alternate construction and destruction is displayed here. "Sailing to Byzantium" offers an escape into art, but an escape that recognizes death as the price to be paid for stepping out of time into "the artifice of eternity." Such a total removal from life's passionate concerns cannot be fully satisfactory. Compare the "drowsy" emperor to the bustling, if somewhat shortsighted, activities of the "young / In one another's arms." The next poem, "The Tower," eschews this escape into art and attempts to work out a compromise between poet and reality, one that will grant the poet's vision some power to influence the very nature of the real, to re-form it.

The terms of that attempted compromise are fairly complex. Coming to Yeats from Wallace Stevens we might be tempted to focus on the poem's insistence that imagination creates not just artistic worlds like Byzantium, but this very world in which we live everyday.

> And I declare my faith:
> I mock Plotinus' thought
> And cry in Plato's teeth,
> Death and life were not
> Till man made up the whole,
> Made lock, stock and barrel
> Out of his bitter soul,
> Aye, sun and moon, and star, all (CP, 196)

Here is the Yeats who sees poetry "calling" a world into existence; stressing the active verbs—*declare, cry, make*—the poet insists that the meaning of things rests in men's memories and desires and that those things are real only

17. On the place of history in Yeats's work, Donoghue, in *William Butler Yeats,* writes: "There are moments in which he [Yeats] is satisfied with whatever the subjective will chooses to do, but there are other moments in which he is satisfied with nothing less than the truth, conceived as independent of his will. . . . Against symbol, therefore, we should place history, meaning whatever the imagination recognizes as distinct from itself. . . . History is a predicate, hopefully to be reconciled to the subject, but it is not the subject's minion" (85–86).

insofar as they carry meaning for us. Poetry and its words grant us access to reality and shape the significances we find in the real. The distinction between sun and moon, between prosaic and imaginative vision, runs through "The Tower." But in order to triumph fully, the poet must unite the two. "O may the moon and sunlight seem / One inextricable beam, / For if I triumph I must make men mad" (CP, 193–94). (In "Nineteen Hundred and Nineteen," Yeats admits this triumph has not been granted to him.) To combine image and reality is poetry's goal, and would be a remaking of the world. The "triumph" would reconcile two things normally quite distinct, but losing the ability to distinguish between the two overwhelms sanity. In part, Yeats wants to celebrate this divine madness, this new form of perception, the poet's frenzy, but his use of the word *mad* is not entirely positive.

A deep guilt runs throughout the poem. The old Irish poet who succeeded in maddening his audience caused their deaths. Further, the poem begins by suggesting that imagination causes pain by supplying images that feed desires an old man is incapable of satisfying. Imagination maddens us, in the sense of frustrating us, and the poet wants to know, when he calls up his varied list of visitors, whether they "in public or in secret rage / As I do now against old age?" (CP, 195). In fostering desires that reality cannot satisfy, the poet causes pain to his audience. The proposed union of imagination and reality might occur only in thought, not in the world itself, and the disjunction between thought and fact is madness—a madness the poet encourages, even causes.

Yet reality has its pains as well, and Yeats's next question (addressed to Hanrahan) suggests a different source of guilt: the poet's deliberate evasion of reality because it is not as spectacular or ideally perfect as the images he cherishes.

> Does the imagination dwell the most
> Upon a woman won or a woman lost?
> If on the lost, admit you turned aside
> From a great labyrinth out of pride,
> Cowardice, some silly over-subtle thought
> Or anything called conscience once;
> And if that memory recur, the sun's
> Under eclipse and the day blotted out. (CP, 195)

Allegiance to the image, an unwillingness to test it against mundane reality, has made the poet "turn aside" from possible success in love, and it is the woman he turned away from that "imagination dwells on most." (At least such is implied, although Yeats does not answer the question directly.) The poet accepts now that it was not the woman, but his own choices that made the love affair unsuccessful. (The relevance or accuracy of such an explanation to Yeats's actual relations with Maud Gonne is hardly important. What is significant is Yeats's understanding of the ideal image's relation to reality, and his guilt about having evaded bringing the two together.) Even now, the "sun" can be "blotted out" by the "memory" of that ideal image of the beloved. Yeats's guilt here involves, in part, the unfaithfulness to his wife involved in dwelling on the woman lost rather than the woman won, but, further, the more extensive guilt of a poet who entices his readers away from the real, offering them moon-struck images of a better world that, in fact, he cannot make substantial. Poetry may very well only feed disillusion with this world without supplying an alternative.

The "will" Yeats writes in the third part of the poem (which includes that declaration of faith with which I began my discussion of the poem) is an attempt to construct that alternative, a construction based on a mixture of Yeats's system (from *A Vision*) and the Irish Protestant "tradition" of Burke and Grattan. However, Yeats leaves the pain of that building effort to the "young upstanding men," while he himself withdraws into the soul, escaping the complexities of both desire and the real, so that all evil and beauty will seem to him only like "a bird's sleepy cry / Among the deepening shades." This acceptance of death at the poem's end carries all the conviction of an old man's weariness. The poet's guilt over his inability to make the image more substantial, and over his continued preference for the image as opposed to the real, hastens his acceptance of death. In declaring his "faith" he has tried to claim that desire so influences perception that the "thing in itself" and the thing as imagined by desiring man cannot be distinguished; thus man might be said to make his world. But that making still springs from a "bitterness" that can only be explained if men do know the difference between image and reality, and see it feelingly. At this point the Civil War poems follow, with their revelation of the image's lack of substance or effectiveness.

Yeats's only defense against this revelation is an insistence on the nobility and "joy" of tragedy. " 'Bitter and gay,' that is the tragic mood," writes Yeats to Dorothy Wellesley (L, 7). "Will, or energy, is greatest in tragedy," so that "it may become a pure, aimless joy though the man, the shade, still mourns his lost object" (E, 449). Yeats still feels the need to assert that his poetry has a truth value, that it reveals something about the nature of the universe and not just something about human psychology. The theory of tragedy allows him to state the insufferableness of the world as experienced, the defiant refusal of imagination to give up its dream of a better world, *and* the inevitable conflict between desire and world. The tragic artist, who can encompass the whole universe of conflict in his art, can experience that "joy" that is, perhaps, not available to "the man, the shade, [who] still mourns his lost object."

There is a suspicion that Yeats cheats somewhat in reaching this affirmation in defeat. He uses the poetic word in two different ways that, in fact, may not be compatible. The word is the means by which the essentially human—desire—is expressed; the word holds the whole conflict between desire and reality within it. The first use of the word makes it represent the human side in the tragic vision; the second use has the word represent the totality. Presumably, the tragic actor plays out his part without knowing defeat is inevitable, but the tragic artist does know that defeat is in store. Yeats's famous statement —"Man can embody truth but he cannot know it" (Letters, 922)—suggests the difficulty here. Only someone who knows the truth can recognize that man embodies it. Yeats grants himself a perspective above the human or, at least, above what he allows to most other men.

But if that perspective is "inhuman," as Bloom claims, it does not yield an inhuman art. Yeats, finally, occupies a position very similar to Rossetti's; the poet is able to locate elusive reality most successfully when something beyond the self opposes the poet's will. And Yeats's need to contact reality is so great that he finds comfort, even "joy," in the experience of frustration. Unlike Rossetti, Yeats is able to transform reality's resistance to desire into the basis of a triumphant art. Yeats does not blame language or the self for man's failure to connect with the real, so he does not continually undermine his own words and impulses, does not hope to achieve a silence which reality would break with its own voice. Instead, words are tied firmly to human, not inhuman, realities in Yeats, the realities of desire and its frustration. The word is either the means by which men speak their defiant desires or the means by which the poet reveals his vision of the tragic impasse. Refusing to yield to reality, Yeats accepts and glories in the full humanity of the word—a humanity that is the word's triumph and its impotence. The early theories of the symbol tried to evade that impotence, but Yeats's later understanding of the poetic word fully admits its "magnificence and penury."

In his acceptance that reality is stronger than imaginative constructs, Yeats joins those other early moderns, Nietzsche and Freud, whose theories of "eternal recurrence" and "the reality principle" also insist on the prior existence of a set reality that men cannot change and that frustrates desire.[18] Nietzsche and Freud are both guilty of the epistemological sleight of hand we find in Yeats. If perception is governed by desire, as Nietzsche and Freud both claim, then how have these two thinkers managed to identify the fundamental features of the real? They grant themselves a privileged insight they do not grant others, in part because the experience they single out as most real is that of frustration, and they see other men as striving to deny just that experience. Tragedy must be the real nature of things, since no man could possibly wish that things be tragic. Later theorists of the imagination in this century will

18. Freud and Nietzsche are also dependent on notions of "instinct" and "human nature," unchanging substratums that allow them to locate the truth about man even while they question the truths men have cherished about themselves.

insist that reality itself is constructed in the union between mind and world,[19] but the first modernists, although they substitute a tragic outlook for the comic hopes of the romantics and Victorians, still hold to the nineteenth-century understanding of the real as constituted prior to and existing independent of any act of mind.

19. Proust is among the most optimistic of modern writers about the power of imagination to shape reality. Postmodernist literature, on the other hand, is likely to stress imagination's inability to influence reality. See my essay, "A la Recherche du Temps Perdu in *One Hundred Years of Solitude,*" *Modern Fiction Studies* 28 (1982–1983): 557–67. In modern philosophy, Alfred North Whitehead most fully articulates the position that reality is constructed in the meeting of mind and world, especially in *Science and the Modern World* (New York: The Free Press, 1967). (But see also Jonathan Bennett, *Locke, Berkeley, Hume: Central Themes,* for another expression of the same conviction. Bennett's criticism of empiricist epistemology is based on its failure to recognize that objects are "constructs.") Whitehead offers his philosophy as a resolution of the persistent Cartesian dualism he calls a "radical inconsistency at the basis of modern thought" (76), namely the simultaneous belief in "scientific realism, based on materialism" and an "unwavering belief" in man's power of thought and his freedom.

Index

203